STAYING CONNECTED

JAMES FERRABEE & MICHAEL St B. HARRISON

STAYING

CONNECTED

How MacDougall Family Traditions Built
a Business over 160 Years

published for
MacDougall, MacDougall & MacTier Inc.
by
McGill-Queen's University Press
Montreal & Kingston | London | Ithaca

© McGill-Queen's University Press 2009
ISBN 978-0-7735-3661-6

Legal deposit fourth quarter 2009
Bibliothèque nationale du Québec

Printed in Canada on acid-free paper that is 100% ancient forest free,
processed chlorine free

McGill-Queen's University Press acknowledges the support of the Canada
Council for the Arts for our publishing program. We also acknowledge the
financial support of the Government of Canada through the Book Publishing
Industry Development Program (BPIDP) for our publishing activities.

LIBRARY AND ARCHIVES CANADA CATALOGUING IN PUBLICATION

Ferrabee, James
Staying connected : how MacDougall family traditions built a business over
160 years / James Ferrabee and Michael St B. Harrison.

Includes bibliographical references and index.
ISBN 978-0-7735-3661-6

1. MacDougall, MacDougall & MacTier – History.   2. Investment advisors –
Québec (Province) – Montréal – Biography.   3. Investment advisors –
Canada – Biography.   I. Harrison, Michael St B   II. Title.

HG5154.3.F37 2009   332.6'20971   C2009-905805-7

Set in 10/13.5 Baskerville 10 Pro by Garet Markvoort, zijn digital

CONTENTS

Foreword: A History to Celebrate   vii
by Bartlett H. MacDougall

Acknowledgments   ix

MacDougall Family Genealogical Chart   xii

Illustrations   xvi

ONE
Setting down Roots   3

TWO
The Making of a Gentleman   25

THREE
Making War and Making Money   39

FOUR
Growth and Depression   56

FIVE

Passing the Torch   72

SIX

Enter Hartland B.   84

SEVEN

A New Century   101

EIGHT

Boom and Bust   114

NINE

War and Peace   128

TEN

The Genesis of 3 Macs   143

ELEVEN

Turbulence and Opportunity   160

TWELVE

Inflation and Volatility   174

THIRTEEN

Irrational Exuberance and the Bubble Economy   191

FOURTEEN

The New Millennium   208

Notes   221

Bibliography   229

About the Authors   235

Index   237

A HISTORY TO CELEBRATE

Foreword by Bartlett H. MacDougall

When an organization reaches a milestone it seems only natural to celebrate the occasion. So it was in September 2008 that MacDougall, MacDougall & MacTier, affectionately known as "3 Macs," gathered in Montreal with their current employees and many of their alumni, with their spouses and dates, for an evening of celebration of our 150 years. It was at this occasion that I announced that a history of the firm was being written to document the role that the MacDougall family and their associates had played in the financial industry in Canada over these many years. The idea had originated with Athol Gordon, a family friend, who made his second career with 3 Macs. Little did I think that there was a story in it, but James Ferrabee and Michael Harrison proved me wrong, and also wrong in another way. It was discovered that we were out by nine years on the anniversary date, a mistake for which I take full responsibility. It seems that our origins go back to 1849, which means that we can now celebrate 160 years in 2009!!

The family tree, included as an appendix, shows that there was always more than one MacDougall family member from each generation who worked in the firm. However, family participation wasn't limited to the MacDougalls. In 2008 we had numerous family members of Watsons, Gallops, Blacks, Westons, Perrys and Berrys, Sears, MacCallums, Rebers, and of course Prices. One way or another, it was the ability to attract high-quality partners or associates that made it possible to grow from a firm of several partners into a corporation with nearly two hundred employees with over half being shareholders.

How is it, one might ask, that this firm has managed to survive in such a mercurial business, when so many others have been acquired, merged to become larger entities, or just closed their doors? There is a theory that "small and focused" or "large and diversified" are sustainable business models, whereas anything in between is vulnerable. From its earliest days the MacDougall firm has been small and focused, and it remains that way to this day. The focus may have changed slightly over the years, but a common thread can be found. The firm has always had an affinity to serve the private client, and this has been the mainstay of the business since its inception.

Just as one generation has followed another into the firm, so too have several generations of private clients been attracted to its services. There is little doubt that this loyalty has been made possible by a high degree of trust, which is of critical importance in an industry that finds itself conflicted in so many ways.

Will the loyalty of current and future clients, employees, and owners allow 3 Macs the privilege of continuing the legacy that the MacDougall family began so many years ago? We think so, as long as there is value in the firm's motto: "integrity, independence, service, and performance."

ACKNOWLEDGMENTS

JAMES FERRABEE

When Tim Price asked me to write a book on the company, I scuttled to the nearest library and dove into the *Dictionary of National Biography*. There was a long article on Donald Lorn MacDougall, the first of this MacDougall family to come to Montreal, in 1840. The article described how MacDougall, his brothers, and their offspring became formative figures in the development of the investment business in Canada and also leaders in sports and military life in Montreal and Canada in both the nineteenth and twentieth centuries.

There is very little written about the financial business in Canada in the nineteenth century and the MacDougalls kept few records. I needed help. Happily, Hamilton Slessor was researching the same period and wrote to 3 Macs for aid. They sent his request to me and that began three years of correspondence by e-mail during which time he did a formidable amount of ferreting information from national and provincial archives, newspapers, and libraries. My part of the book owes much to him.

As well, I am indebted to many members of the MacDougall family, especially Hartland M. MacDougall, Marian MacDougall MacFarlane, Lorna MacDougall Bethell, Merne Price, and, of course, Bart MacDougall, emeritus chairman of the board of 3 Macs. Bart was understanding and patient as he shepherded me through the project. I owe thanks to friends, including Anson McKim and Alexander Reford. Anson was kind enough to read a rough draft and give me wise direction. Alexander, who is an historian as well as director of the Jardins de Métis, scoured the extensive Reford family files and provided colourful background to a crucial part of the story. Cara O'Connell of Bishop's University, Pat Duggan of the *Gazette*, and Jill Harrington spent a great deal of time in libraries digging up information and articles. I am grateful to all of them. The books and articles that proved valuable are listed in the Bibliography.

As a reporter, it took considerable cheek to venture into the formidable field of history writing. I had many mentors who encouraged my curiosity about history, including my Mum and Dad, Roba and Sox; D. Stephen Penton, a magical history teacher in high school; and Donald C. Masters, my university history teacher. I spent a sabbatical year at Massey College, University of Toronto, where I took courses from one of our generation's most respected Canadian historians, Ramsay Cook. That sabbatical and much more I owe to Charlie Peters, the publisher of the *Gazette*, who hired me on little more than instinct and friendship. Edgar Andrew Collard, the editor, took me on as an editorial writer. He was one of a kind – soft-spoken, with a rollicking laugh that came with a delightful sense of humour and knowledge of subjects ranging from hashish to Jane Austen. As a young reporter, I got much more out of the relationships with Charlie and Edgar than I could possibly have given back.

McGill-Queen's Press was welcoming and tolerant to amateurs like me. Editorial Director Philip Cercone supported the project from the beginning and, in the last few months, Anna Lensky patiently steered us through unfamiliar details of publishing, while Curtis Fahey edited the manuscript with sensitivity and skill.

Finally, from the first day to the last, my wife, Di, was on the job. My part of this book is dedicated to Di, who kept the project going with her energy and enthusiasm, common sense, patience, frequent back rubs, and much love.

None of the people mentioned above, of course, is responsible for mistakes of commission or omission. They are entirely my responsibility.

MICHAEL ST B. HARRISON

I wish to thank Sheila Lipari, who kick-started my work on the sections of this book that I authored. Sheila also acted as an invaluable fact checker and spiritual guide when the spirit lagged. Her meticulous corrections of my punctuation and spelling allowed me to hammer away at the keyboard without concerns of showing signs of intelligence.

I also thank Janice Squires, Ian Black, Bob Ross, and Bill Cowen for very useful documentation and memories of the chronology of people and events that influenced 3 Macs.

Of course, I wish to apologize to the many people who have been left out of the account of recent years and hope they understand that it was not my intention to write a telephone book.

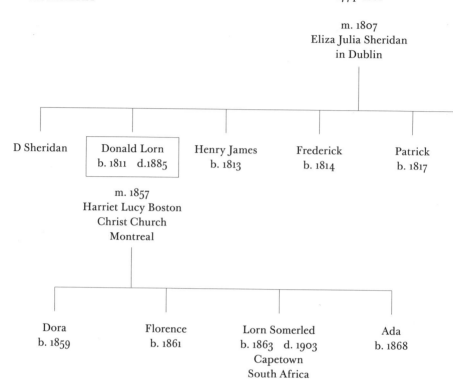

1st FAMILY

Major Peter MacDougall
1774–1861

m. 1807
Eliza Julia Sheridan
in Dublin

D Sheridan

Donald Lorn
b. 1811   d.1885

Henry James
b. 1813

Frederick
b. 1814

Patrick
b. 1817

m. 1857
Harriet Lucy Boston
Christ Church
Montreal

Dora
b. 1859

Florence
b. 1861

Lorn Somerled
b. 1863   d. 1903
Capetown
South Africa

Ada
b. 1868

| Colin b. 1819 | Julia b. 1821 | Hanbury Leigh b. 1823 | Margaret b. 1825 | Alicia Dora b. 1829 |

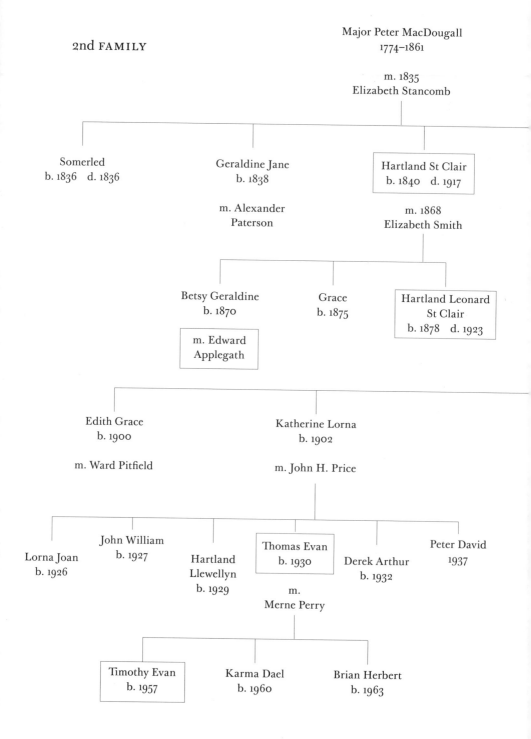

2nd FAMILY

Major Peter MacDougall
1774–1861

m. 1835
Elizabeth Stancomb

Somerled
b. 1836   d. 1836

Geraldine Jane
b. 1838

m. Alexander
Paterson

Hartland St Clair
b. 1840   d. 1917

m. 1868
Elizabeth Smith

Betsy Geraldine
b. 1870

m. Edward
Applegath

Grace
b. 1875

Hartland Leonard
St Clair
b. 1878   d. 1923

Edith Grace
b. 1900

m. Ward Pitfield

Katherine Lorna
b. 1902

m. John H. Price

Lorna Joan
b. 1926

John William
b. 1927

Hartland
Llewellyn
b. 1929

Thomas Evan
b. 1930

m.
Merne Perry

Derek Arthur
b. 1932

Peter David
1937

Timothy Evan
b. 1957

Karma Dael
b. 1960

Brian Herbert
b. 1963

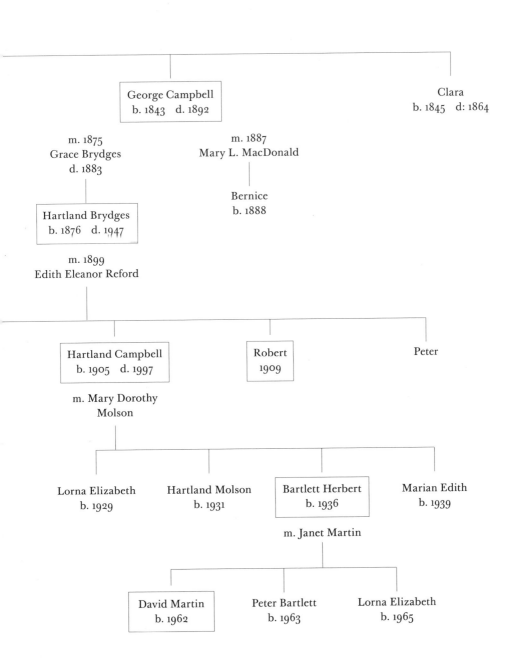

Indicates person employed at 3 Macs

George Campbell
b. 1843   d. 1892

Clara
b. 1845   d: 1864

m. 1875
Grace Brydges
d. 1883

m. 1887
Mary L. MacDonald

Bernice
b. 1888

Hartland Brydges
b. 1876   d. 1947

m. 1899
Edith Eleanor Reford

Hartland Campbell
b. 1905   d. 1997

Robert
1909

Peter

m. Mary Dorothy
Molson

Lorna Elizabeth
b. 1929

Hartland Molson
b. 1931

Bartlett Herbert
b. 1936

Marian Edith
b. 1939

m. Janet Martin

David Martin
b. 1962

Peter Bartlett
b. 1963

Lorna Elizabeth
b. 1965

Major Peter MacDougall, c. 1855.

Donald Lorn MacDougall, 1863. McCord Museum I-7412.1.

Hartland St Clair MacDougall, 1863. McCord Museum 1-618.7.

George Campbell MacDougall, 1870. McCord Museum I-48910.1.

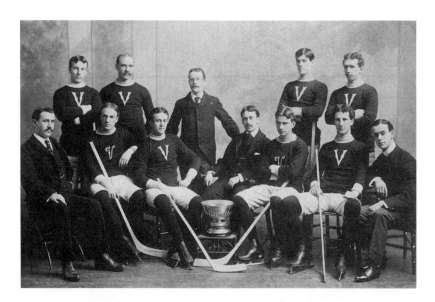

above The Montreal Victorias, 1898. Left to right: sitting, Howard Wilson, R.E. MacDougall, Graham Drinkwater, Paul de Sterneck, Cam Davidson, Ernie McLea, J. Bishop; standing, Frank Richardson, Mike Grant, Watson Jack, Hartland MacDougall, G. Gordon Lewis. On stand – the Stanley Cup. Charles L. Coleman, *The Trail of the Stanley Cup*, vol. 1 (1893–1926) ([Montreal]: National Hockey League [1964]), 44.

facing page, above Metis House, Reford / MacDougall / Price c. 1920
The original owner was Robert Reford. He gave it to his two daughters Edith and Katie, but when Edith married Hartland B. MacDougall Katie turned over her interest to them. It was subsequently given to their two daughters Grace and Lorna. Lorna married Jack Price, and Lorna acquired the interests of Grace. The house burned down in 1974. The property was purchased by Tom and Merne Price and they built a new house in 1986/87.

facing page, below Outremont, home of Donald Lorn MacDougall c. 1870

Hartland B.
MacDougall
playing polo
c. 1925.

Hartland B.
MacDougall
c. 1928.

Left to right: Hartland C. (Tommy) MacDougall, Hartland B. MacDougall, Robert R. (Bobs) MacDougall, Peter L. MacDougall 1940.

HARTLAND CAMPBELL MacDOUGALL

MacDOUGALL, Hartland Campbell—Investment Dealer; President: MacDougall, MacDougall & MacTier Ltd.; MacTier & Co. Limited, Bank of Montreal Bldg., Montreal 1, Que. Born Montreal, Que., March 27, 1905, son of Hartland Brydges and Edith (Reford) MacDougall, both of Montreal, Que. Educated: Bishop's College School, Lennoxville, Que.; Royal Military College, Kingston, Ont. Partner, MacDougall & MacDougall, Montreal, Que., 1928-60; elected to Montreal Stock Exchange, 1927; Governor, 1934-40; Secretary-Treasurer, 1938-39; Vice-Chairman, 1939-40; Governor, Bishop's College School. Served with R.C.A. (Reserve), 1926-40; R.C.A., First Canadian Division, 1940-43; H.Q. Second Canadian Corps (G.S.O. II), 1943; N.D.H.Q., Ottawa, Ont. (G.S.O. I), 1944-45. Married Dorothy Molson, daughter of Herbert Molson, Montreal, Que., April 25, 1928; has two sons and two daughters. Clubs: Montreal; Montreal Racket; Mount Royal; Montreal Hunt; New York Racquet & Tennis. Recreations: racquets, tennis, hunting and golf. Independent. Anglican. Residence: Saraguay, Que.

Hartland Campbell MacDougall, *Who's Who in Canada*, 1961.

MacDougall & MacDougall Christmas Dinner Party, 1953: Left to right: Bill Poirier, Phil Barnoff, Agnes Murphy, P. Bancroft Reid, Caroline McConnachie, George Deveney, Hilda Henderson, H.C. (Tommy) Mac-Dougall, Ruth Waddell, Jock Graham, Janet Gutherie, Tom Price, Odessa Pinkney, Larry Mather, Fiona Bavis, Victor LeDain, unidentified, Pauline Butt, Chris Parsons.

W.S.M. (Stuart) MacTier, chairman, and H.C. (Tommy) MacDougall, president, 1965.

Bishop College School alumni with the 3 Macs in 1985. Left to right: C. Athol Gordon '47, E. Doug Reynolds '65, Alfred M. Dobell '39, W. Stuart Arbuckle '55, H.C. (Tommy) MacDougall '22, Bartlett H. MacDougall '54, Robert G. Ross '51, Thomas E. Price '48, Tim Price '75.

Dorothy Molson MacDougall and H.C. (Tommy) MacDougall, 1988.

3 Macs directors, c. 1993. Standing: Jawaid Khan, Tom Law, Bob Ross, Rick Craig, Tom Aiken, Wilf Dinnick, Bart MacDougall, Ian Black, Athol Gordon, Charles Kennedy, John Gallop, Michael Harrison, Michel Bergeron, Laird Grantham, Jim Perrone. Seated: Phil Barnoff, H.A. (Buster) Jones, Tom Price, John Benson, Joan Neville.

Her Majesty Queen Elizabeth. The Queen Mother on her visit to Canada in 1989 attended by Honorary Lt.-Col. Thomas E. Price Black Watch (RHR) Canada, chairman MacDougall, MacDougall & MacTier Inc. 1976–1996.

Bartlett H. MacDougall, chairman, 2008.

Timothy E. Price, president and CEO, 2008.

Michael St B. Harrison, president and CEO, 1988–2000.

Bartlett H. MacDougall and son David MacDougall, 2008.

STAYING CONNECTED

ONE

Setting down Roots

The propensity to truck, barter and exchange one thing for another is
common to all men, and to be found in no other race of animals.
Adam Smith

The "Three Macs" brokerage firm that has become so intertwined
with the history of Montreal over the last century traces its roots
to the arrival in the city of Donald Lorn MacDougall, a Scott from
Devon, England, in 1840. Within a year, Lorn MacDougall (he, like
a number of other MacDougalls, commonly went by his middle
name) had founded a brokerage business based principally on flour
and grain and, to a lesser extent, timber trading and shipping, a
business that would be firmly established as a fixture of Montreal's
economic life by the end of the 1840s. There were some hard times,
to be sure, in the latter part of the decade, but MacDougall's enterprise survived and by 1850 was poised for even greater success. In
some ways it is a murky story – the sources are fragmentary at best
– but it remains a remarkable one all the same. And it is the foundation of what was to follow.

Montreal was home to a long line of adventurers, first French,
later Scottish, when MacDougall arrived in 1840. From the French
regime to the 1820s, French and Scottish explorers and traders
sketched the outline of what would later be the country of Canada.
They paddled the turbulent river system and rode the lake waves
through Ontario and Manitoba and finally to the Pacific Ocean.
It was clear to them, as it was to their successors through the nineteenth century, that Canada's economic future and political inde-

pendence depended on the efficiency of its water system and, later, its railway lines – in short, its transportation and communication structure. So, beginning in the 1820s, the British and Canadian governments began widening old canals and building new ones. The great St Lawrence could easily handle the fur trade and grain trade in Lower Canada but there was a bigger prize that the mid-nineteenth-century mercantile class in Montreal knew was vital to their future. That was controlling the fertile hinterland of Upper Canada as well as the American and Canadian mid-west. The competition, then as now, came from the opportunistic risk takers of the U.S. east coast.

By the mid-1820s, the first expansion of the Lachine Canal was completed and ships could now bypass the white rapids and the swirling currents in Montreal harbour because the canal cut through the heart of the city. Its four-foot depth could handle the Durham boats and other bateaux hauling the bulk cargoes. But the Americans saw their chance and quickly exploited it. In record time they dug a huge ditch from Lake Erie to meet the Hudson River at Albany, then dredged the Hudson to make barges accessible to New York and its port. The result was a major engineering feat that, starting when it opened in 1825, spawned a commercial bonanza. This put Montreal at a distinct disadvantage. Its harbour, unlike New York's, was frozen for four to six months every year. Montreal was also five hundred miles from the Atlantic, while New York was a hundred feet. The challenges that the Erie Canal threw at Canada and its builders, in fact, plagued them through most of the nineteenth century.

While the commercial struggle for the interior of the continent continued, Montreal quickly became a city of two cultures. Americans seeking opportunity had come north starting in the late eighteenth century; Scots and English at first, and Irish later, sailed west starting shortly after the Battle of Quebec in 1759. They recreated the institutions they regarded as essential to a modern economy and a civilized English community. Those included the Bank of Montreal (1817), McGill University (1821), and the Montreal General Hospital (1822), from which sprouted the McGill Medical Faculty and the Royal Grammar School (1829). Clubs like the Montreal History Society (1827) and the Mechanic's Institute

(1828) served as educational steps towards progress, the universal goal of British society in the nineteenth century.

In 1836 Montreal got its first gas works and two years later the first police force and first synagogue. Next in importance came churches. The working-class Methodists and Baptists built solidly, followed by the Presbyterians and the Anglicans on a grander scale because they tended to be entrepreneurs and merchants. The Roman Catholic Church was the concrete foundation of French Canadian society, as well as the mortar that held together much of the Irish community that poured in during and after the 1840s.

There were significant developments in other areas too. In sports, skating had already become popular in winter, as had tobogganing, and the Scots had imported that curiously awkward game called curling. The Royal Montreal Curling Club, founded in 1807, is the oldest sporting club in North America, and through the nineteenth and twentieth centuries it became the centre from which the sport spread across the continent. Those early Montrealers also counted theatre among the civilizing influences, and so the Theatre Royal was opened in 1825. That same year the best-known English actor of his time, Edmund Keane, diverted the Montreal population with his famous roles from Shakespeare.

Among francophones, many of the main institutions had already been built under the sponsorship of the founding religious order of Montreal, the Sulpicians, the biggest landowner on the island. No English, Scottish, Irish, or French Canadians could challenge the Sulpicians' supremacy. But one could always do business with them, and many Scots, English, and Irish merchants found it profitable to do so.

Montreal also became a comfortable and entertaining stop on a North American tour. A room at Rasco's, the best five-star hotel in town, was six pounds a week, and Montreal was gaining a reputation for its gaiety, helped, no doubt, by the presence of hundreds of British troops who patronized the bachelors' clubs and taverns. In the 1820s and early 1830s, visitors and immigrants alike found their way to Quebec City from England by sail, usually a trip of more than a month, then by steamer boat (owned by the Molson or Torrance family, or both) for a comfortable twenty-one-hour trip to Montreal.

At the start of the 1830s, the population of Montreal was 27,000, at least half of them of British origin. (By contrast, New York's population was 202,000.) The best opportunity for those looking for fertile land was in Upper Canada or the United States. In Lower Canada the best land, quickly farmed out, was in the seigneuries along the river. These lots were either owned by former French noblemen who had likely never seen their land or had been bought by English or Scots in the early nineteenth century. Whoever owned the land, it was still part of the feudal system that not only limited the opportunities for immigrants but also became a source of political agitation. The only way that French Canadians working on the land could get away from the closed atmosphere was to head to the cities, Montreal or Quebec, or the United States. In Montreal, the French were the majority but had little political power. That power was shared by the church and the English.

The keys to the future were well-built transportation links and communications with the other colonies to the west and east, plus the United States and Britain. During the 1830s in Canada, landmark successes were achieved in both fields. The Victorians' favourite word, "progress," could certainly be applied to the building of the first all-steam boat to cross the Atlantic, which was launched in Quebec City in April 1831. The *Royal William*, backed by money from the by then well-established brewery family, the Molsons, was towed to Montreal where the steam engine was installed. It left Pictou, Nova Scotia, amid much anticipation in June 1833, and seventeen days later landed at Gravesend, England. It revolutionized sea travel with its speed, reliability, and safety. Within two years it had taken many days off the sailing time between London and North America, an achievement that, in turn, improved commerce and added a new level of comfort for passengers plying between Europe and North America.

The steamboats were used initially as tugboats to pull ocean-going sailing boats from Quebec City to Montreal. They also brought passengers back and forth, both on business and pleasure, as well as immigrants. The growth in ocean traffic, both steam and sailing boats, was spectacular. In 1838 sixty-five ocean-going ships came to Montreal; three years later, the number had reached 208.

Not long after the first ship completely powered by steam crossed the Atlantic Ocean for the first time, the first railway in Canada opened between Laprairie, outside Montreal, and Saint-Jean, near the U.S. border, a distance of fifteen miles. The £59,000 needed to build the Champlain and St Lawrence Railroad was raised in Montreal, the first taste by the Montreal financial community of the creative use of money. When Canada's first railway was completed, it was a boon for those travelling to the U.S. border, reducing a gruelling seven-hour journey by stagecoach through mud and dust to an hour in the relative comfort of an enclosed railway carriage. The railway era, somewhat delayed in Canada compared with the United States and Europe, nonetheless was launched with champagne and Madeira toasts.

And in 1837, news hit Canada of a new invention that would prove as important to the world as the steamboat and the railway – the first electric telegraph. The telegraph turned the leisurely world the Victorians knew upside-down. It was a first step in the globalization process and within a decade had led to same-day news transmitted across the ocean, while produce prices and other financial news, originating in London or Chicago, could hit the offices of financial traders in New York or Montreal within seconds.

Few people could visualize in the mid-1830s how steamboats and the Iron Horse and, especially, the telegraph would transform the lives of millions, making travel faster and more comfortable and building the foundations of the information age and globalization. And other changes were under way too. By the mid-1830s, politics was intruding into both Upper and Lower Canada, largely influenced by the liberal reformist ideas that had swept through Europe and by the radicalism of Jacksonian democracy, as it was called, that had permeated the United States. Throughout Europe and North America, there were calls for new political institutions or radical changes in the old ones, like Parliament.

Jackson's ideas and those of the reformers in Europe gave impetus to political underdogs calling for action in Canada. In Lower Canada the agitators pushed for the abolition of the seigneurial system; among some French reformers there was an increasing dislike of the English merchant class; and the reformers also found themselves railing against the church, which refused to back radicals like Louis-Joseph Papineau and his cohorts. So in Canada there was no shortage of reasons to grab a rifle and join the crowd as many Patriotes – the name they had assumed – mustered near

Saint-Denis north and west of Montreal and a year later on the Richelieu River to confront the British army and the local militia. In both cases, they were beaten back and several dozen people were killed; some of the leaders were hanged and many exiled to the United States, Australia, Bermuda, and Europe.

One of the most liberal British politicians of that period, Lord Durham, was sent to Canada in 1839 to inquire into the causes of the uprisings, and he reported later in the same year: "I expected to find a contest between a government and a people. I found two nations warring in the bosom of a single state. I found a struggle, not of principles, but of races." It was a more colourful than accurate description of the state of affairs in Lower Canada but it woke up the British government. Additionally, Durham's prescription for the problem caused more political outrage than the description of it. He recommended that Upper and Lower Canada, as the two colonies had been known since 1791, be joined in a united province and that many of the rights given to the French, like language rights in the legislature, be abolished. But he also recommended responsible government, that is, major power and authority in government should rest with the legislature and the cabinet, not with the governor.

Happily, by 1840, the economy in North America was brightening and that was enough to stop further outbreaks of lawlessness. It was clear that more prosperous times were ahead for those who could see into the future. Lorn MacDougall was one of them.

What would prompt an energetic Scot like Lorn MacDougall to come to Montreal? No doubt the names of Simon McTavish, William McGillivray, and particularly Alexander Mackenzie echoed through the Scottish community in Devon. One of the greatest explorers Britain ever produced, Mackenzie had retired to Scotland in the late nineteenth century. Every Scottish boy and many English ones growing up in the early part of the nineteenth century knew him from his book *Voyages from Montreal*. It was difficult not to be caught up in Mackenzie's enthusiasm.

Lorn MacDougall, aged twenty-nine, was looking for a new life when he arrived in Montreal in 1840. The oldest of an extended family born to a major in the British army, Peter MacDougall, he had found his world back home increasingly suffocating. His father's second family came after Lorn had turned twenty-seven, so his half-brothers and sisters were old enough to be his own children. When the family moved from Scotland to Devon, soon after Lorn was born in 1811, his father remained an army officer but there was little prospect that his stipend could educate and launch all his children. The England they all were born into was crowded; London was harvesting disease and the countryside was pockmarked by industrialization. Charles Dickens was recording everyday life in his newspaper articles in the early 1830s. By the end of decade, he was chronicling more sordid details of life in the streets and factories in books like *Oliver Twist* and *Nicholas Nickleby*. So, after reading Dickens, or even without reading him, there were numerous reasons for leaving Britain – the stratified society, the cramped space, and the lack of opportunity for an ambitious, energetic young man.

Lorn, as the son of an army officer, grew up with horses and the military. This was a life for young men with ambition, energy, and a love of the outdoors, just as the church or teaching or politics or the law was for those who aspired to an intellectual life. The major was not a wealthy man but as a British army officer he had privileges. One of those was the opportunity for his boys to attend military school, like the Royal Military Academy, Woolwich. The following is a contemporary description of what was offered a young "gentleman" at Woolwich:

The Royal Military Academy, an elegant and commodious structure, situate [sic] at the south-east corner of Woolwich Common, affords accommodation to about one hundred and thirty young gentlemen, the sons of military men, and the more respectable classes, who are here instructed in mathematics, land-surveying, with mapping, fortification, engineering, the use of the musket and sword exercise ... This department is under the direction of a lieutenant-general, an instructor, a professor of mathematics, and a professor of fortification; in addition to which there are French, German and drawing masters.[1]

There is no evidence that Lorn attended the Royal Military Academy but the fact that he arrived in Canada able to apply for a commission in one of the old reserve regiments suggests that he had received serious military training somewhere. Whether Lorn was trained in England at school or by the reserve, the main component of his training was with horses. He also came out with more than the usual amount of mathematics training, maybe at a bank in Devon or London.

And he likely arrived with a handful of names and a few doors to knock on. He was aware that the Scots continued to dominate in business after the fur trade waned, seconded by the English, followed by the Americans. As one historian has observed, "*grand commerce*, on the whole, remained in English hands."[2] The economy was based mainly on staples, wheat, wood, ashes,[3] and produce, most of it for export. Industrialization was slow to develop though mini-industries were sprouting around the Lachine Canal, where power was being generated for the first time. The one exception was shipbuilding. In 1841 sixty-four ocean-going craft were built in Quebec shipyards.

Montreal's population was then 40,000. For the first time it surpassed Quebec, whose population was 35,000, and far behind, though it would not be for long, was Toronto, with 14,000. (New York's population in 1840 was 313,000.) But it was the population of the Upper Canada hinterland that was expanding rapidly because of the rich soil and abundant land, plus a land-tenure system based on English law rather than the French feudal system, like Lower Canada's. And the climate in Ontario in general and the Niagara area in particular was more temperate than the climate in and around Montreal. To make the point, potential immigrants were told that Upper Canadians were beginning to grow fruit and produce wine in the Niagara area.

The census figures for 1841 and 1851 illustrate the dimensions of the population boom in the 1840s in Upper Canada. Lower Canada numbered 661,380 (510,000 French Canadians and 160,000 English) in 1840 and grew to 863,860 in 1850. Montreal was about 50 per cent English and Quebec City one-third English. The more spectacular and telling increase came in Upper Canada. It shot up from 465,357 in 1841 to 888,840 in 1850 – in effect, doubling its population in ten years and overtaking Quebec, a position from which it has never looked back. A partial explanation of the modest growth in Lower Canada's population was the exodus of French Canadians. Between 1831 and 1844, some 40,000 French Canadians moved to the United States to find more stable jobs and a better standard of living. They had learned that, even when public-works projects created new jobs in Montreal or Quebec City, there was stiff competition from the Irish and English immigrants.

But the main reason why so many immigrants passed through Quebec City and Montreal on their way to Ontario was the opportunity there to buy and work land. The corridor from Toronto to Windsor was especially enticing because the land was flat and rich and there were development projects like John Galt's Canada Land Company that brought immigrants to the Goderich-Guelph area. Wheat was the crop of the moment and much in demand not only in England but in the United States as well. It was also seen by Montreal's merchants as one key to keeping the city's port busy, a chance for them to use their contacts in Britain to fill their trading books and their wallets. The Montreal merchant class wanted to control the Upper Canadian hinterland's exports of wheat and other produce and its imports of manufactured goods and other necessities from Britain.

Despite its small size, Montreal was recognized in North America and Europe as an energetic and ambitious city. John Jeremiah Bigsby, a medical doctor turned geologist, travelled a great deal across Canada and had ended up in Montreal frequently in the previous two decades. This is how he described the city in 1850: "Montreal is a stirring and opulent town. Its inhabitants have always, as the Americans say, been on the commercial 'stampedo.' They are enterprising and active. Few places are so advanced in all the luxuries and comforts of high civilization as Montreal. Some of the show-shops rival those of London."[4] By 1840, the city's reputation as a centre of commerce on the continent was already one hundred years old. One of the main reasons why Montreal was still considered a significant port and seat of commerce was that "remote as the world of Canada might seem ... its people were still in decisive contact with the far wider worlds of Britain and the United States,"[5] and of no one was this more true than Montrealers. Another obvious advantage was the city's location, especially its access to the sea.

During the early and middle part of the century, Montreal was competing with Quebec City for growth and as a seaport. For most of that time, Quebec was the port where the ships left for Europe while Montreal was the forwarding centre of trade between the Canadian and, to some extent, the American hinterland. Barges in various shapes and sizes hauled produce from the west to Montreal where it was loaded on larger boats and tugged to Quebec City. So the shipping business between Montreal and Quebec City was a lucrative one, dominated for many years by the Molsons, later joined by the Torrances. The forwarders who brokered the cargoes from farther up the St Lawrence and inland, to Montreal and then to Quebec City, also found there was money by plying the middle ground in the shipping business. This is how the MacDougalls solidly established themselves in Montreal.

Montreal was much envied by other British North Americans, so much so that Upper Canada's political leaders and commercial interests had pushed since 1791 for the inclusion of Montreal in their province. Hardly a decade went by in the first half of the nineteenth century without Toronto institutions like the Chamber of Commerce passing a resolution requesting the British authorities to merge Montreal with Upper Canada. During the Confederation debates in 1864, yet another request was heard to detach Montreal from its political moorings in Quebec. The idea was, then as now, politically unpalatable. But the pressure from Upper Canada was the first shot in a rivalry between the two cities that echoes through to the twenty-first century.

Lorn MacDougall's entry into the Montreal business world was well timed for someone starting out in the financial business. Banks began to appear in the 1820s. The Bank of Montreal, the first into the marketplace, the Quebec Bank, the Bank of Canada, and a few others opened their doors as private banks but quickly transformed themselves into publicly traded companies – the first in Canada. But, even by the 1840s, there were not enough banks or other publicly traded companies to justify formal, daily trading much less full-time stockbrokers.

Within days of arriving in 1840, however, Lorn was aware of countless other opportunities to jump into the financial merry-go-round. They were spread through the weekly commercial review published by the Montreal *Gazette* between May and mid-November. The following excerpt is typical of the kind of information on offer every Saturday in 1840:

COMMERCIAL

Ashes – A slight reduction in the rates has been submitted to since our last notice ...

Flour – Some sales of Upper Canada fine have been made at 28s.9d to 29d.3d during the week. U.S. flour continues as when last noticed.

Provisions are in good demand and a considerable quantity has been taken up for the Lower Ports. Pork has brought $18 for mess ...

Groceries – Teas continue in good demand and at a slight advance from former prices ...

Exchange – The Banks now draw on London 9 ½, and on New York at 1 ½ per cent premium. Money, however, is still scarce owing to limited amount of paper discounted.

The date when formal trading of stocks began in Montreal has stirred much debate. But, of course, since commercial life started several millennia ago, trading in timber, furs, corn, silks, porcelain, and horses has always found a home, sometimes in a temple, sometimes in a coffee house, sometimes round the water fountain or near a camel herd in the desert. Western tradition and history seems to identify the coffee house as the place where stocks began to be bought and sold. In medieval Europe, the coffee house became a favoured meeting place to trade. Both in London and in New York, it was where trading began. In Montreal, too, the coffee house is identified with the first formal public stock selling around 1832. It evolved in Montreal much like it did in other commercial centres. A time was set once a week and then once a day, usually lasting thirty minutes, for trading. The time was expanded and then rooms were rented, and eventually larger premises were bought.

It would take another thirty years before there were enough publicly traded companies to justify a stock exchange. In the intervening years, though, Lorn MacDougall became the leader of a second-tier financial business that would soon become an essential cog in the maturing financial system. One of the main reasons for his success was his trustworthiness. At the time, most of the business conducted by general brokers was based on trust. As one writer puts it, "trust was central to the granting of credit ... thus the commercial world was structured ... along international chains of personal connections."[6] Lorn quickly built a reputation as someone who could be trusted and who had a finely tuned sense of probity, all of which positioned him well for the leadership role he assumed in the next forty-five years.

Little is known about where Lorn learned about the brokerage business before coming to Canada – if he did – but there is evidence that his first venture into business in the early 1840s turned out to be a failure. It was after he hooked up with John Glass in 1844, already a long-time resident of Montreal, who became a lifetime friend, that Lorn made contacts in the shipping business and started a successful career chartering boats and winning contracts to ship produce to Britain. Glass had worked for Maritime agents since the early 1840s and gained an expertise in this lucrative area of business.

About a year after he arrived, MacDougall was advertising as a "Produce and Bill Broker" on his own and within eighteen months he had set up business in partnership with Glass, the two describing themselves in newspaper advertisements as "Produce and Bill Brokers." As we shall see, the description covered such a wide range of activity because brokers could do virtually whatever they wanted. There was no oversight of their activities.

But oversight was coming. In the early 1840s, Montreal began to create a new governing system. The city was awarded a new charter in 1840 and Peter McGill became mayor. By-laws were produced in 1842, including a modesty by-law that prohibited citizens from bathing in the rivers adjacent to or opposite the city "so as to be exposed to the views of the inhabitants." More important, in 1841 a Board of Trade was officially launched, with Peter McGill as the first president. It was the successor to the Committee on Trade formed in 1822 by merchants whose main purpose was to lobby to extend old and build new waterways into the interior and south to the United States. It met in the "newsroom," previously the first Wesleyan Chapel at St Ann and McGill streets that had outgrown its congregation. From then until the 1870s, when a formal exchange was launched, the Board of Trade more or less watched over the trading activities of brokers.

The Committee of Trade set commission rates in 1822, and again in 1832, and one of the first acts of the new Board of Trade when it was formed in 1841 was to follow suit. Thereafter, rates were set every ten years. For instance, in 1852 some of the charges were listed this way:

On the sale of Merchandise or Produce Foreign 5 % Inland 2.5%
On sale of Bills of Exchange, stocks, specie on the purchase of same with funds in hand:
Foreign ½ % Inland ⅟20%
On sale or purchase of vessels with funds in hand:
Foreign 2 ½% Inland 1 ¼ %

Lorn MacDougall's name appears among the inaugural members of the Board of Trade, an interest that lasted his lifetime (he sat as a council member in 1850 and became treasurer in 1857). He knew that the Board Trade would be a key decision-making body determining not only how the financial system in Montreal developed but also how the municipal government evolved. It was also where decisions would be made to create more efficient trading in flour and wheat. And he wanted to work inside the system rather than outside it.

In that period – for that matter during most of the nineteenth century – government, politics, and business were inseparable. The prevailing belief was that these three sectors "overlapped in wide areas and it was altogether natural that businessmen and politicians should have many connections ... That the state existed to promote the economic development and the interests of business-men ... was not really in question."[7] Of the many examples of individuals who successfully straddled the worlds of government, business, and politics were Sir Alexander Tilloch Galt, Sir George-Étienne Cartier, Luther Hamilton, and Peter McGill. MacDougall was one of the few business people who had no political ambitions. Yet he made sure he was in constant contact with the politically powerful, and he never hesitated to join them in profitable business deals during the next forty-odd years.

When Lorn and John Glass began business, there were few pub-licly traded stocks. The exceptions were banks like the Montreal Bank (later the Bank of Montreal) and the Quebec Bank; the first obtained its charter in 1817 and the second in the early 1820s. In the 1830s the City Bank and the French-owned Banque du Peuple received their charters. A surprise and warmly greeted entry in 1836 was the Bank of British North America, with a nominal capi-tal of £1,000,000. Though its stocks were not traded in Montreal, it acted liberally with its considerable capital but was conservatively administered. That brought a welcome stability to the economy during the commercial and financial crises, the first of which hit in 1837, especially after currency trading was halted during the most violent phases of the rebellions.

Before the Board of Trade began narrowing the meanings of the terms "broker" and "exchange" or "change," in the 1850s, they could mean almost anything. Anyone could call himself an agent or broker before about 1870. In 1842 a few merchants began meet-ing informally to talk over buying, exchanging, and selling pro-duce or bills of exchange or securities. It appeared to one observer that about half-dozen men composed the "board" and they met together when there was reason. Two of them were Lorn MacDou-gall and John Glass.

A "produce and bill broker," like MacDougall and Glass, was a prominent member of the community and had many different tasks:

He handled bills of exchange, discounts, and business of a like character, for it must be remembered that the banking facilities of that period were crude indeed as compared with the present. The banks, for instance, had regular set discount days, once or twice a week, as they considered necessary. The consequence of all this was that business houses that had unexpected calls on them for large sums were compelled to hand the matter over to the broker, who hustled about among men with ready money at hand, and thus was the temporary difficulty tided over.[8]

Apart from the Board of Trade, there were many other occasions to meet individually, of course. Brokers were a close-knit group in a still small city and, to make a living, they needed to talk a lot and walk a lot to find business opportunities.

By the mid-1840s, the Montreal Directory listed three types of business intermediaries: auction and commission merchants, commission merchants, and commission agents. Matching buyers with sellers was necessary, then as now, but to find a seller or a buyer for everything from a cargo of wheat to a 100 weight of duties or a bank loan, the brokers often needed to knock on the door of every counting house and office in the business quarter. At times, in the dead of winter with snow banks piled high, these "traveling salesmen" strapped on snowshoes to solicit a sale or a buy at a person's home. There were no horse-drawn carriages to transport them then and, of course, no telephone. Although the horse-drawn carriage, acting like a modern-day taxi, turned up within a few years, the telephone made its appearance only forty years later.

In 1847 or early 1848, growing out of discussions at the Board of Trade, a committee of brokers was established, and it published the first "Montreal Brokers Circular" on 5 May 1849. The names of two MacDougalls were prominent in the first circular and on the committee (later known as the Board of Brokers). They were Lorn MacDougall and Hanbury Leigh MacDougall, Lorn's brother, aged twenty-five, who became the secretary. There is no family record of when Leigh followed Lorn to Canada but he likely came with his sister, Alicia Dora, six years his junior, about 1845.

The "Brokers Circular" was needed as much to control what brokers did as to publicize their activities. They met on a weekly basis and the main objective of the group was to produce a list of prices for stocks, bonds, produce, and so on. This list began in May and was in circular form and the members furnished copies to their cli-

ents, some of whom were in the United States or Europe. The way
it operated provided business for the board as well as for its members. The business was described this way: "Each of the brokers
was furnished a certain number of circulars free in consideration of
membership, while a great many more were sold in British centers,
such as London, Liverpool and, and, and also to various papers. The
profits arising from the publication of these price circulars were
distributed among the members or carried to the credit of those
who had upon joining elected to pay their admission fee of 100
Pounds Sterling in this manner." The members called themselves
"General Brokers," a refinement that would be refined further in
the next few decades.

But whatever new names were attached to "brokers," Lorn's
main activity remained trading in flour and grain. Annual shipments of wheat and flour down the St Lawrence increased from 2
million bushels in 1840 to 10 million bushels in 1855. In these circumstances, acting as intermediaries between the millers and the
buyers, in particular chartering boats for grain and flour heading
to London, Liverpool, or Clydeside, offered great rewards. The 1
per cent commission that brokers charged was more or less what
their modern-day equivalents charge for managing an average
portfolio.

Nevertheless, wheat, accounting for most of the trade through
the 1840s and 1850s, presented a substantial challenge to Montreal's commercial interests. In the French regime and the early years
of the British regime, Lower Canada grew the bulk of the wheat
even though the soil wasn't suitable. But, by the beginning of the
nineteenth century, Upper Canada had surpassed Lower Canada
in production of wheat and become the bread basket of Canada
and, to a certain extent, Britain. The economy and wheat were as
dependent on each other as a horse is to hay.

It was a volatile business for producers, their agents, buyers, traders, consumers, and governments. Historians chronicle how often
crop failures through the centuries led to economic ruin and political upheaval and the example often cited is the French Revolution.
Examining the figures on exports of flour and wheat to Britain
from Canada in the 1830s illustrates the point. For various reasons,
including crop failures and the high American tariff, exports of
flour and wheat to the United Kingdom in the 1830s varied between

218,000 quarters in 1831 to 5,000 in 1836 and 145,000 in 1840. This partly explains the cause of the rebellions of 1837–38. But misfortune can lead to opportunity. Since Lorn MacDougall and his then partner John Glass described themselves as "produce" brokers in the early 1840s, they saw clearly where the money could be made.

MacDougall and Glass were probably the first brokers to charter vessels and also become agents for British shipping companies. Their first charter may well have been on 23 June 1843 when they hired the vessel *George Glen* to move 2,000 barrels of flour to Liverpool. A few years later, MacDougall and Glass served as maritime agents to charter the *Mary Brock*, headed to London with 4,000 "minots" of wheat from Collis, Ross and Company, and 2,523 barrels of flour from Buchanan and Company. It was a roaring and profitable business in good crop years and the major business for Montreal brokers in the 1840s and through the 1850s and 1860s. The next step was to make agreements with the shipping companies that were beginning to appear on the scene. That was not long in coming.

Timber trading was also a major money maker, even though much of the traffic went through Quebec City. To make money for shipowners, however, the ships had to be as full coming from England to Canada as they were topped up by timber on the trip from Canada to England. Montreal merchants saw the opportunity and eagerly tried to fill dozens of ships coming from Britain to Canada. From the 1820s, they brought biscuits, tobacco, liquor, and innumerable other high-end products as well as the latest in men's and women's fashions. But the need for Canadian staples in Britain and Europe far exceeded the amount of goods the young colony of Canada could absorb. The result was that many ships sailed to Canada empty, making it more expensive to ship via Montreal. American coastal ports picked up this trade because the United States was expanding exponentially and its need for British machinery and other goods could fill many North American–bound boats. Nevertheless, the spring arrivals in Montreal were much anticipated and they came just in time for the summer selling season in Montreal, Kingston, Toronto, and the hinterland of Upper Canada. Some of the happiest customers at the more fashionable Montreal stores in summer were Americans, especially from the south, travelling north to escape the heat.

Lorn MacDougall and John Glass terminated their formal relationship in 1849 and Lorn then set up a partnership with his brother Leigh as general brokers, under the name of MacDougall Brothers, the first of many times that designation would appear. Such brokers cast their net widely, as one advertisement in the Montreal Directory of 1843–44 illustrates:

> GENERAL SHIPPING and COMMERCIAL AGENT, CUSTOM HOUSE and STOCK BROKER, Montreal – Sells or purchases, as agent, GOODS and PRODUCE of all kinds; keeps a Register of REAL ESTATE and all PUBLIC STOCKS for sale; purchases Stocks for those requiring them; receives and forwards to and from Britain and elsewhere; Merchandise or Goods of any kind; attends to all kinds of Custom House business and Agency of any nature (Charles E. Anderson).

Stocks like those we know today were rare. To quote one commentator: "In those days, anything like an authentic quotation for a stock or bond was unknown in Montreal, the business being of such an irregular nature, it was next to impossible to establish the actual selling value of a security until offered, since it was mainly established by the law of supply and demand at the time of the transaction." The emphasis was on bonds and debentures of government. In 1840 the first of the commercial columns began to appear in the Montreal *Gazette* but stock prices were seldom mentioned. Still, in 1842, this stock list included:

> Eight chartered banks
> 1 insurance company
> 1 gaz company
> 1 railway
> Bonds from the Port of Montreal, the Chambly Canals and roads being built to and from the canals

The oil to keep business moving was currency and the currency situation was barely controlled chaos whether it involved trading ashes or wheat or city bonds. Until the late 1850s, British pounds and U.S. dollars were prime currencies but so was the Mexican and Spanish gold dollar. The need for circulating currency, for purposes of liquidity, explains why banks were promoted so vigorously and created so fast. This need had been met during the War of 1812 when army bills were the prevailing currency. But when the war ended, they were called in, creating a serious shortage of money circulating in the system. The Bank of Montreal and other banks were quick to pick up the slack and print their own currency. While that brought some stability to the currency situation, the multi-currency internal trading system created inefficiencies. Every bank and merchant broker, as a matter of routine, became a foreign currency trader. MacDougall and Glass, no doubt, seized this opportunity, among many others.

Marketing has always been a key to good business. The term was not widely used in the 1840s and 1850s, but Lorn MacDougall understood what it meant and was one of the early traders to advertise, beginning in 1842, when, as we have seen, he described himself as a "Produce and Bill Broker." For several years, Lorn MacDougall and his partner innovated again by providing weekly updates on the markets for the *Gazette*. Again, the prices of publicly traded stocks were published infrequently. The emphasis was rather on the price of wheat, flour, timber, and ashes, as well as freight rates and commission charges. After MacDougall and Glass parted company in 1849, the tradition of "marketing" continued with MacDougall Brothers.

The first part of the 1840s was prosperous. After the rebellions and political upheaval of the late 1830s, the economy bounced back and so did the confidence of the commercial classes. In 1843 there was a strike by workers at the Lachine Canal, with mainly Irish labourers on one side and Scottish contractors on the other. The rancour created a self-conscious and independent wage-labour workforce for the first time and marked a watershed in the history of labour relations in Canada. The same year, the capital of the new United Province of Canada, incorporating the old colonies of Upper and Lower Canada, was shifted from Kingston to Montreal. Two more canals, the Chambly and Cornwall, opened.

The arrival of new immigrants continued apace: in 1842, 44,374 came; in 1843, 27,153; and in 1846, 32,152. That year was one of the most prosperous of the decade. An observer coming to Montreal in

1846 remarked that "the city with its dark stone buildings and iron shutters, gave an impression of ancient grandeur." But the glow didn't last. To the surprise of most Canadians, economic depression blew in with the next strong wind. There was little warning of how many sacred cows would be slaughtered in the next few years, not only by the United States but also and especially by the British government of the day. The moves in Washington and London pummelled the mercantile class in Montreal, especially those involved in the timber and wheat trade. Lorn MacDougall was one of the most prominent of these traders-cum-brokers and his business suffered.

The first piece of bad news came in 1845 when the U.S. Congress passed the first of the Drawback Acts that eliminated the American tariff on Canadian-bound and European-bound goods transshipped through the United States either to Europe or from Europe. Congress was feeling the pinch of competition from the St Lawrence canal system because staples like timber and wheat were bypassing the Erie Canal. If tariff costs to British or Canadian shippers who preferred to transport goods through the United States could be eliminated, these shippers might be encouraged to use the Erie Canal route rather than the Montreal one.

The same year, 1845, the British government began to face up to the rising potato famine in Ireland. Above all, the Irish needed wheat to feed the starving people there ... wheat from anywhere. The imperial preferences up to then – the Corn Laws – favoured Canadian wheat and timber exporters but the British saw free trade as the only way out of the political and humanitarian disaster about to engulf them. It meant dismantling the old mercantile system that had built an empire. These were desperate measures for desperate times.

Suddenly, it seemed, Canadian traders were dumped in a lifeboat to make their way as best they could in the cold North Atlantic. By 1847, depression infected the American economy, spilling quickly into Canada. Britain and Europe were already fighting hard times, the worst being the destitution and human tragedy taking place in Ireland. The British answer to starving Irish was to bundle them in boats – the sick, the dying, the old and young – and point the ships to the St Lawrence River. When they arrived, thousands were already dead in what came to be known as the "coffin boats." They spilled onto Grosse Île, about thirty miles downriver from Quebec, many beyond aid. The rest made their way to Quebec City and Montreal. Clergy and doctors died at Grosse Île trying to minister to the desperate souls.

Montreal mayor John Mills became a victim when he visited the sheds on the Montreal waterfront. So did the Roman Catholic archbishop of Toronto, Michael Power, trying to comfort the dying in their last hours. In Montreal, the newly formed police force tried to keep order. The burning of tar in the streets was ordered to rid the air of infection. In all, more than 90,000 people sailed up the St Lawrence that summer of 1847, more than double the number of the previous record year, 1843. About 20 per cent died before they reached shore or soon after. Some 5,000 of those are buried at Grosse Île; another 15,000 succumbed at Montreal, Kingston, Toronto, or along the river and lakeshore route west.

The great migration of the dead, the half-dead, and the dying was the worst humanitarian tragedy North America had seen until then and its effects – some good, some bad – lasted for years. It left both private charities and public finances in a disastrous state, with so much money needed to provide food, shelter, and clothing. It left Montreal and Quebec filled with homeless. It also left a residue of willing working men who contributed heartily to the economic boom of the next decade and beyond. The only permanent damage seemed to be done to the already tenuous relationship between Britain and Ireland, exacerbated by a group of boisterous Irish nationalists in the United States who badgered British North America off and on for the next twenty years.

All the while, politics in the Union were taking an alarming turn. The new governor general, Lord Elgin, promoted the British policy of encouraging cabinets to take responsibility for their own actions, and a spate of controversial bills came before the Legislative Assembly when it met in early 1849. The most controversial for the Montreal English was the Rebellion Losses Bill, an expenditure of £100,000 to compensate those who said they had suffered material damage during the 1837–38 rebellions. (One of those claiming damages of £12,000 was Dr Wolfred Nelson, one of the rebels, who in the mid-1850s became a mayor of Montreal!)

The bill was scandalous to many because the amount of compensation was more than double the £40,000 paid out in Upper Canada years earlier. In addition, and this was difficult to forgive, most of the money would compensate rebels and come from a government already deeply in debt.

The night in April that Lord Elgin, still in his mid-thirties, spirited, bright, and bilingual, drove from his official residence outside the city to sign the bill, an angry crowd gathered at the parade square, Champs de Mars, carrying torches. Elgin's carriage was pelted with eggs and other missiles, and then the assembly itself was torched. Neither the police nor the military could keep order. Elgin made it home that night but the fallout was just beginning. English Montrealers saw the Rebellion Losses Bill as the first indication that Britain was abandoning responsibility for Canada. And the consequence of Elgin's action was that the radical majority in the two Canadas would no longer be an adjunct to power, but in control. Yet, if there had been public-opinion polls in 1849, they probably would have shown that the real cause of the disaffection was not Elgin's action but the economic depression. In any case, the reaction among the commercial class in Montreal was swift. Its proposal, tinged with a strong dose of desperation, was that Canada should ask for annexation to the United States.

The proposal generated political heat but was largely concentrated in Montreal and largely, though not exclusively, with the English. The culmination of these efforts in the fall was an Annexation Manifesto, signed by 325 people, including a future father of Confederation, Alexander Tilloch Galt, and a future Conservative prime minister, J.J.C. Abbott, as well as apolitical businessmen like D. Lorn MacDougall. Although the manifesto caused much noise, within a few months it was forgotten in a resurgence of economic activity that started in 1850 and that revived the fortunes of Montreal's business class, including MacDougall himself.

TWO

The Making of a Gentleman

In 1849, the accumulated sense of failure was so oppressive that it drove men to repudiate their unavailing loyalties and to destroy the cherished system that had failed them.

Donald Creighton, *The Empire of the St. Lawrence*[1]

The tumultuous year of 1849 shook the confidence of Montreal and its business people at many levels. Whether or not every one of the 57,000 Montrealers knew it, by 1850 the dream of the city becoming the outlet to the Atlantic, and therefore northern Europe, for all of the mid-west of North America, had disappeared down the barges on the Erie Canal. In short, New York was winning out. It had more than 510,000 people, ten times the population of Montreal, and its economic advantages could not be matched by its rival to the north.

The year 1849 marked the end of Montreal as the political capital of British North America. It also demolished the illusion that Britain would ever again give Canadian goods preferential treatment, as well as discrediting once and for all the desperate idea of annexation to the United States. But Montreal was not dead. The dream simply needed reshaping. Indeed, Montreal began the new decade with many positives. Although it would never again be the national or provincial capital, the city continued to be the bustling epicentre of business and commerce in Canada, a status it would retain well into the twentieth century. Its pre-eminent role in the country's political, social, cultural, and sporting life was just as well established.

Happily, 1850 signalled the beginning of a new period of prosperity along with changes in the economic model. Gold had been found in California and it stirred a whole continent to contemplating riches, not only on the west coast of the United States but wherever the precious mineral was found. So startlingly had the morale changed among the commercial men, including the 325 who had signed the Annexation Manifesto and those who had marched with torches to set the Parliament Buildings alight, that by 1851 many of them were greeting and meeting the once hated governor general, Lord Elgin, as if the battles of the previous three years had never happened.

Lord Elgin had little to do with it, but the recovery was both fast and broad-based. In 1848 customs revenues, which were the major source of income for the government, totalled £304,338; by 1851, they had doubled to £708,700 ; and two years later, in 1853, they hit £986,597. The amount of wheat and timber flowing through the St Lawrence system had shown astonishing rises, all the better for the brokers, including the MacDougalls, whose principal business was still in trading staples.

If Montreal had failed to become the centre of continental commerce, the merchants and brokers had succeeded in building up solid connections with London, Glasgow, New York, and Boston, as well as Toronto and Quebec City. The New York and London stock exchanges became models, and as they evolved, especially into self-regulation, so did Montreal. Their contacts – and Lorn was known to have one of the best lists in the city – improved, especially after the telegraph opened with New York and Montreal in 1847.

The role of the broker-merchant class was also evolving. Through the 1830s and 1840s, one merchant might find himself informally buying and selling ashes, timber, grain, currency, bonds, stocks, drygoods, insurance, and much else. That was about to change. By the mid-1840s, there were discussions at the Board of Trade about finding a suitable place to meet "on change." At the meeting in April 1846, it was resolved that "a committee be appointed to ascertain whether a suitable place can be found for the use of merchants who desire meeting daily on change, and to report thereon at the next meeting." First, the Montreal News Room was recommended, then they settled on the Exchange News Room, which was used one half-hour every day, around noon, except Sundays. But, at least for the first few years, it shut down when the port was quiet from November or December through April. In fact, after operating through 1848, there appears to be have been no site chosen for formal meetings through 1849, a recession year, though informal meetings were likely held. Then, in 1850, the board settled on the Merchants News Room.

As the brokers' business evolved, an equally important change was taking place in how business was organized. Partnerships, the main mode of doing business at least from the eighteenth century, started to face competition from the joint stock company. In 1850 the Canadian legislature passed its first law authorizing joint stock companies. Called the Companies Act, it was refined during the 1850s, with the regulations becoming more specific about the duties and responsibilities of stockholders and directors. The major change, of course, was that stockholders no longer bore the full liability but instead had limited liability. And the main result was that the Canadian economy was starting to shift away from a reliance on the staples of timber, wheat, and fish to large scale industrialization. This meant manufacturing, mining, mechanical, and chemical businesses, all needing capital. About $100 million in capital poured into Canada in the 1850s compared with $35 million through the 1840s. Most of it represented railway building but the spin-offs were enormous and enriching.

Until then, the major capital projects, like the canals and roads, were financed by either the British or the Canadian government. The railway era would be financed differently. By 1850, Canada had 66 miles of railway compared with 9,000 in the United States. But, by the late 1840s, one of the largest projects, the St Lawrence and Atlantic Railroad, had been launched, with the goal of providing Montreal with a winter port by building a railway to the border of Maine which connected with one coming from Portland. At the same time, another railway, the Grand Trunk, aimed at linking Montreal with Ottawa and Toronto.

The railway era in Canada was the work of thousands of labourers and many dodgy schemes to raise finance locally because the British and American markets had dried up. With the major merchants and financiers of Montreal, including Alexander Galt and Lorn MacDougall, providing a determined team, the St Lawrence and Atlantic was completed in 1853. MacDougall owned seventy-two shares but the vast majority of the hundreds of shareholders in 1853 held fewer than ten shares. It was a popular cause and many Montrealers found themselves shareholders – perhaps for the first time – including the Anglican bishop of Montreal, Francis Fulford, who owned two shares. It was difficult at any one time to know how many shares were outstanding or what they were worth because of the many refinancing schemes. Meanwhile, looking west rather than east, the important railway connection between Montreal and Toronto was not completed until 1856.

What the railways did for Canada internally the steamships did for the country's trade, particularly with Europe, in everything from wheat to shoes. Montreal's harbour was the hub of this activity, in fact the engine of the city's economy and a spark plug for the Canadian economy as a whole. It was in the 1850s that the steamship began to take over from the sailing ship, at least on transatlantic trips. The Allan brothers were the quickest to sense the importance of the steamship in transporting both people and goods, and while their reputation was slow to grow in Canada, the same was not true in Europe and the United States. The first steamship to sail the Atlantic under the Allan banner, also known as the Montreal Ocean Steamship Company, was the *Canadian*, which left Liverpool on its maiden voyage on 16 September 1854. The cost for the trip was 18 guineas or $80, about $1,000 today. By 1859, Toronto residents could get to Britain even in winter by first taking the Grand Trunk to Montreal and then the St Lawrence and Atlantic to Portland, Maine. An advertisement in a Toronto newspaper on 24 November 1859 read:

Montreal Ocean Shipping Company,
Carrying the
Canadian and United States Mails
Calling at Cork

The Royal Mail

S.S. Hungarian
Capt. Jones
Will sail from Portland, on

Saturday, the 26th November,
Immediately after the arrival of the train of the previous day
From Montreal

Passage from Toronto to Liverpool or Cork:–
First Cabin $78 to $87, according to Accommodation
Steerage $19.

Meals not furnished to passengers until after embarkation.
Toronto, Nov. 18, 1859.

While the first steps towards the industrialization of Canada were taking shape along the Lachine Canal, frenetic activity was under way in other areas. A week-long industrial exhibition displaying Canada's wares was opened in October 1850 at the Bonsecours Market. The estimate was that 20,000 to 30,000 people turned up – If true, about half the population; the week ended with a dinner for 800. The idea of the Industrial Fair was to preview the most innovative products to be shipped to the Grand Industrial Exhibition of 1851 in London, the showcase for the Empire at the height of the Victorian age. Its chief organizer was Prince Albert, the tireless promoter of British inventions and industry. Two hundred boxes were shipped to London as part of Canada's contribution.

On a more sombre note, the first meeting of the Mount Royal Cemetery was held in 1850. Lorn MacDougall was one of the organizers. A new cemetery was needed because the old one was filled with thousands who had succumbed to cholera in the previous five years. The first burial two years later was of the Reverend William Squire, general superintendent of the Wesleyan Methodist missions in eastern Canada, who died of cholera three days after attending to a merchant from Upper Canada who was stricken with cholera in one of the local hotels.

The first four years of the 1850s saw hectic construction activity in and around the city. By 1854, Canada had built 2,000 miles of railway and the first stone was laid for the Victoria Bridge. It was the year of the Reciprocity Treaty with the United States, which ushered in more prosperity and shifted the country's trading ties from an east-west to a north-south axis. All this was leading to a more sophisticated financial system and economy with less and less interference from Britain. And the first fortunes were being made. One of them was made by Peter Redpath, who opened the Redpath Sugar Refinery in 1855. Another was that of Hugh Allan, whose Allan's Steamship Line was operating four steamships from Liverpool, with an average crossing time of twelve days and twenty-three hours, which itself was revolutionary. A third fortune belonged to Alexander W. and John Ogilvie, whose first flour mill opened in 1856. As important as these enterprises were, a milestone of the mid-1850s was the first discovery of oil in Ontario.

After nearly ten years of dithering, commission hearings (at which Lorn MacDougall testified), and international negotiations, Canada adopted its own decimal currency on 1 January 1858. Finally, the pound-shilling-and-pence disappeared in favour of Canada's own dollar, worth 100 cents. The change streamlined the day-to-day operations of business both internally and externally. Business people no longer needed four pockets to keep track of currencies.

The frenetic construction activity partly shielded Montreal from the worst of the 1857 depression that hit Europe and North America. Among other effects, the depression dried up state coffers and raised the unpleasant prospect of governments failing to meet debt payments and other obligations. It forced political and business leaders to think about new political and business relationships. One such leader was Alexander Galt. In 1858 Galt delivered one of the seminal speeches of Canadian history when he outlined a plan for a confederation of the British North American provinces. Here, at last, was a serious basis on which to build a new country in the top half of North America, the ultimate step towards self-determination. That plan took nine years to realize, nudged on by a civil war in the United States and an historic compromise between French and English Canadians that has endured to this day.

Montreal was an exuberant city in the late 1850s, overflowing with new immigrants and celebrating freshly minted successes. One such success was the opening of the Toronto-Montreal railway line by the Grand Trunk in late 1856. Another was the completion of the Victoria Bridge in 1859, an engineering masterpiece. The next year, 1860, this became the excuse for the grandest celebration to that time in Canada, the first royal visit to Canada by the then Prince of Wales, Prince Albert, who officially opened the bridge named after his mother.

Business was booming. Through the 1850s, more than 3,000 persons were pouring into the city a year, so that, by 1861, Montreal counted 90,000 persons, double the size of Toronto. The stunning growth in population was caused mainly by the need for so many people in the metal business. For instance, in 1858, the labour force working on the Victoria Bridge numbered 3,040 men, more than 2,000 of them artisans of all kinds. They were backed up by 6 steamers, 723 barges, and 4 locomotives. It was said at one point in the late 1850s that there were between 10,000 and 15,000 men working on the Grand Trunk line from Toronto and on the Victoria Bridge.

The first train from Toronto to Montreal turned out to be a grand warm-up for the visit of the Prince of Wales four years later. Montreal officials, grandiose and generous as ever, sent out 7,000 invitations to people from across Canada. Many of them from populous rural areas of Ontario decided to travel to Toronto, hoping to catch the train to Montreal. The "Celebration Special" left shortly after dawn on Monday, 27 October 1856 filled to overflowing. As the train inched away from the platform, pulled by two steam engines, hundreds of disappointed invitation holders were left on the east-end siding. For those lucky enough to make it, the ride took a gruelling fifteen hours, and when the ten cars of weary Torontonians steamed into a station in Pointe-Saint-Charles, it was the signal to start the celebrations, even if many of the visitors could not find a bed.

With or without sleep, on Tuesday a long parade, which took fifty-five minutes to pass at any one point, marched through the main streets of the city. Floats and marchers were a varied lot, emphasizing the importance of both public and private institutions and organizations. Naturally, the Montreal firemen showed off their latest equipment, shined up for the occasion; there was a float built by masons, then a profession much in demand; the Montreal India Rubber Company showed off a rubber boot several feet high; and the printers and bookbinders and the Montreal Horticultural Society were among the other professions and groups of one sort or another who displayed their wares. Finally came the Indians of Caughnawaga, resplendent in painted faces and headdresses.

That afternoon, Montrealers and their guests boarded a twenty-seven-car train to ride to the opening of the Montreal Water-works, several miles to the west and south in the city's suburbs. They then attended a military parade and display at the Champ de Mars, mostly made up of British soldiers. But the evening ball at the new Bonsecours Market was the highlight of the two days of festivities. There is no record that Lorn MacDougall was there but he had many friends and lots of business interests in Toronto and it is likely he was a guest because everyone who could afford it and wanted to – some 7,000 to 8,000 people – came to the hall that overlooked the waterfront. As they arrived, they saw the main source of Montreal's wealth, a maze of sailing ship masts and the round funnels of new steamboats docked in Montreal's port.

Such was the crush of people that dancing did not begin until 1 a.m., but the delay didn't discourage the merry-makers, who whirled through the reels and the waltzes well into the early morning. One of them was Mayor John Beverley Robinson of Toronto, who, at some point, lost his gold watch to an expert pickpocket. Montreal's reputation as a party town was firmly established.

When the noise of the celebration faded away, Montrealers turned to watching the first bridge being built across the St Lawrence River. The foundation stone of the Victoria Bridge was laid in 1857 and the inaugural passenger train crossed the one and a half miles of water on 17 December 1859. The project cost $7 million, all paid for by the Grand Trunk Railway. The famous railway engineer Robert Stephenson designed it and London contractors Jackson, Peto, Brassey and Betts built it. It was an engineering feat to be proud of and it was built to last, which it has to this day.

One of those participating in the celebrations and now an established member of the business community was Lorn MacDougall.

He had already spent fifteen years in the city and was a recognized member of the business community, even if the business of trading produce, livestock, and, increasingly, stocks and bonds was little known outside a tight circle.

Beside the hard work, he was lucky enough to be sailing on the wind of change. The mid-1840s to the mid-1850s was a time of startling transformation for Canadian business. The world was getting smaller through communications and transport revolutions. Montreal was connected with New York by telegraph in 1847 and to Europe by undersea cable in 1858. In 1840, the year he arrived in Montreal, annual shipments of flour and wheat down the St Lawrence amounted to two million bushels. By 1855, it had reached ten million bushels.

MacDougall was already well experienced in chartering the ships that kept the wheat flowing across the Atlantic. Being a broker in the shipping business, then as now, can reap hefty rewards. He knew the Allans of the shipping business and the Ogilvies in the flour business well enough for them to become friends as well as business partners, to the profit of both. A significant sign that commission trading was now a fully integrated part of the city's commerce was the daily reporting in Montreal newspapers on prices and quotations of commodities, exchange, and securities.

By the first years of the 1850s, MacDougall had assumed leadership of the brokering industry, whether that was trading wheat or flour or ashes or debentures or stocks. Aided by the Board of Trade, he established regulations for brokers and guided the evolution of the different types of brokers as the decade wore on. Brokers, meanwhile, got their own building in 1855, known as the Montreal Exchange.

MacDougall was one of the leaders in persuading the legislature to adopt the Canadian dollar and its decimal currency in place of the then chaotic system of multi-currencies. There were two assumptions underlying the presentation he and others made to the legislature in 1855 in support of adopting the Canadian dollar. The first was that Canada was coming of age industrially and financially in the 1850s and that, like Britain and the United States, it had thrown off the business methods that had ruled in British North America and other British colonies for more than 100 years.[2] And second, Canada, for good or ill, was becoming a much more North American country, less and less a European one, and more and more engaged financially, industrially, and even socially with the United States.

By the mid-1850s, besides his leadership role in the business community, Lorn MacDougall had also achieved considerable financial success. With a solid financial cushion to support him, he began to stretch his interests in many directions. Financially, he was an early investor in the St Lawrence and Atlantic Railroad, the largest enterprise ever undertaken by the United Province of Canada, even if it would benefit one part of the union more than the other. And in 1856 he founded the Canadian Marine Insurance Company along with Hugh Allan, J.J.C. Abbott, and Louis Renaud, a prominent French Canadian businessman. From the beginning of his active business career, he formed partnerships with individuals and with groups until the joint stock company became common in the 1850s. The earliest partnership was the one with John Glass and his brother, Leigh, in the 1840s and 1850s. Meanwhile, there was a MacDougall Brothers in the late 1840s and early 1850s, which was made up of Lorn and Leigh. In 1858 MacDougall Brothers popped up again, also with Lorn and Leigh.

By the early 1850s, Lorn had moved to Côte Sainte-Catherine, an area on the north side of Mount Royal, and taken over an estate named Outremont with a large house which he rented. One reason why he moved to the outskirts of the city was that he needed land to reorganize the Montreal Hunt Club, which he had helped to found and of which he was the grand master in the 1850s. The hunt was run from Outremont but ranged over the whole surrounding area. Another reason for the move was his plan to resettle much of the MacDougall clan, including his father and his half-brothers and half-sisters, in Montreal. From the 1850s on, Outremont became the family gathering place. Lorn lived at Outremont for two decades, as did Leigh, though intermittently. The head of the clan, Major Peter MacDougall, then aged eighty-one and a widower, arrived in 1855. An avid member of the Montreal Hunt Club, he lived at Outremont until his death in 1861 at the age of eighty-seven. At the time of his arrival in Montreal, the two youngest sons, Hartland St Clair and George Campbell (both known by their middle names), plus at least two daughters, including Geraldine Jane, were also settled there. In 1858, at the age of twenty, Geraldine married Alexander Thomas Paterson at St George's Church in Montreal. Another daughter to come to Canada, Alicia Dora, was married in 1851 to an officer of the British garrison in Montreal. She and her husband were destined to spend most of their lives in England.

St Clair and Campbell made Outremont their home until they were launched on their own careers. St Clair arrived at age fifteen needing education and work. There was plenty of work at Outremont caring for the horses and dogs. Over the rest of his life, he was never far from horses. Though he wasn't prominent in the Hunt, he played polo and belonged to the Polo Club as well as the Jockey Club. Campbell, the last and youngest of the MacDougall brothers, who was three years younger than St Clair and thirty-two years younger than Lorn, was in his early teens when he arrived at Outremont. He took much of his formal education in Montreal, first at high school and later, according to family accounts, McGill University. Also a skilled a horseman, he would later win trophies for riding at New York horse shows.

The Outremont estate was very much in the countryside, at least forty-five-minutes by carriage to Montreal (today it is a twenty-minute drive in good traffic). Living so far from the centre of the social life could put a crimp on the activities of bachelors like Lorn and Leigh. But a social life can develop around horses and it helps when friends live in the neighbourhood. One of those friends was John Boston, who was a lively presence in the city for sixty years, many of them as sheriff. After emigrating from Scotland at the age of sixteen in 1802, he trained in the law. But he became just as well known as a businessman and was a director of many of the major enterprises then operating, like the Bank of Montreal, the St Lawrence and Atlantic Railroad, and the Grand Trunk Railway. In short, he was a good man to know because he knew everyone and possessed both "urbanity" and the "Midas touch," in the words of his biographer in the *Dictionary of National Biography*. For all those reasons, Lorn was obviously happy to have him as a friend and neighbour. But there was another reason too. Boston fathered several daughters and one of them, Harriet Lucy, attracted Lorn, who clearly was one of the most eligible, best-liked, and richest bachelors in Montreal. They married in 1857 when she was a mature twenty-six and he was forty-six.

If Outremont seemed remote, it was also healthier. Montreal was an overcrowded city in the late 1850s, filled with workers building the railroads and the Victoria Bridge. Living conditions in the east and west end of the city along the waterfront were notoriously unhealthy, with open sewers running beside the streets, few indoor toilets, and a climate that guaranteed at least four months of severe cold. The working people lived under the menace of diseases like smallpox, cholera, and typhoid as well as the threat of fire and flood. In July 1852 a fire destroyed 11,000 houses, and in February 1858 many of the homes of people living near the river fell victim to a freak winter flood. Spring floods were not so much freakish as an annual visitor. No wonder those who moved up the economic ladder also moved up the hill to the dry and bountiful lands at the foot of Mount Royal.

The 1850s was a gay time in Montreal and both Lorn and Leigh now had the space and money to devote time to social, sporting, and family matters. The social scene was lively, "including a busy round of balls and assemblies, as might be expected of the largest city in the colonies." Bachelors organized balls, so they could check out the marriage market and, of course, manipulate it to their own ends. Canadian society was not nearly as stratified or social conventions as rigid as they were in Victorian Britain, and this was reflected in relations between the sexes. The abundance of space meant more opportunity for the young to date and talk and get to know each other. And all this social action was much easier in the countryside than in the city, especially when riding was involved. "Rural bachelors were much more free of restraint than the urban male," comments a social historian of the day.[3]

In 1857 Lorn and Leigh signed up with about ninety other notables in the city to incorporate the St James's Club, a men's club modelled on the British ones that so dominated the social, business, and political life of London.[4] One of the early visitors to the club was Sir William Howard Russell, the well-known British war correspondent, who took advantage of a lull in the American Civil War he was covering to come to Montreal in the winter of 1862. According to Edgar Andrew Collard, the editor of the *Gazette* who wrote extensively about eighteenth- and nineteenth-century Montreal, Russell gave this description of the club a few years after it opened: "I need not say that it was with satisfaction I exchanged my railway van for a comfortable room in the house of Mr. Rose at Montreal ... I dined at the club, where we had an agreeable party, enlivened by the fervent conversation of some Southern gentleman of the little colony of refugees which find shelter in Montreal under the British flag."

The 1850s was a remarkable decade in British North America, as it was in Britain. And much progress had been made from the previous century. An author of the Victorian age pointed out that in 1730, for every four children born in London, three failed to reach their fifth birthday. One hundred and twenty years later, medical science and public-health improvements had almost reversed the equation, so that roughly three out of every four children born in London reached their fifth birthday. Montreal kept up with advances in medicine made in London because it had its own hospitals, whether supported by public subscriptions, like the Montreal General, or by the church, like Hôtel Dieu.

Many other advances, all dating to the previous decade, continued to make life far easier and more efficient. For instance, the telegraph brought people who lived across oceans, thousands of miles apart, and cities, hundred of miles apart, closer together, while also speeding up business, especially the financial business. The ocean-going steamer brought reliability and more comfort to travel between Europe and North America and rendered the mail more reliable. The railway between cities like Toronto, Kingston, Montreal, and Quebec City was a joyful improvement on spine-jarring stagecoaches and chilly sleighs that could take more than thirty-six hours between Toronto and Montreal, although sleighs were faster. One sleigh operator advertised that he could make the Kingston to Montreal journey in two days travelling all night, but the train reduced that travel time to six hours by 1856.

And in North America, the larger cities began experiencing new forms of entertainment not unlike what Britons and Europeans were enjoying. Such diversions as private and public dancing, riding to the hunt, skating, attending the theatre, and participating in a newly formed Art Association were available. There were also

tours by writers and poets like the American humorist Mark Twain
and the English romantic poet Elizabeth Barrett Browning, and
explorers and geographers, many coming to speak to students and
faculty at the still young McGill College.

Of considerable importance to the city in the 1850s was the opening of the new Christ Church Cathedral late in the decade, which
became a compulsory stop for visiting royalty and other notables
because it was a fine example of the revivalist Neo-Gothic style.
Church attendance, while not compulsory, was certainly a social as
well as a religious event on Sundays for Protestants and Catholics
alike. Mark Twain, among others, drew notice to the proliferation
of churches in Montreal. And there were all sorts, Methodist, Pres-
byterian, Baptist, Anglican, and, most especially, Catholic, cater-
ing to both English and French. It was not only a duty for most
people to attend church but part of their education. "A young man
brought up in careful home might have heard, whether written or
read aloud, 1000 sermons," notes a student of Victorian England.[5]
Perhaps this is a slight exaggeration but not much. For Victorian
parents, fixing the moral compass of their children when they were
young and then reinforcing it as they grew older was one of their
main responsibilities.

Montreal was a fashion centre then, as now. Its stores attracted
many customers from the United States (especially during the Civil
War) and Upper Canada because it was a pioneer in introducing
the latest fashions to spruce up dancing parties, salon suppers, and
public receptions, of which there were many, not to forget church
services. "Bloomers" made their entry onto the streets and into
the salons of the city in 1851. Tight at the ankle and billowing on
the sides, Amelia Bloomer's invention was a welcome addition to
the mid-Victorian woman's wardrobe and, likely, to men's view of
women.

Lorn MacDougall and his friends made the most of the 1850s,
a charming and richly rewarding period in Montreal. A century
later, an expert on the Victorian age gave the 1850s high marks:
"Of all the decades in our history, a wise man would choose the
eighteen-fifties to be young in."[6] The MacDougalls took full advantage of the 1850s – in Montreal.

THREE

Making War and Making Money

… We're going to conquer Canada – because
we ain't nothing else to do.

Fenian fighting song

By the time Albert Edward, Prince of Wales, stepped from the ship
Kingston onto Montreal Island on Saturday, 25 August 1860 – a
step that was delayed one day by torrential rain – Montreal had
dressed up as never before and few times since. St James Street
was decorated like a birthday cake, complete with newly installed
gas lights. The centrepiece of the street, then as now, was the fine
nineteenth-century banking hall that was the headquarters of the
Bank of Montreal. With its grand Corinthian columns celebrating Mammon, it stared across Place d'Armes, the oldest square in
the city, at the twin towers of Notre Dame Church which, just as
grandly, celebrates the glory of God.

The church bears the unmistakable imprint of the founders of
the city, the Gentlemen of St Sulpice, the order of secular priests
started by Abbé Jean-Jacques Olier. With godly guidance they
unofficially set the tone, and many of the rules, by which the city
functioned from the 1650s to the 1950s. In 1860 they also owned a
great deal of the land on which the city was built, and on which it
has expanded to the present day.

The prince, only nineteen, was Queen Victoria and Prince
Albert's eldest boy. He was young, impressionable, and full of
energy. It was his first trip away from home, where his German-
born father rarely let him out of his sight. But he took to the job
with enthusiasm. As Stephen Leacock put it in *Montreal: Seaport
and City*: "Albert Edward was prepared to attend everything, open

anything, shut anything, dedicate anything, review soldiers all day and pretty girls all evening, pray and be prayed at, dine for two hours and dance it off in eight."[1] On his Montreal visit, and later in Ottawa, Toronto, and, eventually, Washington, he seemed to do it all and relish it. He was whisked from place to place in the city with few chances to catch his breath or snatch much sleep. The highlight was a dance in the Crystal Palace, a huge, temporary structure built in the fields of what is now Peel and Sainte-Catherine. It was 300 feet in diameter and festooned with 2,000 gas lights illuminating a gallery where 3,000 persons were seated, many of them young ladies on display and ready to dance with the prince if called on. Quite a few of them got their chance because the prince arrived at 10 p.m. and danced until 4.30 a.m. the next morning.[2]

There was a flush of pride from Halifax to Toronto after the visit of the Prince of Wales, along with a sense of real accomplishment and progress, especially in Montreal. But it soon dissipated in the roar of the guns of the defiant, budding Confederate army that bombarded Fort Sumter in the harbour of Charleston, South Carolina, on 12 April 1861. This was the signal of the start of the American Civil War, one of the most horrific wars the world had ever seen. It was a war that would have a profound effect on the United States and the people of British North America.

In fact, Canadian historians agree that no other decade in the nineteenth century had as much impact on Canada as the 1860s. It was a time when the bulging United States was in a state of high anxiety. For its neighbours, the difficulty was dealing with the unpredictability from month to month because the splintering Union's mood shifted from looking inward in fear for its own survival to looking outward at grandiose schemes to expand its borders, the dream of "manifest destiny." Naturally, Canada offered a rich and tempting piece of real estate and the idea of invading Canada surfaced on many occasions in Washington, sometimes more, sometimes less, seriously. And whenever it did, the Canadian body politic shuddered.

The complicating factor was Britain, then the protector of the scattered colonies of British North America. It was perceived by many in the United States to be in sympathy with the eleven breakaway states in the Confederacy and against the forces of the Union.

The leaders in Washington, led by the Republican secretary of state, William Seward, made no distinction between Britain and British North America. And he knew that the most effective way of punishing the former was to tweak the latter.

One result of the frequent threats from Washington was to galvanize both Britain and British North America to action. The effect was that the idea of a union of the British colonies moved from the shadows to the top of the political agenda in both countries. But, before Confederation became a sealed deal in 1867, the people of British North America were shaken several times by the prospect of imminent war. In the early 1860s, Lorn MacDougall, hardly ever idle, began planning to help protect Canada, if the country ever needed it. The plan was centred around the Montreal Hunt.

Even before the Civil War began, Montreal was booming and bursting at the seams. The great public works projects of the 1850s, the opening of the railway link between Toronto and Montreal and the Victoria Bridge, were completed. Trains shunted noisily through the city, heading west to Toronto on the Grand Trunk that had its headquarters in Montreal. Montreal was also the headquarters of the St Lawrence and Atlantic Railroad that rolled east to Sherbrooke, near the U.S. border of Vermont and New Hampshire, then to the winter port of Portland, Maine.

The harbour was the busiest in the colonies and getting busier. The shot of adrenalin was delivered by the railway building of the 1850s, plus the new steam-powered transatlantic service, which together positioned Montreal as the main depot for goods coming to and from the east and west, and even the south through Portland. In six years from 1854 to 1862, the annual tonnage arriving at the port leaped from 64,000 tons to 258,000. By 1863, the port had eight grain elevators capable of discharging 24,000 bushels an hour. It was common by mid-decade to count eighty-six ships a day in the port and by 1869 the stevedores worked round the clock, aided by lights, to keep up with the hectic port activity. The visitor did not see the statistics. What he saw was a huge assemblage of vessels that stretched for miles along the waterfront. The scene hinted at a richness that lay behind the port. "Palatial hotels, horse (street) railways, regular lines of omnibuses, clean, well-watered streets, all proclaimed to the visitor the power and opulence of Montreal," says an historian of the period, Peter Waite.

Sharing that power were people like William Molson and his family, whose fortune came from beer they had made for nearly one hundred years and whose business interests had spread into banking and shipping. And there was the Allan family, led by one of the three brothers, Andrew, later Sir Andrew Allan, whose fame through his shipping line was spreading through Europe and the rest of North America. The Molsons and Allans, like the Redpaths and Ogilvies, took on civic duties at the Board of Trade and in the education and charity fields. The people who managed thriving businesses, rather than owning them, also wielded much power, people like T.B. Anderson of the Bank of Montreal and Thomas Paton of the Bank of British North America.

The Scots were the envy of many and the enemy of some in mid-century Montreal. As a group they were by far the most successful compared with the Irish, the English, and the native French Canadians. And it was largely because, over the centuries, the Scots put so much emphasis on education. It was their superior education that vaulted them to leadership roles in many fields, whether it was finance or politics or business or the military or education itself. Two of the earliest Canadian universities were McGill and Queen's, both products of the Scottish system.

It is impossible to generalize about the relationship between the Scots and French Canadians over the period from the beginning of the fur trade to late in the nineteenth century. There is strong evidence that many of the Scots employed French Canadians as servants as well as Irish and Scots and they spoke mainly French with them. At higher levels in business, Scots were often associated with French Canadians in major ventures like mining for silver or potash and banks.

Indeed, if the money was largely in English and Scottish hands in the 1830s, more and more French Canadians joined the club in the 1840s and 1850s, and beyond. In the 1830s, most of the capital for major works was raised in Britain or by governments. Afterwards, however, the importance of local capital grew, and, while most professionally ambitious French Canadians continued to gravitate to the law, there was a growing number who found their calling in business. Entrepreneurs like Augustin Cantin, the largest steamboat builder in Montreal in the 1840s and 1850s, Joseph Masson, one of the wealthiest merchants in the 1850s, C.S. Cherrier, later to become president of the Banque du Peuple, Louis Renaud, and, by the 1870s, L.-J. Forget, who became a prominent financial man over the course of the nineteenth century, invested in projects started by their English-speaking counterparts, just as the latter invested in francophone enterprises.

The fact that there was so much money to be made in Montreal explains why partnerships between English/Scot and French Canadian businessmen could take form despite the cultural barriers between the two groups. It also explains why so many French Canadians trekked into the city from rural areas between Montreal and Quebec City, and why immigrants crowded into the city from Europe. One non-English, non-French group that witnessed significant growth was the Jews. In 1851 there were 181 Jews in Montreal, an increase from 107 in 1837, and there were nearly 400 by 1858 when a new synagogue was built on de Bullion Street. Names like Cohen in the brokerage community and Joseph and Hart in the business and legal communities popped up frequently, including in the formation of sporting and business clubs.

There were also names from the political world who easily moved back and forth between business and politics, like Alexander Tilloch Galt, who started in business in Sherbrooke in the 1830s and 1840s, then became the MP for Sherbrooke and later the financial genius behind Confederation; the Montreal mayor and future prime minister J.J.C. Abbott; Sir George Étienne Cartier, like Galt a Father of Confederation but also a lawyer and general counsel for the Canadian Pacific Railway; and Luther Hamilton Holton, prominent businessman and Liberal.

The financial business was evolving quickly from its fledgling condition in the 1830s and 1840, when almost anything that could be traded, from wheat to lumber to bills of exchange and currency, came under one broker, to a new level of sophistication defined by a division between those selling commodities and those selling financial instruments. In 1853 a bill was passed to incorporate the Montreal Exchange, and, starting in 1854, Montreal had its own exchange building where these trades took place, overseen by a Board of Brokers which had moved into the Merchant's Exchange Building as the Exchange moved out. Taking a cue from New York, where pressure mounted for more regulation of trading, especially in stocks, Lorn MacDougall, among others, helped establish the Corn Exchange in 1862, trading mostly commodities. The same year, the Board of Brokers became the Board of Stock Brokers. Lorn was elected its first president, and later he became the first chairman of the Montreal Stock Exchange (MSE) when it was formally founded in 1874. It was a sign of how much influence he had in the evolution of the brokerage business during the preceding twenty years.

While not one of the merchant princes, Lorn knew them all and did business with them all, often joining partnerships in manufacturing, mining, and insurance ventures, all very successfully. And slowly, under his influence, the business of trading in financial instruments became more mature and more widely accepted as an integral part of the financial community, as it had become in both London and New York. Although the company books are not available to confirm it, Lorn clearly handled many of the investments of Monteal's leading figures. Obviously, it became an article of faith with the first MacDougalls that playing by the rules and using discretion about revealing the accounts they held, and those they didn't, was paramount.

Lorn, for example, found himself as secretary treasurer of the Lake Huron Silver and Copper Mining Company and in that position reported to the commissioner of crown lands in 1863 that "an amount of not less than three thousand one hundred and seventy pounds has been expended thereon by 'The Lake Huron Silver and Copper Mining Company.'" The late 1850s and 1860s was when mining started to become a driver of the stock exchange. It was in part a serious search for precious metals and other metals used in the burgeoning industrial sector in North America. And part of it was attractive, then as now, to investors who saw it as a casino that one day might lead them to the illusive jackpot. Throughout his career MacDougall was a partner in ventures searching for silver and copper in the Lake Huron district as well as Quebec. He set up the Oxford Mining and Smelting Company in 1863 with

Alexander Galt, among others. Then there was the Kennebec Gold Mining Company in the Beauce area of eastern Quebec bordering on Maine, and the Gaspé Lead Mining Company. All these enterprises were pulled together by investors from Montreal and occasionally from Britain.

Lorn and others also saw opportunities in peat mining through the Canadian Peat Fuel Company and later the Montreal Plumbago Mining Company in counties around Montreal. These companies generally had a capitalization of $30,000, $40,000, and up to $100,000, and typically with initial shares selling for $100 or $200 – not exactly penny stocks. And Lorn saw opportunities, too, in investing in infrastructure in his own city, which, at that time, was almost all privately owned. In 1858 he participated in the formation of the Montreal Mountain Boulevard Company and a few years later, in 1861, the Montreal Railway Terminus Company. The latter was born the same year the street railway began laying track. By 17 August, a contract was signed for six miles of single track, eight passenger cars, a stable, and a shed. The street railway was an instant success, carrying more than 1 million passengers in 1863 and 1½ million in 1864.

Lorn MacDougall's most ambitious and creative investment vehicle of this time was the Montreal Investment Association. It was formed in 1865 with a captialization of $1,000,000, divided into 5,000 shares at $200. Under the act that created it, the association resembled one of the first mutual funds, with extremely broad powers to buy and sell in the marketplace: "The Association may acquire, hold and dispose of public securities, stocks, bonds or debentures of any corporate bodies, the bonds and debentures and any other evidence of debt of Government, municipal debentures, or debentures issued by the Government of Canada in exchange for those of any town, city or municipality of this Province." In addition, it could act as an agency and trust association, which meant that it could hold, invest, and deal in mortgages and buy and sell real estate, although it had to sell any real estate within five years of buying it.

At the height of the boom of the early and mid-1850s, MacDougall Brothers consisted mainly of Lorn, who had turned forty-five in 1856, and his younger brother Leigh, then thirty-three. But partnerships were born and then broken up within months with no bad feelings. The scene resembled nothing so much as musical chairs. In most cases, changes appeared to be motivated for strategic reasons, and sometimes, in the case of the growing MacDougall clan, for family reasons.

In 1856, for instance, Alexander Budden and Leigh MacDougall formed a general brokerage and produce partnership while Lorn announced that he would continue MacDougall Brothers on his own account. He remained on his own (though usually in the office next door to his brother) until Thomas Davidson joined Lorn to form MacDougall & Davidson in 1861. Thomas Davidson was the son of David Davidson, the chief cashier of the Bank of Montreal. The family was as well connected as anyone could be in the financial community because the Bank of Montreal was not only the premier bank in Canada but was operating in New York in the 1860s with remarkable success. By the late 1850s, the average size of Canadian banks was larger than any American bank and the Bank of Montreal was the largest and most powerful player in the New York money market using immense sums. Naturally, the Bank of Montreal dominated the banking scene in Canada as no other bank has done before or since. It was also the best-known Canadian institution outside Canada. (That may be one reason why Jefferson Davis, the president of the Confederacy, felt confident in leaving his personal papers in the vaults of the Bank of Montreal when he was sent to Fort Munroe as a prisoner of the Union after the Civil War.)

In 1861, when the Civil War was less than a year old, the British and Canadian governments awoke with alarm to the possibility of an attack from south of the border. The annexationist talk in official Washington added to the anxiety. But it was the *Trent Affair*, in the winter of 1861, when Southern diplomatic agents were seized aboard the British steamer *Trent*, that brought Britain and the United States uncomfortably close to war.

Montrealers were spooked and immediately took measures to defend themselves, including making earthworks to cover the pillars that held up the Victoria Bridge on the south shore at Saint-

Lambert. Surveys were begun to build entrenchments round the city. British troops were shipped into Montreal and to other points that were vulnerable to U.S. invasion, including Niagara. At the same time, the Canadian government recruited some men for the old militia regiments but the emphasis was on recruiting a new volunteer force, known as the "active militia" and manned mainly by weekend soldiers, whose main purpose was to augment the imperial garrison. The populace obviously took the threat of invasion seriously because volunteer regiments began sprouting in Montreal and Toronto, among other places, sometimes financed by individuals. One of those in Montreal was the Royal Guides, forty in number, which was essentially the Montreal Hunt Club in uniform. They were headed by Captain Lorn MacDougall, an enthusiastic member of the Montreal Hunt for many years. Another volunteer regiment was the 3rd Battalion, Victoria Volunteer Rifles, in which Lorn's half-brother, Hartland St Clair MacDougall, became a lieutenant in the early 1860s. St Clair then obtained, in 1864, a first-class military certificate, a program run by the British army garrison stationed in Montreal. It was a major accomplishment for a lowly, twenty-three-year-old lieutenant, because such certification was usually reserved for field grade officers, majors or lieutenant-colonels. Because of the impression he made in winning the first-class certificate, in 1866 St Clair was promoted to major, then lieutenant-colonel, and was briefly the commanding officer of the regiment.

Yet another of these regiments was the 5th Battalion, Royal Light Infantry (today's Black Watch of Canada), of which George Campbell MacDougall served as an officer from 1866 until 1871. In 1875 the Royal Light Infantry would be reorganized into the 5th Battalion, Royal Fusillers, and St Clair was appointed captain with the rank of major.

After the initial flurry of excitement prompted by the 1861 threats, Canadians got back to business while still keeping a close eye on the tumultuous events south of the border. Complicating relations with the United States at this time was the fact that Montreal and, to a lesser extent, Toronto were safe havens for both Union army deserters and Confederate sympathizers, even though the majority of the population of both cities supported the Union. Matters came to a head in October 1864, when twenty-five Confederate soldiers, dressed as civilians and using Canada as a base, raided three banks in St Albans, Vermont, fifteen miles across the border, and fled back to Canada on stolen horses with a reported $200,000. American authorities captured some of them and the rest were seized in Canada by a posse of detectives and constables. They were immediately clamped in jail in Montreal. But the provocative act was not so much the raid as the action of a Montreal magistrate the following 14 December when he released the prisoners for want of jurisdiction. The reaction was quick and angry in Washington and through the northern states. The new sense of hostility to Britain and Canada was best illustrated by an editorial in the New York *Times* which stated: "We were never in better condition for a war with England." This time Canadians took the words more seriously, realizing that when the Union troops won against the Confederate forces, which by 1865 it was becoming more and more evident they would, there was little to prevent them from making an about-turn and swallowing Canada.

But there was a more immediate threat and that was from the bizarre organization known as the Fenian Brotherhood, an amalgamation of earlier Irish American militant societies in Britain pledged to securing Irish independence from Britain. The Fenian Brotherhood was founded in 1858 in Britain and 1859 in the United States, and was made up of Americans of Irish origin, of which there were many thousands. Its method of operation was to rouse young Irishmen in the northeast of the United States, arm them with rifles, and send them across the border in raiding parties. The noise was so loud in the U.S. border states that the Fenians began attracting the attention of the British and Canadian authorities, as well as the police and military in the United States who regarded them as a nuisance.

Until the mid-1860s, though, the Fenians were an unknown quantity to Canadians and British political and military leaders, even to the Americans. But, when the Union troops were demobilized, thousands of young, restless Irish Americans flooded into the northern states with little to do. Many of them were boys barely out of puberty but ready to raise hell in any way they could, up to and including murder. As for their motives, one of their marching songs probably best summed it up:

We are the Fenian Brotherhood, skilled in the arts of war
And we're going to fight for Ireland, the land that we adore
Many battles we have won, along with the boys in blue
And now, we're going to conquer Canada – because we ain't
     nothing else to do.

"Canadian Fenianism was never really dangerous," says a military historian.[3] But there is no doubt that, at the time, the idea of an uncontrolled mob of armed and highly motivated young men roaming the northern border of the United States, even if they turned out to be a rag-tag and disorganized gang, was frightening in the contemplation. One of the unknown factors that caused much of the anxiety was whether or not the American authorities, either on and near the border, or in Washington, would support the putative invaders. By the late summer of 1865, after a visit to Quebec by Lieutenant-General Ulysses S. Grant, the victor in the Civil War, that question was answered, although not widely broadcast. Grant had quietly assured the British authorities that the United States had no ambitions to conquer Canada. Yet that didn't inoculate the population in Canada from "fever fits of apprehension" that continued to break out.

One of those "fits" came in the spring of 1866 when rumours spread that the Fenians were planning to attack Canada on 17 March, St Patrick's Day, the same day the Americans proposed to terminate the Reciprocity Treaty. It never happened but in early April the Fenians started planning a foray into New Brunswick, specifically, Campobello Island, in a bay on the border between the two countries. When the threat became known, the British quickly sent warships to the scene and the militia in Nova Scotia and New Brunswick mustered. While the activity continued for most of April, the only achievements were "a couple of acts of stealthy incendiarism, and the strengthening of the case for federation in New Brunswick."[4] But the seemingly minor events in New Brunswick sent chills through Canada East and Canada West (the later provinces of Quebec and Ontario) when, on 9 April, a group of Toronto Fenians were arrested in Cornwall, near the Quebec border, on their way to Maine.

That wasn't the end of it. The Campobello raid had repercussions in the Fenian movement, which was momentarily humiliated by the fiasco. They tried to regenerate the enthusiasm of the Brotherhood at a meeting in Buffalo, New York, close by the Canadian border, in late May. This precipitated a call in Canada West for a volunteer force of 30,000 to aid the British troops. ("The cities of Canada in the first days of June, 1866, were in the grip of such excitement as they have seldom known. 'Nothing like it since 1837,' said a dispatch from Montreal ...'"[5]) A mini-battle followed on a small strip of land on the Niagara peninsula on 1–2 June that was bungled by an inexperienced British army officer in Toronto. The major engagement occurred near Ridgeway on the 2nd, when a detachment of volunteers, attempting to join up with the main group of British soldiers, met the raiders and drove them from their first position. As a result of an order from Toronto, the Canadian troops became disorganized and abandoned the field to the Fenians. By the next day, the British regulars and Canadian volunteers had regrouped, but the Fenians were then back on the American side of the river, where they were intercepted by an American gunboat. They were released a few days later. On the Canadian side, nine were killed on the battlefield or died of their wounds, including three University of Toronto students, and about thirty were injured. About the same casualties were suffered by the Fenians.

Meanwhile, farther to the east along the border with New York and Vermont, where the main thrust of the Fenians was expected, a quick raid by a group of Fenians in early June caused about $15,000 worth of damage before about 1,000 of them fled back across the border. On 6 June, across Lake Champlain to the west, there was a serious threat to the town of Huntingdon. But a reinforcement column of volunteers marched to the area quickly and discouraged the raiders. Two days later, though, intelligence reports from the border area of Vermont raised an alarm that precipitated a general mobilization in and around Montreal. The Royal Guides, which in 1863 were given the honorary title of "Governor General's Body Guards," were ordered to the Missisquoi Bay area along with the Rifle Brigade, the 25th King's Own Borderers, the 7th Royal Welsh Fusiliers, and local volunteers. Meanwhile, the Royal Light Infantry was ordered to Hemmingford.

Saturday, 9 June, was an exciting day for Montreal, the day military activity reached a high point. The Royal Guides, with their horses, embarked on a train at Bonaventure station with a unit of the Montreal Cavalry, a spectacle that one historian describes as follows: "As the Royals and the Cavalry moved off, they were enthusiastically cheered on their way by Montreal Mayor Henry Starnes, Montreal Militia Commandant John Doyle, and some 5,000 Montrealers who had crowded Bonaventure Station all day long as carload after carload of troops pulled out of the station."[6] That same day, the first wave of troops to advance on Saint-Armand from Saint-Alexandre were disappointed to find that the Fenians had already decamped. "All day Friday the Fenians had tramped back across the border, furious that the American officers had arrested most of their leaders and seized their arms and ammunition. Their only comfort was the booty they had lashed to their backs or conveyed on plundered horses."[7] When the Royal Guides appeared, finding Saint-Armand clear, they moved on with the combined regular-volunteer force to Pigeon's Hill. There they found what has been described as "perhaps a couple of hundred [Fenians] all told, racing for the border."[8] The Guides, well trained from their weekly outings with the Montreal Hunt, took flight after the fleeing men, easily jumping over the rough barricades set up by the Fenians. Despite the best efforts of the Royal Guides, who raced to the border to cut off the retreat, most of the Fenians escaped back over the border and were quickly arrested by waiting American officers. Still, some sixteen prisoners were rounded up by the Royal Guides. The other regiments moved to secure Pigeon's Hill and the surrounding area but saw no action because the Fenians had retreated so quickly.

Captain Lorn MacDougall of the Royal Guides had led the charge after ordering the troops to draw their sabres. One of the troopers later described the action: "As we neared them our Captain ordered a charge telling us to use only the flat of our swords and in a minute or two we were among them slashing right and left. I saw fellows tumbling head over heels as they were struck. Quite a number of the Fenians emptied their guns, and I heard the zip, zip of bullets about my head. In the running fight we reached the boundary line. There a company of U.S. regulars was stationed and as fast as a Fenian tumbled over the line he was seized and disarmed."[9]

The Royal Guides were the only troops to come in contact with the Fenians on the eastern front in 1866. When they returned to Montreal with their sixteen prisoners, it was a day for great celebrations not only in Montreal but also in Toronto and other places through Canada West and Canada East. And, in a review of the combined military force at Champ de Mars in Montreal on 23 June, the Guides and their commander, Captain MacDougall, were accorded the place of honour, even ahead of the regular imperial troops.

The Royal Guides' action at Pigeon's Hill, short and small though it was, boosted the morale of the colonies. It signalled to people from Halifax to Niagara that they could defend themselves and inculcated a new sense of pride and self-confidence. The British, too, were impressed and very relieved as well because the successful repulse of the Fenians gave them the excuse they needed to pull out their troops. Four years later, most of the British troops were gone, leaving Canada to its own military resources.

Although the military action against the Fenians did not wipe out the threat, Canadians had learned that the band of brothers was ineffective and toothless when it came to invading. Not for the first time, their actions did not live up to their words. The other lesson from these cross-border skirmishes was that the Americans regarded the Fenians as a nuisance and were determined to shut down their operations and tame their more exuberant leaders. In a broader context, the threat of annexation and invasion from south of the border was clearly receding. And that was the most welcome relief of all. It meant that Canadians, and especially Montrealers and Torontonians, could get back to their main occupation, which was to grow the economy, whether it was in the factories, in the banking halls, fields, and forests, or on the rivers. Then, as now, public mood has much to do with economic growth and the mood of the British colonies in 1866 was more upbeat than it had been since 1861.

The events of the 1860s – the Civil War, the Fenian raids, the surly mood of the United States that led to the revocation of the Reciprocity Treaty of 1854 in 1866 – spurred Canadian political leaders and their overseers in London to negotiate a plan for a union of the British North American colonies. Although the idea was floating on the periphery of politics during the 1850s, the serious negotiations began in 1864 and ended when the British Parliament passed the British North America Act in March 1867. Confederation came into effect on 1 July of the same year.

After Confederation, new priorities were urgently needed. The most urgent was securing the "north-west," that is, the land from Manitoba through to the Rockies over which the Hudson's Bay Company had held suzerainty for a century, to say nothing of British Columbia where mighty rivers flowed that had gold in them. What was at stake was no less than the filling out of a country before the expansionist Americans marched in. This would require the building of rail ties, starting with central Canada and the Maritimes but then extending across the west. These were to be critical years.

By the late 1860s, the two younger MacDougall brothers were either in the financial business or were training for it. Campbell began his career at the Bank of Montreal, the centre of action in the city's – and country's – financial life. His progress helped by Lorn and Leigh's contacts in every corner of the bank, he took up a position with the Bank of Montreal in New York in the 1860s and capped his banking experience in that city with work at a brokerage firm before returning to Canada about 1866. St Clair, after taking his turn in the military during the Fenian scare, went into business on his own. His first advertisement as a broker appeared in 1865, with the address 19 Saint-Sacrament; Lorn was right beside him, at 18 Saint-Sacrament. From the beginnings of Campbell's and St Clair's careers, Lorn was a major influence on them, as was Leigh. Both older brothers were generous with their knowledge and support.

For ambitious young men with an eye on a financial career, there were many places to train at the time, including the banks – especially the Bank of Montreal, the behemoth of the period – and the brokerage houses. But Campbell and St Clair didn't need to go far from the family businesses. It so happened that Lorn and Leigh were set up in two different partnerships for much of the 1860s that complemented each other rather than competed. St Clair and

Campbell skipped between the two, picking up what they could as they went.

From 1861 through to 1867, Lorn ran the firm of MacDougall & Davidson, who listed themselves as "stock and bill brokers" and were members of the Board of Stock Brokers, of which Lorn was the chairman. Leigh was a partner in the firm of MacDougall & Budden, who styled themselves "produce brokers" and were members of the Corn Exchange. By the mid-1860s, Lorn MacDougall had added a new business. His company was the agent for the North British and Mercantile Insurance Company. The two family companies covered a wide range of businesses, and the more the better while the younger brothers were learning.

These were years of growth and expansion, as much for the financial sector as for the manufacturing one. By 1867, there were 33 chartered banks with about 123 branches in Canada. Their assets accounted for 78 per cent of the assets of financial institutions in Canada while 28 building societies accounted for 9 per cent of the assets. So the banks had become a solid cornerstone of the economy. They were formed and run under the Scottish tradition that tended to be much more conservative than the brasher American tradition with loose controls. That is why Canadian banks were better able to survive through economic downturns than American ones. As for the brokerage business, it was breaking down into more traditional trades as we know them – those who deal in commodities and produce and those who deal in stocks, bonds, and so on.

For this world of finance, London was an important connecting point. Despite their ties to New York, Canadian financial people were keen to establish a presence at the centre of the Empire, whether to watch over the trading of Canadian stocks on the London Exchange, make contacts in the insurance business, or simply pick up on the ever-changing shifts in mood and trends in the financial district. Another good reason to be established in London was that, by 1870, the Bank of Montreal had set up a substantial branch office there. Its success was ensured by what had happened in the mid-1860s.

In anticipation of Confederation in 1867, London was where the increasingly pressed Canadian government was borrowing most of its money. If it wasn't London banks which were financing the provincial government, it was the Bank of Montreal. Toronto banks were struggling. In 1863 the Toronto-based Bank of Upper Canada, until then the government's agent, signalled that it could not meet a loan payment. Luther Holton had been recently made the government's chief financial minister after Alexander Galt left office in 1862. Holton, with solid connections in London, knew how desperate the situation was at the Bank of Upper Canada. He also knew that the most financially stable and the shrewdest bankers in the province of Canada were in his own city. He began negotiating with the Bank of Montreal.

The result shocked and angered Toronto business circles, but it was no surprise to others in government and business. According to the agreement with the government, the Bank of Montreal became the "the Fiscal Agents of the Province of Canada, and ... the Provincial Account should be transferred from the Bank of Upper Canada on the 1st of January next (1864)." This was a bold move by E.H. King, the general manager of the bank. He was betting heavily that the Confederation dream would become a reality. When Galt returned to the finance minister's job in 1864, the chances of Confederation's success rose sharply. But more bad news came in October 1867, a few months after Confederation, when the Commercial Bank of the Midland District of Ontario failed. Galt's resignation as finance minister came soon after.[10]

In the end, King was right that Confederation would prove a political and financial success. Except for the bank failures, it led to boom economic times between 1867 and 1873. Legislation was proposed and passed rapidly, creating confidence and encouraging expansion that became profitable for bankers as much as for brokers, manufacturers, and shippers.

By mid-1869 Canada was witnessing an era of unprecedented progress and expansion. No one was in a better position to experience this progress than the MacDougalls of Montreal.

FOUR

Growth and Depression

Rouse ye Sleepers, time for dreaming /
When our daily journey's done.
Snowshoeing song

As Confederation slowly began to consolidate, the economy grew commensurately. The Atlantic provinces, including Prince Edward Island, which joined Confederation in 1873, turned into sizeable markets for Ontario and Quebec goods, as did Manitoba, which joined in 1870, and British Columbia, which joined in 1871, though trade with those new provinces took longer to develop. Key to this growth was the financial sector. Total assets of the financial sector in 1870 represented 31 per cent of the gross domestic product (GDP). (For comparison purposes, by 1910 those assets accounted for 80 per cent of the GDP.) In the same year, 73 per cent of the assets of all financial institutions in Canada were controlled by the more than thirty active banks. They had more than 120 branches and a paid-up capital of $33.4 million. Their shares provided credit for business people and, besides being a savings vehicle, created wealth for those who invested in the more solid ones like the Bank of Montreal and the Bank of British North America. The MacDougalls were heavy investors in the banks on their own account and their clients, and profited handsomely over the next decades.

The banks were not totally trustworthy in the eyes of many Canadians. There had been three insolvencies between 1859 and 1862, one in 1865 and two in 1866. In addition, in 1863 two bank charters had been withdrawn, and, two years later, eight charters that had been granted were not used. Yet, despite these confidence-crushing events, the Canadian banking system set up branches that offered a more solid and more reliable road to growth than the more free-wheeling American system that offered a bank in every hamlet.

Throughout the nineteenth century, Montreal was the banking centre of the country and, for most of that time, the Bank of Montreal was the largest bank with the most heft in government and business circles. It was also reaping the highest profits. The annual meeting of 1872 illustrated how profitable it was. The sum available for distribution, after profits and additions from premiums on new stock, amounted to $2,238,996. From that came bonuses and dividends of 16 per cent for happy shareholders.

For Lorn MacDougall, stocks were of more interest than commodities – even though he was never far from the commodities game because his brother was in it – and his aim was to create a stock market in Montreal on the model of New York and London. Since Montreal already had a building known as the Montreal Exchange, the transition would be relatively simple. In fact, even though business was slow, the Board of Stock Brokers, with Lorn MacDougall as president, held regular daily meetings through the 1850s, 1860s, and early 1870s. In 1874 it was formally transformed, by a provincial act of incorporation, into the Montreal Stock Exchange. The names on the provincial charter were few and familiar. D. Lorn MacDougall was the exchange's chairman, a position he would hold until the end of his life, and its other members were Charles Geddes, one Colonel Frost, J.W. Taylor, George W. Simpson, T.M. Taylor, and St Clair MacDougall. A seat cost $1,000 in 1874 and jumped to $2,900 in 1877 and $5,750 in 1883.

During the slow years of the 1860s, Lorn MacDougall had tried some incentive marketing to bring in business to the Board of Stock Brokers. For instance, the fee charged for listing a company was used to buy champagne for the members, and any dispute between members was settled with a fine that also was used to buy a case of champagne. There is no word whether champagne was a successful marketing tool but one commentator has said that, bubbly or not, something was working: "In 1870, the volume of shares in the Bank of Montreal was about five times greater than in 1860. Five brokers had a significant volume of trades in 1870: Ford and Tait, Burnett and Thomson, MacDougall and Davidson, Robert Moat, and Prentice and MacDougall ... some of the same brokers also began to participate actively in new stock issues. The Consumers' Gas Company initial public offering in 1873 listed as its brokers: MacDougall and Davidson, Dunn Davies & Co. and F.L. Hart."[1]

In Toronto, the process of creating an incorporated stock exchange took longer than it did in Montreal. One reason for this was that Toronto, perhaps because it was closer to the frontier and less under the influence of the relatively conservative Scots who dominated the financial community in Montreal, had a more free-wheeling spirit. But there was also no doubt that Toronto was closer to New York geographically and spiritually. The brokers in Toronto preferred regulating themselves when it was to their advantage, and forgetting about any regulations when it wasn't. In any case, it took longer for traders there to agree on a regulatory regime.

No doubt, the lack of regulation and then the bank failures of the mid-1860s set back the creation of the Toronto Stock Exchange (TSE). By 1865, some regulations were put in place but they were largely cosmetic. It was not until 1871 that a reorganization was begun, with daily lists, daily meetings, and a common meeting house. The move was applauded. The *Monetary Times*, a Toronto weekly, commented: "We are glad to learn that stock brokers of Toronto have organized a stock exchange of which the following firms are members: Pellatt & Osler, Campbell & Cassels, Blaikie & Alexander, Philip Brown & Company, H.J. Morse & Co., Forbes and Lownsborough, B. Phipps, Wm Paterson & Company, Hime and Baines, Robert Beatty & Co., Hope & Temple, H. Joseph. Clarke & Fields, Edgar J. Jarvis." The *Times* added, with a touch of boosterism: "The institution is to have daily meetings at 11.30, the proceedings of which will be in most respects similar to those of the stock exchanges of principal cities on the continent. The membership fee is fixed at $250. It cannot be doubted that Toronto has acquired sufficient importance as a stock and share market to justify such an organization, and give good hope of its success." The 1871 improvements led to incorporation under a special act of the Ontario legislature in 1878. Most important, commissions were established that year of ½ per cent on stocks and debentures, and ¼ per cent for transactions of more than $2,000. The exchange had twenty-one members by 1878 while Montreal recorded twenty-six members a few years earlier.

From the beginning and for many years thereafter, Montreal brokers were more active than their Toronto counterparts. Toronto brokers listed fifteen issues in 1857, eighteen in 1865, and thirty-four in 1872. In comparison, Montreal announced eighteen issues in 1857 and sixty-three by 1874, the year the Montreal Stock Exchange was incorporated. Of those sixty-three issues in 1874, twenty-one were by banks; nine were government and municipal bonds and debenture issues; and the remainder were divided among railroads (four), mining (three), shipping (three), gas (one), and assorted industrial (ten).

By the 1870s, Montreal and Toronto had been linked to New York by telegraph for some years, which helped both exchanges because Canadian stocks were sold widely in New York. Of course, Montreal and Toronto could not match New York and London where, by the late 1860s, those exchanges were trading $3 billion and $10 billion annually.

As important as business was, it was never all-consuming for the MacDougalls. Sports of every variety attracted them, from hunting to skating, snowshoeing, racquets, and golf.

Lorn's interest in skating dated to 1862 when he acted as one of the promoters of the Montreal Skating Rink. Snowshoeing was even more of a passion for the MacDougalls. Beginning in the 1840s with a small group of English Montrealers, it expanded through the 1850s and 1860s until it became the most popular winter sport in the city. By the 1870s, dozens of clubs had formed and their membership had branched out from the English and professional classes to the French and working classes. Almost any day, and certainly most nights, snowshoe club members could be seen walking the streets of the city before they mustered and headed off on treks over the mountain. They were easily recognizable by their distinctive uniforms, made up of a knitted toque, a blanket-like coat that was tied with a flowing sash, leggings, and moccasins on which they strapped the snowshoes. The songs they sang when they gathered at their club houses after the long "jog" recalled the old days of the French regime, when winters were harsh but the men were hardy, and of those later times when Indians accompanied the fur traders on their winter expeditions to the North-West. One such song went:

Rouse ye Sleepers, time for dreaming
When our daily journey's done.
Bind the snow shoes,
Fast with thongs too,
See that all is right and sure.
All is bliss to, naught's amiss to
A brave North Western voyageur, oh ...

CHORUS

Tramp, tramp on snow shoes tramping,
All the day we marching go,
Til at night by fire's encamping,
We find couches in the snow.
On, on let men find pleasure
In the city dark and drear.
Life is freedom, life's a treasure,
As we all enjoy it here ...[2]

Campbell MacDougall, who spent the greater part of his youth in Canada, became an accomplished snowshoer. The challenge of climbing the seven hundred feet up Mount Royal on four-pound snowshoes, or competing for trophies in hurdle races of two miles, or conquering a marathon run of twelve miles around the mountain, tested both his athletic ability and his endurance. He won at least one of the major snowshoe races in the city in the 1870s.

Snowshoeing and skating drew people from all corners of the city, as well as attracting the attention of governors general, visiting royalty, and other notables from Europe and the United States. Their appeal was enduring. In a guidebook written for tourists and sportsmen in the early 1890s, one of the country's best-known English poets of the time, Charles G.D. Roberts, told how skating and snowshoeing continued to get top billing in Montreal's sporting scene, especially during the famous carnivals that took place in the 1880s: "Perhaps the best skaters and snowshoers in the world are the sons and daughters of Montreal. Her Winter Carnivals, with their ice castles stormed by torchlight. Their gay skating tournaments and masquerades, their unrivaled snow-shoe parades, have become world-famous. The climax of the Carnival is the assault upon the ice-castle, which, illuminated within by electric light, flames with white and ghostly radiance, recalling the dream palaces of Kublai Khan."[3]

Then there was racquets. The main instigators of this sport were the British military, who brought the game from England to satisfy their hankering after summer recreation in Montreal. The officers of the various regiments made up the backbone of the membership but from the earliest days it was never exclusively a game for the military or the English. From the early 1840s, Leigh and Lorn took up rackets at various makeshift courts built in the commercial part of the city. One of the first courts, built about 1836, was described as an uncovered wooden structure, 84x80 feet, located at St Peter and Craig streets and counting among its first members Sir Louis Hippolyte La Fontaine and E.-E. Lamontagne. Leigh MacDougall is listed as one of the top players in the 1850s, as was his brother-in-law, Captain (later General) Thomas Gallwey of the Royal Engineers. And, from the 1850s until his death in the mid-1880s, Lorn MacDougall was also a member and a keen player.

The MacDougalls also were involved in one of the historic chapters of sport in Montreal, this one involving golf. On 4 November 1873 a group of eight men met in the office of Sidey Brothers at 301 Common Street, near the Montreal docks. The group included stockbrokers Arthur M. Cohen, Frank Bond, and St Clair MacDougall. They agreed that day to form the Montreal Golf Club and the first day of play was set for 7 November on what it is now known as Fletcher's Field. They negotiated a rent from the city of Montreal of $100 a year.

Unknowingly, and in a somewhat makeshift fashion, the sixteen charter members had established the first golf course in North America, under rules established at St Andrew's in Scotland. But it did not resemble the grounds at St Andrew's because, on days set aside for members' play, Saturdays and Wednesdays beginning at one o'clock, the course did not belong exclusively to them. In fact, the red-coated gentlemen players shared the nine holes on the mountainside with the public out for walks and picnics. The first golf balls were not a danger to the passersby. They were made of goose feathers and were stitched into painted leather sacks. Slowly, however, early forms of rubber replaced the feathers and, as a consequence, the hickory-handled clubs with simple metal bases, bearing such odd names as "niblick" and "mid-iron," could send the ball soaring. It became necessary for polite players whose shots had gone astray to shout "fore" to forewarn those wandering on the course.

The Montreal Golf Club was not a casual venture. From the start, the entrance fee and the annual subscription was set at $5. The caddies received ten cents for nine holes and twenty cents for eighteen holes. A year after Queen Victoria awarded the "Royal" title to the club in 1884, a terrible smallpox epidemic hit the city and the caddies were required to have certificates of vaccination – still new and still controversial as a form of prevention.

Early on, the members established trophies and the most coveted, the Club Belt, was won in 1880 by J.G. Sidey, in whose office the club had been founded; his winning score of 114 was described by the record keeper as "very good play considering the grass." Years later, in 1896, with the city encroaching on the slopes of the mountain, the club would relocate to Dorval at the west end of the island. But "Dixie," as the Dorval site was known, was also the victim of an expanding city, so in 1959 the club moved farther west to Île Bizard. One of the eighteen-hole layouts at Île Bizard, the Blue Course, is recognized today as one of the finest courses in North America. The Royal Montreal, as the club is known, has hosted the Canadian Open Championship nine times and in 2007 received world recognition when it hosted the President's Cup, the match-play competition between the best golfers of the United States and the best of the rest of the world.

The post-Confederation boom ended in 1873 and a serious depression began in 1876 which lasted until 1879. In fact, from the 1870s to the 1890s, Canada's economic growth sputtered along at a steady but not spectacular rate. Even though growth was slow, one or two

sections of the economy managed to thrive while others were struggling. There was no reason for gloom.

But there was a malaise through the country in the 1870s, and
it continued beyond that decade into the 1880s. Canadians were
nervous watching the explosive expansion of the United States
after the Civil War. As the American frontier pushed towards the
Pacific Ocean, nervousness was replaced by a combination of awe,
envy, and fear about what was happening. There was reason for all
three.

From the late 1860s until the end of the century, thirty million
people passed through the east coast ports of the United States,
one of the largest migrations in history. The flocks of people arriving in the United States, and the industrial and agricultural development that they sparked, produced astonishing numbers. In 1861
the U.S. population was 31.5 million; by 1900, it had hit 75 million.
In 1870, 53,000 miles of railways were built. By 1900, the figure had
quadrupled to 200,000 miles, a figure that represented the total
mileage of railways in all European countries.

Meanwhile, in the same period, Canada's population grew from
3,600,000 million to 5,370.000. The country attracted 1,500,000
immigrants but lost close to 2,000,000 to the gravitational forces
pulling from the United States. Most of those who left were
Canadian-born, including a large number of French Canadians
who moved to work in the fast-growing mills of the northeast.

Starting in the 1870s, Canadian politicians and businessmen
knew what they were facing and the realization dictated what their
priority would be. It was no less than survival and survival meant
building a transcontinental railway that would make possible the
exploration and development of the land between Manitoba and
British Columbia. As a consequence, most of the country's commercial and political energy, as well as financial resources, were
dedicated to building the railway. It would be a major political,
financial, and moral victory when the first passenger train made
the cross-country trip from Montreal to Vancouver in 1886.

The building of the Canadian Pacific Railway (CPR) was done so
quickly it is understandable that it left scars of resentment across
the land, some of which last to this day. One of the most emotional

struggles involved financial control of the syndicate that built the railway. It became an issue early in the planning and remained one to the end. It was, of course, pull-and-push between the financial and political interests in Toronto and Montreal. But the tug-of-war between the two Canadian cities, in fact, had started long before the CPR negotiations began.

The rivalry surfaced as far back as the Constitutional Act of 1791, which replaced the Quebec Act of 1774 and divided what was then known as Quebec into Upper and Lower Canada. The British, who wrote the act, ignored pleas from the leaders of Upper Canada to include Montreal in that province rather than in Lower Canada. Agitation continued until the Union Act of 1840 created one Province of Canada out of Upper and Lower Canada. There was a political contest over where the capital should be located and Montreal lost out after the Parliament Buildings in Montreal were burned by Tory mobs in 1850. The political stalemates created by the Union Act in the 1850s and 1860s led to Confederation in 1867, when Upper Canada and Lower Canada were recreated as Ontario and Quebec.

There is little doubt that the urban rivalry between the two cities from 1840s to the twenty-first century has been a significant factor in both the economic and political development of Canada. And the main emphasis in this rivalry for the last 170 years has been on financial matters, including the role of the federal government.

We have seen how riled the business community of Upper Canada became over the transfer of the government account from the Bank of Upper Canada to the Bank of Montreal in 1864 and the subsequent failure of the Bank of Upper Canada and the Commercial Bank. When a few years later the Bank of Montreal refused to accept the notes of the Royal Canadian Bank, the Toronto *Globe* thundered: "A more diabolical act of treachery than this, is impossible for the mind to conceive." The Hamilton *Times* was equally upset: "We fear the Bank of Montreal has the government in its power and is disposed to play the tyrant."

Those comments reflect the tone of the debate between the two business communities for decades. And the fact that Toronto was to lose the next round was even more galling. This was the contest over who would control the building and financing of the transcontinental railway. The group Prime Minister Sir John A. Macdonald initially formed in 1873 to build the railway involved both Toronto and Montreal businessmen. But it collapsed when the Pacific Scandal led to the defeat of the Macdonald government in the election of 1873. The consortium headed by George Stephen that finally secured the charter in 1881 was closely identified with Montreal and represented three of the most powerful institutions in the country, the Bank of Montreal, the Hudson's Bay Company, and the federal government.

Outside the financial field, Toronto and Montreal competed for the hinterland of Ontario. In the 1860s, Montreal still saw the Ontario hinterland as ripe for exploitation and struck hard with a new weapon, the travelling salesman. In the 1870s, Toronto struck back with its own salesmen who spread through rural Quebec and by the 1880s into the Maritimes.

Montrealers were worried by the successes of the businessmen from Ontario. The competition was, like most economic wars, about jobs and investment in industries from clothing manufacturing to shoes to railway engines and even nails. In 1871 Montreal, with its population of 115,000, enjoyed a sizeable advantage over Toronto, with only 56,000, even though Ontario had a larger population than Quebec. And Toronto was forced to compete for investment and jobs with cities scattered through the province like Hamilton and Kingston. But, with or without competition, the two cities were separated by distinctive attitudes resulting from geography and the backgrounds of the two peoples. Outsiders saw the differences clearly. "The wild and rabid Toryism of Toronto was appalling," was the acid comment of Charles Dickens, who toured Canada in 1842.[4]

Toronto was much more closely aligned with New York because at least half the population looked to New York as its spiritual and business centre. But making New York its principal focus for business was a dream. New York was going its own way and was far ahead in terms of resources and much more sophisticated in its financial and business dealings. Yet, even with the rivalry between Toronto and Montreal, the capital structures of the two cities became and remain close, while the peoples and attitudes of the two cities were as different then as they are now.

By 1881, Montreal's population had reached 155,000, with the French enjoying a majority of about 60 per cent. Toronto's population was then 86,000, of which 80,000 were English, Scots, or Irish. The result was a much more homogeneous population than Montreal's. It was a tight, English-speaking community with close ties through family and sentiment to Great Britain. "Not only was the area British, it was also Protestant. On both counts the city was hostile to French Canada and to a lesser extent Roman Catholics in general," says one historian.[5] In other words, there were many reasons for Torontonians to resent Montreal and Montrealers.

Through the 1870s, the MacDougall name was prominent in financial circles in both Montreal and Toronto, though the nature of Lorn MacDougall's business was changing. These ads appeared in December 1873 in Toronto's *Monetary Times:*

MacDougall Brothers
Stock Brokers
Member of the Stock Exchange
Buy & Sell Stocks and Bonds in Canada
The United States and London
St. Francois Xavier Street
Montreal

MacDougall & Davidson
Brokers
North British and Mercantile Insurance Bldg.
Montreal
Members of the Stock Exchange
Correspondents: Bank of Montreal, London,
Messrs. Morton Rose & Co., London,
The Bank of Scotland in Edinburgh, Glasgow
and Dundee: Messrs. Gammon & Co., New York

The MacDougall Brothers mentioned in the first ad above was not the earlier firm consisting of Lorn and Leigh but a new company formed by the two youngest MacDougalls. After working on his own in the early 1860s and later creating a firm called MacDougall & Prentice, St Clair joined with Campbell to create a new MacDougall Brothers, which installed itself at 68 Saint-François Xavier, just a few strides from MacDougall & Davidson at 72 Saint-François Xavier. MacDougall Brothers, as they advertised, sold stocks and bonds with and through New York and London as well as Montreal and Toronto. The contacts both brothers acquired, especially the people Campbell met through the Bank of Montreal, gave them an advantage when the Montreal Stock Exchange opened that year. St Clair, as we have seen, was a charter member of the MSE.

By the early 1870s, Leigh was dividing his time between England and Canada, working in the office of one brother or another while in Canada, and probably working on behalf of both of them while in London.[6] As for Lorn, he had now spent more than thirty years in the financial business. In his mid-sixties, with his brothers dealing mainly in stocks and bonds, he continued along the diversification track he had set out on a decade earlier, with the decision of MacDougall & Davidson to become agents for the North British and Mercantile Insurance Company. In 1875 MacDougall and Davidson also became agents for the Scottish American Investment Company.

And diversification did not end there. In 1872 Alexander Galt led a group of prominent Montrealers, including Lorn MacDougall, John Molson, James Rose, and Edward Rawlings, in forming the Accident Insurance Company of Canada. Lorn became a director of the company, and Edward Rawlings was made manager and secretary. The MacDougalls' interest in the company was not short-lived. In 1890 MacDougall Brothers held ten shares of Accident Insurance.

Also in 1872, the same group that was behind Accident Insurance, with the addition of John L. Blaikie, William Gooderham, and A.R. McMaster of Toronto, Donald McInnes of Hamilton, and James G. Ross of Quebec City, started the Guarantee Company, with which the MacDougalls would be associated until well into the twentieth century. Lorn MacDougall was one of the directors, and Edward Rawlings was the manager. The announcement of the company's formation stated: "The business of this company is solely that of granting *bonds of suretyship* for faithful discharge of the duties of

Employes in all positions of trust. In this it takes the place of private suretyships." The Guarantee grew out of several other failed attempts at replacing personal fidelity bonds, which, because they could be obtained only from friends and relatives, were an awkward, costly, and inefficient way of bonding those who required it for their job, mainly employees who handled large amounts of money. Guarantee was the first company in North America to offer fidelity bonds and it was successful from the start. It began operations out of an office at 237 St James Street, with authorized capital of $100,000 (of which $15,525 was paid in). In the first year, it issued 559 policies and reported a surplus of $5,539. Almost twenty years later, in 1890, a shareholders list showed that St Clair, who was long closely associated with Guarantee, held thirty-six shares of the company for his own account, while MacDougall Brothers held another sixty shares for its account and 792 shares under the category of "special." One can only speculate whose shares were in the "special" account, but it may be that MacDougall Brothers was holding the larger amount for Lorn's estate.[7]

All these interests, along with the "correspondent" or agent function that MacDougall & Davidson assumed for the Bank of Montreal, London, and private bankers in New York and London, make it clear that their business was flourishing. Lorn had reached the status of financial sage and he was not only acquiring new agencies but was much sought after for his advice and business acumen. In 1876 he was given the singular honour of being appointed a member of the Canadian commission for the International Centennial Exposition in Philadelphia, which marked the 100th anniversary of the signing of the Declaration of Independence. The exhibition provided the United States a chance to show the rest of the world its industrial achievements. According to one commentator, up to this point, not only did Europe view America as an "aspiring country," but U.S. citizens themselves felt inferior. After the fair, many experts revised their opinions, vowing that that American industry was overtaking the British, even going so far as to say that the British had more money but the Americans had more brains.

Now that he was approaching seventy, Lorn MacDougall moved back into Montreal in the late 1870s to what was described as a "sumptuous $10,000" (about $220,000 in today's money) house on

Sherbrooke Street. The MacDougalls were doing well, but parts of the Canadian economy were being hard hit. Exports hit a low level of $72 million in 1879, fully 20 per cent down from 1873. Exports of lumber products fell by 50 per cent between 1873 and 1879. Beginning in 1875, commercial failures began to rise noticeably and the paid-up capital of banks fell by more than $6.5 million between 1875 and 1879.

Prominent Montrealers who were directors of banks under stress found themselves in trouble as well, in some cases with the law. The Mechanics Bank suspended payment in May 1879 owing to the refusal of Molson's Bank to extend further accommodation, it was noted in the financial press. Although this was the second time the institution has failed within three years, and liabilities were listed as $294,000, it did not cause as much ruckus as the bankruptcy of the Consolidated Bank. Not only were large sums involved – it was reported that $3,500,000 disappeared from the time the bank opened in 1876 until 1879 but there were prominent names attached to the Consolidated Bank, including Sir Francis Hincks, a one-time minister of finance.[8]

Canadians were becoming much more conscious of the activities of the financial sector of the economy, no doubt the result of wider knowledge of how the banks operated. The stockholders and depositors also began to realize that directors sometimes took on their jobs while closing one eye to what was happening inside the bank – and leaving it all to the chief cashier or general manager – or simply abandoning their role as trustees or watchdogs.

When the depression hit severely in 1879 – including and especially in Britain – the newspapers and magazines targeted the iniquitous stock exchanges, including the relatively new ones at Montreal and Toronto, as a main cause of the financial malaise. The cause was taken up in the Canadian House of Commons by a Montreal MP, Desirée Girouard. In proposing a bill to regulate stockbrokers, he charged that stockbrokers "speculate in stocks for their own profit ... It is also known that the operations of the brokers are secret. Their doors are closed, and no ordinary mortal has any access to their proceedings. The result of these speculations and combinations among brokers has been great depression in hard times and great inflation in times of prosperity."[9]

No doubt, there were shenanigans when some brokers stretched credulity with the difference between their "bid" and "ask" quotations, but, like most transactions in the small financial world Canada had become, you dealt with those you trusted. And the MacDougall brothers had a reputation for being, above all, trustworthy.

Through all these years, the MacDougall clan continued to grow. Lorn and Lucy had started producing children in the late 1850s and 1860s, first Dora in 1859, Florence two years later, Lorn Somerled in 1863, and Ada in 1868. St Clair married Elizabeth Smith in 1868. Their first child, Betsy Geraldine, was born in 1870; in 1896 she would marry Edward Richard D. Applegath, who later entered the financial business, working for MacDougall Brothers. Betsy and Edward's first child, Grace, was born in 1875, followed by their only son, Hartland Leonard St Clair, in 1878. He, too, was trained in the financial business and worked during the First World War at MacDougalls.

Montreal photographer William Notman showed Campbell as a handsome and confident young man in the early and mid-1860s. His social as well as his sporting life were obviously full. By the mid-1870s, he was living on Sherbrooke Street, which was just beginning to open up as a prime residential area.

On the same street was the residence of one of the city's best-known railwaymen, Charles John Brydges, an Englishman who had come to Canada in 1852 out of impatience with the slow promotion system in British railways. He began work as managing director of the Western Rail Road Company of Canada, work that took him everywhere in Upper and Lower Canada as well as the North-West. That and later work as the general manager of the Grand Trunk and the Hudson's Bay Company won him a multitude of contacts, from Prime Minster Sir John A. Macdonald to the men who built the Canadian Pacific – in short, most of the men of action at that time. Brydges was known as a tough administrator, authoritarian but very solicitous of the men working on the railways and in the shops. When he left the Grand Trunk in 1874, he was given a substantial 4,000-guinea golden handshake as well as a $10,000 bond from his Quebec friends, led by the Grand Trunk employees.

Campbell MacDougall was less attracted to Brydges than to his daughter Grace. They were married in Montreal in 1875 in St Martin's Anglican Church. A year later, on 10 March 1876, their first child, Hartland Brydges MacDougall, was born. More than any of the children of Lorn and St Clair, Hartland would keep the family financial business thriving through to the middle of the twentieth century.

FIVE

Passing the Torch

We seem to penetrate into a spirit-world and
hear the very ghosts of sound.
Melville Bell

One of the most exciting technological breakthroughs of the late
nineteenth century, the launching of the telephone, came in 1876,
within a few days of Hartland Brydges's birth. His Uncle Lorn,
assisted by his uncle St Clair and his father, Campbell, won a major
role in the first $500,000 stock issue by the Bell Telephone Com-
pany of Canada. It was the epitome of forty years of work for Lorn
and, at age sixty-nine, solidified his reputation as the leader of the
Montreal's financial community. It was also an historic moment for
Canadian capitalism.

Alexander Graham Bell received a patent for his "electric-
speaking telephone" in Brantford, Ontario, in March 1876. The
next year, he assigned 75 per cent of the Canadian rights to his
father, Melville Bell, a phoneticist and expert on defective speech.
Bell Sr then presented the new technology in a series of lectures.
His description of the new invention, quoting his son, offered a
bold prediction: "The day is coming when telegraph lines are laid
on to houses just like water and gas – and friends converse with
each other without leaving home."[1] While he was renting the new
product for $40 a year, in a marketing coup, he built a telephone
line in Ottawa for then Prime Minister Alexander Mackenzie,
between his office and the governor general's residence, Rideau
Hall, several miles away.

Melville Bell knew that he was selling a product not a service
and immediately saw that the biggest hurdle to building a service was putting together a network of wire through cities. The

second hurdle was posed by two major Canadian telegraph companies, Montreal Telegraph and Dominion Telegraph, which announced that they would compete to build networks. The result was that Montreal streets were a maze of wires and poles as both companies rushed to set up their separate systems.

In 1879 Bell Sr decided to sell his rights to the telephone in Canada to National Bell of the United States, which, in turn, chose the Bostonian Charles Fleetwood Sise as general manager. Sise arrived in Montreal in March 1880 and set to work. By late April, the Bell Telephone Company of Canada was incorporated under federal legislation. The names of Alexander Melville Bell, Thomas Davidson, an old friend and partner of Lorn MacDougall's, and H. Gordon Strathy, among others, had appeared on the petition for the act of incorporation; however, the names of Charles Sise, the general manager, or Alexander Robertson, the president, had not.

A taste of the problems Sise would encounter for years was telegraphed in the House of Commons debate on incorporation. Said one MP: "It seemed ... a very high-handed act, after a Legislature had incorporated a city and conceded to it certain powers – the inhabitants of that city not being able to till the soil without permission of the city; not being able to plant a tree without authority – that persons outside of that city should be allowed to come in and break up the soil for the purpose of laying down their wires. If permission of this kind was granted to telegraph companies and telephone companies and horse railways, citizens would never know when they were safe."[2]

By July 1880, the Montreal *Witness* prophesied a "telephone war" when negotiations broke down between the Montreal Telegraph Company, the Canadian District Telegraph Company, and Bell. But, by the end of the year, Sise had bought out the two other companies and claimed that Bell offered service in Nova Scotia, New Brunswick, Quebec, Ontario, and Manitoba and had interests in British Columbia. In all, it served 2,100 customers, including 546 in Montreal, 353 in Toronto, 230 in Ottawa, and 181 in Hamilton. It had 150 employees. But that was only the beginning and Sise needed capital.

The first share issue for $500,000 came out in December. The offer was for 5,000 shares at $100 each. The prospectus was published prominently, in a 6x10-inch box, in the newspapers beginning on the 16th. There was no mistaking its importance to the financial community and the population as a whole. At the top of the announcement, Andrew Robertson was listed as president, C.F. Sise as vice-president and managing director, and C.P. Sclater as secretary-treasurer. Robertson and Sise were listed as directors along with Montrealers Hugh Mackay, Thomas Davidson, and the Honourable J.-R. Thibaudeau. Two Bostonians, W.H. Forbes and T.N. Vail, plus R.A. Lucas from Hamilton, completed the directors' line-up.

A prospectus, then as now, is an attempt to persuade potential investors to buy shares and also to build confidence in the company with shareholders and the general public alike. This was all the more important for a company like Bell, which did not have a long history in Canada. So, in bold letters, the directors publicized the company's bankers, counsel, and broker as, respectively, the Bank of Montreal, Strachan Bethune, and D. Lorn MacDougall, whose office was then at 11 Hospital Street.

In text running five hundred words, the company elaborated on the patents it owned, the property rights and goodwill it had amassed, and the other companies it had acquired, including ones in London, Hamilton, and Windsor, Ontario. It said that the company "will have the exclusive right to use in Canada any improvements or future inventions applicable to Telephony of A. Graham Bell." It added: "The Company owns and is now operating more than 2,000 miles of wire, with over 2,000 subscribers, and has, in addition, some 200 private lines one-quarter mile to five miles in length." Listing thirty-one Bell exchanges or agencies in thirty-one towns and cities from Nova Scotia to British Columbia, the company asserted that "the Private Line Service connecting two or more points with each other, where there is no Exchange System, is increasing rapidly, and is also used to connect points in the Dominion with points in the United States." Then the potential of the company and its service was laid out: "The demand for Telephone Service increases so rapidly, and the uses of the Telephone appear so illimitable, that the Directors have authorized the sale of a small amount of Stock, which will be sold, fully paid and at par of $100 per share. Subscriptions for Stock will close on the 21st instant."

From the time the prospectus first appeared on 16 December, inquiries were directed to the Bell Company on Hospital St, or D.

Lorn MacDougall at 11 Hospital Street, or MacDougall Brothers at 69 Saint-François Xavier Street, at the corner of Hospital. Lorn MacDougall's name stood alone among the brokers although he was still a partner in MacDougall & Davidson at 72 Saint-François Xavier. Choosing MacDougall and Davidson for separate appointments to the board of directors was a testament to their connections and their reputation for competence in the financial community.

As the primary broker, this was one of the most rewarding deals Lorn MacDougall had won in a long career. The sale of Bell shares caused so much excitement and generated so much publicity for the telephone that it was clearly a shining moment, not only for Lorn MacDougall, but also for the Montreal financial community which only six years before had opened a stock exchange. Bell became one of the most successful companies in Canada. By 1915, when C.F. Sise retired at age eighty-five, after thirty-five years running the business, the number of subscribers had grown by 100 times – from 2,100 to 237,068. It had 2,235 shareholders and 8,000 employees, many of whom had or would become shareholders themselves.

While Bell was enjoying a successful launch, the rest of the Canadian economy was moving ahead slowly compared with the hectic activity across the border. The American economy hadn't stopped to take a breath after the Civil War. Thousands of immigrants poured into the east coast cities looking for a chance to share in the land giveaway and other rumoured riches of the western frontier. By 1880, the United States had a population of thirty million, compared to four million in Canada, stretched thinly from Halifax to Victoria.

For more than ten years, the Canadian government had laboured on two fronts to push Canada into the mainstream of North America and start to build an industrial nation. The first front was the National Policy, developed by Macdonald as a counter to the high-tariff American industrial system. Canada, too, needed tariffs to protect its industries and the National Policy was sold by Macdonald and accepted by the Canadian voters in the late 1870s. The second front was the launching of a transcontinental railway that would tie the country together and provide a launching pad for immigrants to settle the empty expanses of western Canada. Immigrant workers were also needed in the east to help build the new industries in cities and towns that would manufacture everything from clothing to steel and cement.

The National Policy was easier to carry out than the railway was to build, but, through the genius of a partnership of money men attached to the Bank of Montreal, with wide contacts in London, and engineers who bashed through forests and under and between mountain ranges, the railway was finally finished to the west coast by 1885.

The year 1885 was a notable year for Montreal and the MacDougalls as well. For the Lorn MacDougall family, it began in early February with plans for a big wedding for their second daughter, Dora Lucy, at Christ Church Cathedral where Lorn and his family had been members for decades. The newly built cathedral of the Anglican community in Montreal commanded a central position on Sainte-Catherine Street, which was fast developing as the new street for shopping. The imposing neo-Gothic, block-long cathedral seemed to encourage grand shops and high-end customers. It was easily accessible from St James Street, the financial and commercial district, requiring just a short ride up Beaver Hall Hill. It was also accessible to the mountain and Sherbrooke Street – the famous Golden Mile – where many of the country's wealthiest and most influential families lived.

But the wedding that was so meticulously planned never came off. The groom, a Montreal gentleman by the name of Walter Wilson, not only did not show up on the wedding day, but he unexpectedly skipped town for New York. He had postponed the wedding once the previous October, but plans were not nearly so advanced then. The young man was described as living in "princely style" and was much in evidence on the social circuit. There appeared to be security in the fact that he was known to the MacDougall family and that his brother, Reid, had already married the MacDougall's other daughter, Florence. Although his behaviour was haughty, no one sensed that he would cause such a scandal in his own city.

The aborted wedding, of course, fed the gossip columns of newspapers in Montreal, Toronto, and other Canadian centres, but the news also reached New York. The New York *Times* printed the story on 8 February 1884 under the headline: "Deserted At The Altar": "The entirely unlooked-for postponement under very peculiar circumstances of a marriage in fashionable circles has caused a sensation in the highest circles of Montreal society. The contracting parties were Mr. Walter Wilson, a well-known young gentleman, and Miss Dora Lucy MacDougall, eldest daughter of D. Lorn MacDougall, a well-known banker and broker." The correspondent was told that "shortly before the hour fixed for the ceremony yesterday afternoon two of the groomsmen went to Mr. Wilson's residence, according to the agreement, to accompany him to the church. Judge of their surprise when they found that he had left the city without giving any intimation, either to Miss MacDougall or her father."

Opinion was divided as to whether Dora MacDougall sensed there was something wrong when she and Walter had met earlier in the week. But Walter's friends were furious after joining with him in many celebrations during the several weeks prior to the wedding in the most prestigious clubs, including the St James' Club. He was described by his friends in the Montreal *Star* on 9 February 1884 as "probably one of the most fastidious and extravagant men in Montreal." The party at the St James Club was said to be "one of the most recherché spreads ever given at the fashionable uptown Club house." Not only was he feted but he received numerous costly wedding presents from his personal friends. The friends were not amused, as they told the Montreal *Star*: "'The indignation,' remarked a member of the Club today to the writer, 'in our circle is very great and I certainly shall have a meeting called to have him blackballed.'" The final indignity to his friends, not to say Lorn MacDougall and his family who were left with some 500 presents to return, was that they had paid for the various prenuptial parties. The *Star*'s account added: "The numerous gentlemen who entertained Wilson on Monday last have resolved to send the bill for the supper to the firm of Walter Wilson & Co., accompanied by a note stating that while the supper was obtained by the fugitive under false pretenses, they refuse to pay the bill." The *Star* story concluded by quoting Walter Wilson, then in New York, as saying that the reasons why the wedding did not take place were of a purely private nature and had been fully explained. "There is not an atom of truth in the rumors circulated in Montreal he was already married or was in any financial difficulty whatsoever."

A February wedding, if it had gone ahead, would have overlapped with the annual winter carnival that Montreal had begun staging in 1883. The Ice Palace on Dominion Square, ninety feet square and with thirty-foot towers at each end, the whole lit by electric lights at night, was a spectacle to behold. When snowshoers invaded the palace with their torches and fireworks crackled through the crisp night air, Montrealers believed that there was nothing like it to be seen anywhere in the world. It was exhilarating winter recreation for those who showed up by the thousands for the Ice Palace events. A masquerade ball on the huge skating rink appeared like a fairyland.

But with spring came the inevitable floods that inundated the harbour and the housing along the Lachine Canal. And this year, 1885, Montreal also had to endure something that had afflicted it many times in the past, an outbreak of smallpox. That was bad enough – thousands fell victim to the disease – but what made it even worse was the social, economic, and even political unrest which accompanied the epidemic. Ironically enough, this unrest was triggered by the opposition of many to a measure that would have stopped the disease in its tracks.

Around the end of the eighteenth century, after an estimated 400,000 people were dying a year in Europe of smallpox, hope appeared. It came in the form of experiments in Britain which showed that farm workers were becoming immune to the disease. The idea of a vaccination formed out of cowpox horrified much of the population. But, when members of the British royal family decided to inoculate themselves with the vaccine in the 1820s, substantial opposition subsided. The first moves towards compulsory vaccination came in 1837 and then in 1853 the Smallpox Compulsory Vaccination Act was passed. The idea quickly spread to the United States, where most states required vaccinations against smallpox in the 1840s and 1850s. Smallpox was all but eliminated in the United States by 1897.

In Montreal, vaccination was promoted by the civic and health authorities and many of the doctors – English and French. Yet, by the 1870s, hundreds of Montrealers, mainly but not exclusively French Canadians, still kept the door firmly shut to any vaccinator even while the death toll was rising in the city. The fact that vaccination clearly was controlling smallpox elsewhere did not convince the holdouts. Nor did the efforts of a new mayor, Dr William Hingston, who was determined to tackle the many public-health problems that beset the city, from bad water and runaway animals to smallpox. Outsiders were beginning to notice that Montreal was behind the times. A story in the New York *Times* on 11 December 1874 set out the issues Hingston would face after he took office: "The Montreal (Canada) STAR gives statistics from the Health Department, showing the deaths in that city in eleven months to be 5,290 of which 661 were from small-pox. This is only for the city proper. Outside the city limits there have been 1,029 deaths, of which 129 were from small-pox. This makes the death rate of Montreal 46 per 1,000, 15 per 1,000 more than New York, and twice as heavy as London. The STAR calls on the Catholic Clergy to advocate vaccination, in opposition to the French doctors who oppose it."

It was a disease that spread more quickly among the cramped shanties by the Lachine Canal than among those people living higher up the mountain on Sherbrooke Street. It was highly contagious and so could travel from house to house as quickly as an infected person could walk between them. Myths abounded and one of them was that the English were bent on eliminating French Canadians through vaccination. It was a notion that even Dr Hingston, so respected in the community, such a committed Catholic, and so fluently bilingual, could not dispel. He did everything possible to change people's minds, including distributing 25,000 bilingual handbills through the city. "Why does the disease visit Montreal so severely?" he asked. "We nurse it. In Quebec City, Three Rivers and Toronto no one writes or rails against the principles of vaccination."[3] It was a frustrating time for Hingston and his many supporters.

When smallpox was still killing dozens in August 1876, during Hingston's second term, the Montreal *Herald* expressed that frustration in desperate, even hysterical language: "The reason for this has been that many of our inhabitants not only object to vaccination but entertain the most dangerous notions on the subject of its contagious character. It is no wonder that in certain quarters of Montreal, smallpox is as common as dirt."[4]

By the late 1870s and early 1880s, it appeared that smallpox was subsiding when, suddenly, in 1885, it reappeared. This time, vaccination was made compulsory and a fine of $20 was imposed on those who refused or or, for whatever reason, failed to comply. Many in the city still opposed vaccination, with French Canadians leading the way – in spite of the fact that their doctors and leading politicians supported the measure. By mid-August, 120 persons had died in one ward in the city and the rate of infection was rivalling that of 1875. In addition, in August, the first prominent English Canadian, former finance minister Sir Francis Hincks, died of smallpox. The city was not only being hurt by the deaths but was being shunned and feared.

There was no official total of those who contracted smallpox that year but the unofficial count was 4,771, with more than 3,000 deaths recorded. After 1885, resistance to vaccination began to disappear and Montreal joined the rest of the North America and Europe in accepting vaccination as the only way to fight the horrendous disease. By the end of the century, it had virtually disappeared as a killer disease in Montreal and Canada.

It was a sad November for the MacDougall clan. On 14 November 1885 the New York *Times* announced in bold, large letters: "D. Lorn MacDougall, a stock broker, managing director of the North British and Mercantile Insurance Company and at one time President of the Stock Exchange, died at Montreal yesterday of paralysis. He was 76 years old." (In fact, he was seventy-four.) The Montreal newspapers fully covered his life and death in the next days. There were descriptions of his accomplishments and tributes to his character from many of his friends and from newspaper editorialists, as well as from the clergyman who led the service at Christ Church Cathedral.

The day after Lorn MacDougall's death, the Montreal *Herald and Daily Commercial News* reported: "The entire community was both surprised and greatly grieved, yesterday, on learning of the death of this esteemed gentleman; for although he was known to have been invalid for some months past, due mainly to general debility at a ripe old age, the immediate cause of death was a stroke paralysis at three o'clock yesterday morning from which the sufferer did not rally." The *Herald* and others chronicled MacDougall's career, pointing out that he was the first stockbroker to open an office in Montreal in the 1840s and that he had eventually founded the Montreal Stock Exchange, of which he was chairman until the year before he died. And the *Herald* said that the main reason for his success in the financial field was his independence.

The people with whom MacDougall had worked most closely at the Montreal Stock Exchange recorded their appreciation of his high character, his never-failing large-heartedness and liberality, and his uniform courtesy and kindness to those with whom he was brought into contact. The Montreal Stock Exchange and the Montreal Board of Trade passed resolutions praising his life and accomplishments. Flags flew at half mast all day as a tribute to his memory at the offices of Bank of Montreal and six insurance companies, as well as the Montreal Exchange.

For all that, Lorn MacDougall was not widely known outside the financial community. He had many friends among those who served in the federal Parliament and the Montreal city council, and who crossed easily between political life and business, but he never stood for public office, though clearly he was asked to do so. His world was above all that of business, and he prospered in it to an extent that likely surprised even him. Once he entered into partnership with John Glass in 1844, there was no stopping him as he forged a business career that was as varied as it could be in Montreal at that time. He found himself involved in "change," that is money transactions, and also in "trade," which could mean anything from shipping ashes to Europe to organizing shoes and other manufactured goods to be sent to the Maritimes after Montreal began developing as a manufacturing centre.

Through it all, he focused on building a reputation for honesty in a business where taking shortcuts and overcharging was the norm. The brokerage business, to some, was the unacceptable side of business and the people involved in it were often regarded as less than honest brokers. Lorn spent much of his life trying to right this impression. In the 1840s and 1850s, the only way of building up a business and a reputation was through person-to-person meetings. There was no telephone. That made even booking office meetings or lunches difficult because it was necessary often to send messengers in carriages to make a simple meeting possible. Lorn did not mind; in fact, he excelled at the personal side of business, building contacts that would last a lifetime and winning the respect of all as a man of integrity.

In many ways, Lorn MacDougall could call himself a banker. In the late 1840s and 1850s, when banks were not as spread out through the city as they would later be, brokers like Lorn became informal lenders to individuals they knew. In business, they often financed produce shippers; in later years, as we have seen, he and Thomas Davidson became "correspondents" for British and American banks in Montreal.

And, when it came to his own investments, Lorn favoured the banks. The one he knew the best was the Bank of Montreal. He was never a director but he knew all the senior officers and watched closely every move they made. In the last few years before he died, his portfolio included, of course, the Bank of Montreal as well as the Canadian Bank of Commerce, the Bank of British North America, and the Molson's Bank.

Outside business, Lorn was known for his generosity. Indeed, for him to lease a huge house, employ servants, and welcome many of his siblings into his life was itself a humanitarian act. Montreal, bitterly cold and buried in snow for six months of the year, was not Devon. Yet, by the early 1850s, Lorn's business connections and his success as a "broker" – in the broadest meaning of that word – provided a comfortable life for everyone, including his father Major Peter, who spent the last six years in Montreal, and his much younger brothers, Hartland St Clair and George Campbell, when they came as teenagers in 1855. In every case, Lorn gave them shelter and acted as their father, adviser, business partner, and friend. It was a disparate family brought together by Lorn and nurtured by him and his wife, Lucy. The brothers and half-brothers remained friends for the rest of their lives.

Lorn and Lucy helped many different charities in the city, from orphanages to relief for those hard hit by the flooding that hit the low-lying areas of Montreal almost every year. In sports, he revived the Montreal Hunt Club in the 1850s both financially and in membership and led it as master of the hunt for four years. He played racquets when the sport was beginning in Montreal in the 1840s and 1850s. He answered the call to arms when the Fenians threatened Montreal in the 1860s, forming his own regiment, the Royal Guides, who were among the very few army units which saw action. He helped form the Montreal Skating Rink and encouraged that sport as well as snowshoeing, which was the most popular winter sport from the 1860s to the 1880s.

His had been a very active life involving business, sport, the military, and, not least of all, looking after a family that had come from England in mini-waves during the 1840s and 1850s. At his funeral in Christ Church Cathedral, presided over by the Right Reverend William Bennett Bond, the bishop of Montreal, the Reverend J.G. Norton eulogized MacDougall as a man loved and honoured by all who knew him. "You who have known him so long need no one to tell you of his honorable, upright life, his kindly courtesy to all, and his liberality to all good works ... his independent thought and action."

In short, he was a gentleman.

SIX

Enter Hartland B.

He is well connected but not rich.
Robert Reford

After Lorn's death, an office under his name was kept open by his son, Somerled, listed under D.L. MacDougall Stock Brokers, 1 Hospital Street. Somerled worked there until 1890 when he moved to New York. After that, there is no listing under his name in Montreal. In the late 1890s, he left the business and sailed to South Africa where he died in 1903, just forty. There is no record of how he died though one might speculate that it was in the South African wars, in which many Canadians participated with enthusiasm. He was Lorn's only son.

After Somerled left Montreal, it seems that most of Lorn's business, including the insurance business, was taken over by MacDougall Brothers, still comprising St Clair and Campbell. They were in their mid- to early forties, with reputations that followed on Lorn's for integrity and knowledge of the various businesses. They kept up their contacts, too.

It was helpful that, by 1885, St Clair had become secretary-treasurer of the Montreal Stock Exchange and, a few years later, its vice-president and finally president. It appears that having a MacDougall on the executive of the MSE was good for business at MacDougall Brothers and reassuring for the other members. It kept the MSE's reputation at a high level because St Clair and Campbell's contacts were not only extensive in Canada but reached to Toronto and also to London, England, and New York as well as other east coast cities that had exchanges, like Boston, Philadelphia, and Chicago.

The next MacDougall destined to play a dominant role in running the family business was Hartland Brydges, the son of Campbell. He made his mark as a football and hockey player, a tennis player and golfer, and an internationally recognized polo player.[1] He lived during a remarkable seventy-year period. He grew up in the horse-and-buggy era, but before he died he saw the first jet plane fly, the passenger car mass-produced, and radio and gramophone recording that changed leisure time. He also saw train travel common across North America and luxurious boats plying the North Atlantic that brought Europe to Montreal's doorstep. Hartland would take full advantage of the trains and sleek ocean liners, making frequent trips to the United States and to the United Kingdom to play polo and to promote business.

Following his birth in 1876, the first part of Hartland's life was spent on Sherbrooke Street where his father lived. As a very young man, he knew horses and, even after his Uncle Lorn moved from Outremont into Montreal in the early 1880s, Uncle St Clair and his father, Campbell, maintained horses and continued to play for the Polo Club. Campbell also indulged his love of good horses by buying and trading them. Horses, in short, were in the family.

Then tragedy entered Hartland's young life. His mother, Grace, died suddenly in 1883, when he was only seven years old. This left Campbell a widower. Although he obviously could count on the extended family to help with the raising of his son, it could not be a long-term arrangement.

Montreal provided lots of sporting activities for a young person growing up in the 1880s and 1890s. There were cricket and baseball clubs but neither was widely played at the time. The bicycling club boasted seventy members, a rackets group counted forty members, and the lawn tennis club had sixty members who used the lacrosse grounds every day except Saturday. A newly popular sport was football, which numbered three clubs. Hartland would have been introduced to golf at the still-new Montreal Golf Club on Fletcher's Field, on the side of the mountain, because his Uncle St Clair was one of the founding members and a director. At one time or another, he played nearly all these sports during his active sporting life, as well as polo.

The most popular game for the average Montrealer, and one that Hartland also likely played, was lacrosse. There were nine clubs in the city, the best-known of which were the Montreal Club, with grounds on Sherbrooke Street, and the Shamrocks, with grounds on Sainte-Catherine Street. One of the features of lacrosse for the fans was that the teams included many Indian players. Their games against white opponents drew big crowds.

Lacrosse and football, among other games, were played by members of the Montreal Amateur Athletic Association (MAAA). Hartland joined the football crowd at the MAAA with much enthusiasm and became a star fullback. An older Montrealer recalled Hartland's prowess in a letter to the editor shortly after his death: "Hartland was the greatest of all backs, and there has been none better among the touted players of today. No runner ever got past him. He did not tackle in the usual dive for the knees, but threw himself at the coming runner and grabbed him in an embrace that tumbled both to the ground ... The game was faster then, with more variety; much internal passing, more running, drop kicks and no time out. And when a runner was tackled, a dozen others did not pile on him. And the same teams played the entire game; no changing every few minutes."[2]

From age seven to twelve, Hartland attended Eliock School on what was then called Dorchester Boulevard. In 1888, at age twelve, he was sent to Bishop's College School (BCS) in Lennoxville, ninety miles east of Montreal and two hours by train. It was then a boys' school attached to Bishop's College, which had been founded in 1843 at the confluence of the Massawippi and St Francis rivers.

At BCS, Hartland met a fellow boarder and sportsman who became a teammate in school sports and later with the Montreal Victorias hockey club and, later still, the "second" MacDougall in MacDougall & MacDougall which they formed in the early 1920s. His name was Robert E. MacDougall. For years, Hartland and Robert (commonly known as Bob) were thought to be brothers when, in fact, they were not related.

Once he got to Bishop's, Hartland thrived. It was a school modelled on the British boarding school, more specifically on Rugby School, where the legendary Thomas Arnold presided in the 1830s and 1840s, at the height of the Victorian age. It was Arnold who introduced the prefect system to British schools and, like many British innovations, that system ended up in Canada, including at BCS. Hartland MacDougall became a prefect in his last years at the school, 1893–94. Later generations considered him the "prototype" of "Head Prefects," so widely did his reputation spread. In a book on the school written some decades ago, this is a description of eighteen-year-old Hartland just as he was becoming a prefect: "Hartland MacDougall demonstrated his athletic prowess and superb sense of sportsmanship as a member of all first teams, and this may have had a powerful influence on his nomination as a Prefect. In office, MacDougall gave himself wholeheartedly, as he did on the field and rink, to the job of prefecture. His kindness, sagacious advice, a devotion to ideals and his untiring pursuit of the desirable objective were not forgotten with his departure from Lennoxville, but were remembered and evaluated by his contemporaries as much as fifty years later with something akin to reverence."[3]

On 31 March 1892, when he was mid-way through BCS, Hartland was hit with another personal tragedy: his father died at the young age of forty-nine. "Very well known as a sportsman," one account read, Campbell was "an expert rider and was owner of some fine horses." The company built up by Campbell and St Clair "gained an extensive clientage that made business one of large volume. Though he died young, he had achieved distinction in his line of business and as a sportsman had gained wide friendship among many of the most distinguished citizens of the province."[4]

Back at BCS, hockey had become the favourite sport of both the headmaster of the time, H.J.H. Petry, and the boys. Petry was well aware how hockey games kept up the morale at the school during the long winter months. It also kept up spirits in the small industrial towns surrounding Lennoxville, whose teams played against the boys at BCS. In many cases, the BCS boys found themselves shorter than their opponents but they made up for it in speed and agility. The school history notes: "Certainly, of the school's activity every season in Townships hockey made it possible for BCS to get a high level of competition year after year, as was true of no other sport. Travelling by two-horse, open sleighs with buffalo robes' insulation against the chill, school teams played their away games as far afield as Cookshire, an hour and a half's run. Stanstead was somewhat longer."[5]

BCS became known far and wide for its excellent hockey teams. "Championships of the Eastern Townships, a galaxy of stars amongst his prefect nominations and, probably most of all, the famous team of 1893 spread the reputation of BCS hockey as far away a Winnipeg and the Atlantic seaboard."[6] The school produced three superstars of Canadian hockey in that period. Ernest McLea, Robert MacDougall, and Hartland MacDougall became mainstays of the Montreal Victorias, who dominated the then very young national hockey scene in the 1890s.

The first game of hockey, legend says, was played at the Victoria Skating Rink in Montreal in 1875 with nine players to a side. In increasingly more refined versions, it proved to be a popular sport in the 1880s, based around the winter carnivals of those years. The Montreal Victorias first played in 1883 during the winter carnival; they took their name from the Victoria Skating Rink that had been built in the 1860s. The Amateur Hockey Association of Canada, founded in 1887, ran hockey until 1898. The game was quite different from today's game. There were six players to a side, and the game was played in two periods of thirty minutes each. Often the players were on the ice for the whole game. There was sudden-death overtime.

The first Stanley Cup was presented by the then governor general, Lord Stanley, in 1893 to the MAAA. But, in the last part of the 1890s, the Victorias dominated the league, which was then made up of the Victorias, the Montreal Hockey Club, the Montreal Crystals, the Ottawa Hockey Club, and the Quebec Hockey Club, and nearly monopolized the Stanley Cup, winning the trophy from 1895 through 1898. The three BCS "old Boys" – McLea and the two MacDougalls – played a prominent part in the triumphs of the Victorias in those years, when the team was "pitted against the best clubs and the toughest transients in the game, strapping giants in Winnipeg, Ottawa, Montreal and Quebec City, who travelled from one to another Cup-hungry organization with money to bid for hockey fame."[7] The BCS men were not big considering the "strapping giants" they were up against in hockey (and football too). For the record, Robert MacDougall was 5'7, 158 pounds; Hartland MacDougall was 5'10", 155 pounds; and Ernie McLea was 5'10" and 149 pounds.

However, despite their small size, the rough-and-tumble style of hockey they played became the pattern for the modern game. Robert MacDougall was a star forward on the Victorias and Hartland played an increasingly more prominent role in the five years he played. He began as a substitute, first in goal and then on defence. His citation at the Canadian Sports Hall of Fame, where he was inducted in 1976, the 100th anniversary year of his birth, states: "In 1898, his final season with the club, MacDougall played in all eight games for the undefeated Victorias and scored three goals. He was a member of the Victoria teams that won the Stanley Cup in 1895, 1896, 1897 and 1898."

One of the most exciting games took place in Winnipeg in December 1896. It was provoked by the Victorias after they had been beaten earlier in the year by the Winnipeg team in a challenge match. The Victorias wanted a rematch and they finally got it in Winnipeg on 30 December. Montreal won the game 6–5 after overcoming a 4–2 deficit at half-time. And it was BCS's Ernie McLea who got the winning goal. Along with Hartland MacDougall and Robert MacDougall, that team included a star from McGill named Percival Molson.[8]

The year after he left BCS, in 1895, Hartland went to work for the Bank of Montreal, as his father had done in the 1860s. The bank was the largest in Canada and the financial agent of Canada in England. The federal and most provincial governments rarely made a major move without consulting it. The bank had total assets of $50,000,000 (in today's money about $1.1 billion) and forty places of business, mostly in Canada but also in New York, Chicago, and London where it was the respected financial face of Canada.

Hartland was joined at the Bank of Montreal by his friend Robert E. MacDougall. The new job allowed Hartland to play hockey for the Victorias and football for the MAAA. Within two years, he had travelled to England where he had uncles, including Leigh, both to

put him up and introduce him to contacts and explain the sometimes arcane workings of the "city," London's financial district.

It is part of the MacDougall family lore that Hartland, then twenty,
first attracted the attention of Edith Reford by offering to stable
her horse. To be sure, there was no shortage of stables attached
to Robert Reford's houses. There were stables at or near their city
residence on Drummond Street just above Sherbrooke Street, close
to where the Ritz Carlton Hotel and Holt Renfew greet customers
today. Other Reford stables were at a model farm he built at Sainte-
Anne de Bellevue at the extreme west end of the island, and also
at a summer house he owned at Beaurepaire, in the western part of
the city on Lake St Louis. Then there was an establishment he built
at Metis Beach, 375 miles northeast of Montreal on the south shore
of the St Lawrence.[9]

From the beginning of their relationship in 1896, one of the
strongest bonds between Hartland and Edith was a love of horses.
And, from the beginning, the Reford family took a keen interest
in the MacDougall boy, none more than the formidable Robert
Reford. A Victorian businessman who had emigrated from Belfast
in 1845, Reford built up a series of companies from ocean shipping
to lumber and rice milling, as well as a family of three boys and
two girls. He presented a gruff exterior and a moralistic manner,
constantly lecturing children in letters that were cajoling, criticiz-
ing, and encouraging in equal measure. His favourite themes were
education, religion, and success. Reford's wife, Kate, known in the
family as "grumbling Kate," also handed out criticism in large dol-
lops. Clergymen and Protestant missionaries were looked on with
favour, but Reford told the staff not to allow them into the house
in his absence for fear that they would leave with too generous a
donation.

As sternly as he sometimes treated his children, he accommo-
dated their spouses in every way. In August 1896, when he first
learned that Hartland and Edith might be interested in each other,
he wrote to his wife, who was in Metis: "The Hotel [at Metis] is I
think going to be an uncomfortable place for him and I wondered
if you would like to ask him to stay with you and use Lewis's room.

Think the matter over and do as you think best."[10] It is doubtful whether Hartland would have been offered a bedroom in their Montreal or even Beaurepaire house, but rules were far less rigid in the country, especially in such a big house so far away.

"He seems a nice kind of fellow. Is Edith fond of him or he of her?" asks an anxious father in the same letter. "When I asked her about it all I could get out of her was 'ridiculous' – there is nothing between us. He certainly I think goes down to see Edith. She might do better and she might do worse."[11] In October 1898 they became engaged to be married, and Reford seemed pleased at the prospect of being a father of the bride at age sixty-eight and with his son-in-law to be. He wrote to his brother in Toronto: "You will be surprised to hear that my girl Edith has become engaged to be married sometime next spring to a Mr. Hartland MacDougall who we have known for a long time. He is well connected but not rich."[12] To his sister he wrote that Hartland was "a very nice fellow ... I hope it will be for their happiness."

The wedding was held on 26 April. "She got an awful lot of presents," her father commented, "some of them splendid ones. I send you today's Gazette with list of some of the presents, guests ... it was quite a grand affair and I am glad it is over. So is Kate who is used up." The *Gazette* write-up went on for a full column, listing dozens of the hundreds of guests and describing their presents for their readers. The story read:

A fashionable wedding took place yesterday afternoon at St. George's Church, Mr. Hartland B. MacDougall, and Miss Edith Reford being the contracting parties.

The Right Rev. Bishop Bond officiated, assisted by the Very Reverend Dean Carmichael. The bride wore a magnificent gown of cream duchesse satin covered with chiffon and embroidered with silver bow-knots ... the four bridesmaids, Miss Katie Reford, Miss Beatrice MacDougall (half-sister of the groom), Miss Stearns and Miss Cora Brainerd were dressed alike in gowns of white sun-rayed chiffon, blue chiffon sashes and hats of white tuile, trimmed with blue choux and pink roses. Mr. Bartlett McLennan was his best man, and the ushers were Mr. Andrew Reford, Mr. J.D. Paterson and

Mr. W. Angus ... later Mr. and Mrs. MacDougall left for New York by the evening train.

The guests included the Molson family, Mr and Mrs Montagu Allan, Mr and Mrs Charles Meredith, and a full complement of the MacDougall and Reford families. Then there were the presents. As the *Gazette* reported:

> The wedding presents were numerous and very handsome. Mr. Robert Reford, Mr. Lewis Reford, Mr. and Mrs. John Thomas Molson and Mr. Vanneck gave cheques: Mrs. Robert Reford, a magnificent diamond brooch with pearl-shaped pearl necklace ... Mr. Andrew Reford a saddle and toilet articles in silver; Mrs. Campbell MacDougall (the groom's step-mother), cabinet of silver ... Mr. Dwight Brainerd, pedigreed wire-haired fox terrier ... Mr. Bart McLennan and Mr. Bertie Ogilvie, traveling cases ... Miss McLennan, Tiffany glass vase; the maids in the Reford household, silver pudding dish. There were many other valuable gifts, including the handsome vase presented by the Montreal Football Club.[13]

Alexander Reford, a great-great-grandson of the father of the bride, said of the *Gazette* article: "It was like the modern-day *Hello!* magazine without the pictures.

Wilfrid Laurier, who succeeded John A. Macdonald as prime minister in 1896, was as different from his predecessor as a bartender was to a clergyman. Macdonald loved telling stories and hearing them. Laurier liked neither. Macdonald enjoyed his sherry in medium or large quantities, depending on the occasion, and he revelled in smoking the odd cigar. Laurier neither drank nor smoked. Their politics would be different, too.

The 1890s marked the beginning of the mass migration into Canada, mainly from Europe, which of course helped the Reford shipping interests, among others. By the late nineteenth century, there was little free land left in the United States and much in

Canada. And there was finally an efficient transportation system in place in Canada – mainly the Canadian Pacific Railway (CPR) but also the Grand Trunk and Intercolonial Railway – to get the thousands where they wanted to go, whether it was to farm in the western plains or to work in the newly industrializing cities.

While the plains were filling up, there was opportunity for workmen in the growing industrial cities of Montreal and Toronto and, to a lesser extent, Trois-Rivières, Sherbrooke, Windsor, and Winnipeg. There were so many jobs in the rapidly industrializing areas around the cities that the haemorrhaging of French Canadians to New England in the 1870s and 1880s stopped, and those workers headed where jobs were becoming plentiful – in Quebec and parts of Ontario.

And, by the 1890s, city life was being transformed by the electric light and the bicycle, among other things. The author and educator W.L. Grant wrote in 1894 about the latest technological development. "Montreal was the first port in the world lighted by electricity. The result is continuous labor. The electric lights are placed at intervals of about two hundred yards, from the mouth of the Lachine Canal to Hochelaga so that the whole harbour is lit up."[14] Electricity would play a dominant role in the growing industrial base in Canadian cities, providing the energy to make steel and rail cars, motor cars, and paper. The biggest change seen on the streets of the city was the sudden sprouting of the modern bicycle, complete with Dunlop's new pneumatic tire. The tires were developed in 1890 and, by mid-decade, as soon as spring arrived, the new bicycles appeared by the thousands, gliding along the streets with ease, speed, and grace, a new way for city folk to enjoy freedom, even in the suburbs.

Newspapers had become much thicker, reflecting the new type of pulp and paper, and in 1896 the Eddy Match company was advertising that it produced 28,000 matches a day. Cook's said it would take a Canadian to Europe and back on a sixty-day tour for $575. Skis and even golf clubs were also being advertised.

Canada's place in the world was changing. Confederation was, at best, a shaky coalition of provinces and so was regarded by most Canadians, until the 1890s, as an experiment whose outcome was uncertain. At the same time, Canadians watched with trepidation the evolution of politics and society in the United States from the 1860s on. Their view of the United States was combination of worry, envy, and disdain. The worry centred on American military and economic power, which could crush Canada if the United States so willed. The envy was directed at the record of the United States in eating up the land west of the Mississippi and building a continent-wide country in a matter of a few decades that was robust and rich. The disdain was reserved – as it always has been in Canada – for the "style" of Americans, so many of whom seemed so rich and so ready to bulldoze anyone in their way, the roughrider mentality.

By the mid-1890s, Canadians had begun to see the possibilities for growth in their own country after twenty-five years of mediocre economic performance. Suddenly, the cloak of gloom was replaced by a vision of a future filled with light and promise – the twentieth century could be Canada's. Then, as the 1890s gave way to the new century, Canada began changing in other ways. The rural society of the eighteenth and nineteenth centuries, which grew produce for Canadians and as well as Britons to eat, was being taken over by a more urban and industrialized society. Labor unions began to spring up. Farmers revolted over the new emphasis on the cities.

No one was immune from the major shifts transforming the basis of society. Even the horse lost its key place in industry, commerce, and the everyday life of Canadians in the years leading to the First World War, its job being taken over by the motor car and then the truck. Everyone had to think differently in their daily lives and their work world from the 1890s on, and that included the world of commerce and finance. Among other changes was an enormous expansion of total output during the first two decades of the twentieth century.

In 1900, when Hartland MacDougall was learning the financial business from the inside, the stock exchanges were run by the "call" system, which ran like this. There were actual "seats" on the exchange. Against three walls were arranged individual small desks and each was armed with a book and a pencil. Starting at 10 o'clock, the secretary would mount to his desk and proceed to "call" the listed stocks from A on, allowing an interval to secure a "bid and asked" and to permit trades, which each member would note in his book for the information of his office. When the "call" was over, open trading would be permitted until the time for the next "call." This may seem cumbersome, but the fact remains that, at the turn of the century, the exchange was expanding rapidly, as reflected both in the growth of the stock list and in the increased turnover: "In 1902, the membership was increased to total sixty ... the period till the outbreak of the First World War was again one of steady expansion ... the stock list had increased at that time, to 182 issues and the number of members to 75."[15] There was so much confidence in the future of the country and the exchange that the directors decided to construct a new building in 1904.

In the same era, Montreal's underbelly was made up of slums, with little or no sanitation, creating a shack-like area below the mountain that had become a civic embarrassment. While a reputed 70 per cent of Canada's wealth resided in the Golden Mile just below Mount Royal, Montreal needed an major injection of money to clean up its muddy, fly-infested shanty towns of the lower half of the city. The long process of cleaning up and washing down had started in the mid-1880s.

It was Hartland's mother, Grace Brydges, who was one of the first to recognize the need for help near the yards of the Grand Trunk Railway of which her father, C.J. Brydges, was managing director. She was instrumental in obtaining land from the Grand Trunk to build a church in 1871 in the heart of Point-Saint-Charles, then known as "The Point." It opened in 1871 as a regular church of the Anglican diocese of Montreal and attracted the attention of Grace's friends from the city on the hill who were willing to help. The church has since been known as Grace Anglican Church, after her.

Also understanding the pressing need for change was Montreal mayor Raymond Prefontaine, who in 1897 proudly compared the city in that year to its state in 1884. The difference was the massive amount of infrastructure that Montreal had built in a thirteen-year period. In 1884, 13 miles of streets were open, with less than half of them paved. In 1897, 178 miles of streets were open and 26 ½ miles were paved. Brick sewers amounted to about 7.5 miles in 1884 and 104 miles in 1897. In the same period, the population had jumped from 172,000 to 250,000. It all had financial implications.

In fact, thirty years before the city fathers of Montreal discovered that infrastructure could be financed by selling bonds to eager buyers, in London, Paris, or New York, other cities were peddling bonds. While big banks were underwriting these bonds, smaller brokerage houses were also underwriting smaller issues from smaller municipalities. One of the first small houses to do that was MacDougall & Davidson in 1869. The bigger story of the development of bond trading involved, of course, the larger banks, which led the way. And among the leaders, as one might expect, was the Bank of Montreal.

Bonds and debentures sold by small municipalities and big governments started well before Confederation. Brokerage houses bought some of the smaller issues, selling them to insurance companies (which they, in turn, sometimes represented) and banks.

Then the banks, led by the Bank of Montreal, which was well established in New York by the mid-1860s and in London by the beginning of the 1870s, jumped in. Many of the bonds that were not sold privately were listed on the stock exchanges, or the comparable institution before the MSE and TSE were legally established.

Historically, the major financing for the canals from the 1820s to the 1850s was done by the British government on a government-to-government basis. But, by the time the railways and other public services like streetcars and waterworks came along, the municipalities sought the money on the competitive markets, which at that time were mainly London and less often Paris and Montreal and Toronto. The major financing was largely done through the banks and mainly in London with private banks or brokers. That is why British private banks often had "correspondence" relationships with brokers in Canada. MacDougall & Davidson, as we have seen, acquired several "correspondent" agreements with British private banks.

The next step in the creation of "global" bond market was to tie in the United States where there were large pools of money ready to finance public works as well as private investment, in both Canada and the United States. Here, an institution was needed to bridge the gaps in knowledge and style between London and New York. This is where the Bank of Montreal stepped in. That bank first became an underwriter of bonds in 1874 in London, with an 800,000 sterling issue for the province of Quebec in participation with Morton Rose & Company. Soon after it underwrote a 750,000 sterling city of Montreal issue and then a 500,000 sterling subscription to a Dominion of Canada loan.

In 1879 the bank tried some innovative financing that allowed it to become the first to tap the New York market for Canadian bonds. It came in with a $3,000,000 province of Quebec bond issue that it syndicated and that was payable either in sterling or U.S. dollars. It was the first foreign issue sold in New York on its merits and the historic financing got much attention. The Canadian press saw it as an advantage for Canada to have a choice of markets. The next step wasn't far away. In 1882 apparently one-half of a $1,500,000 province of Quebec loan was taken up by Montreal broker M. Wurtele and the other half by another Montreal broker, L.-J. Forget.

In the next twenty years leading to the turn of the century, the relationships between the public and private banks in Canada and London and New York grew closer. The financings became more sophisticated, and brokerage houses like G.A. Stimson, Hanson Brothers in Montreal, and A.E. Ames began specializing in bonds. By the late 1890s and early 1900s, the Central Canada Loan and Savings Company, formed in 1884, was fast building a reputation as the most influential bond company. The most important employees of Central Canada Loan, including G.H. Wood and J.H. Gundy, applied in 1901 for a licence to form Dominion Securities. Here was a clear sign that the banks were facing more and more competition from big and growing bond houses.

As Dominion Securities was being formed, Max Aitken of Halifax came to Montreal with the object of reshaping Canadian industry by reorganizing, amalgamating, and investing in new enterprises under the name of Royal Securities. The diminutive Aitken, better known after he emigrated to England as Lord Beaverbrook, laid siege to Montreal's business community by taking over businesses. The best remembered of these moves was the consolidation of thirteen cement companies to form the Canada Cement Company.

Along with Aitken, from the beginning of the new century, new immigrants swarmed into the cities. They found hydro replacing coal and steam as an energy source. The new west was attracting farmers whose efforts produced huge grain crops, especially wheat, that fed the world. Montreal and Toronto both doubled their populations between 1891 and 1911 – Montreal from 219,616 to 490,504; Toronto from 181,215 to 381,833. The country's population nearly doubled between 1901 and 1921, from 5.3 million to

10.3 million. Meanwhile, Winnipeg's population leaped by more than five times from 25,699 to 136,035 in a twenty-month period. Part of Winnipeg's growth could be attributed to wheat. In 1896 wheat production stood at 7,855,274 bushels. Five years later, it was slightly more than 25,000,000 bushels, and by 1911 the production topped 75,000,000 bushels.

New industrial production techniques, more sophisticated financing, and new technologies, like electricity and the telephone, made industry more efficient and helped to build an industrial base. A few figures will illustrate. In 1901 a total of 55 companies with a total capitalization of $7,662,000 were formed with Dominion charters; in 1911–12, 658 companies were formed, with a total capitalization of $447,626,000.

Just after the death of Campbell in 1892, a major blow to Mac-Dougall Brothers, St Clair, then approaching his mid-fifties, began searching for help and decided on his nephew, Alexander Paterson, whose father had married St Clair's sister, Geraldine. Paterson, then thirty-two, joined the firm in 1893. He came from a well-established family, his father, Alexander Thomas Paterson, being part of the mercantile house of Gillespie and Moffat. Geraldine, two years older than St Clair, married Alexander Thomas Paterson in 1858.

Young Alexander was educated in England and returned to Montreal to join the Bank of Montreal at the age of seventeen. He left there three years later in 1881 to join his father's firm, where he spent the next twelve years before beginning work with MacDougall Brothers. In 1897 Paterson was made a partner. By 1900, and the first few years of the twentieth century, MacDougall Brothers was crowded with family. Besides Paterson, Hartland Leonard, St Clair's son, then in his early twenties, joined the firm. Then, in 1900, E.R.D. Applegath, a son-in-law, married to his daughter Betsy, moved into the offices. Hartland Brydges, two years older than his cousin Leonard, spent a year at the firm in 1900–01 but may have found it overcrowded, because he soon joined Charles Meredith & Company. By 1904, Paterson himself had decided to move on. He bought a seat on the Montreal Stock Exchange and begin his own firm, which he headed until he died in 1931. The Paterson family is very much a presence in Montreal through the well-known lawyer, political activist, and former Bishop's University chancellor Alex Paterson.

During these hectic times, St Clair was voted chairman of the Montreal Stock Exchange in 1894–95 and again in 1897 out of respect for his long service in the brokerage business. With the turn of the century, he had accumulated three score years, a hefty reputation for efficiency and his contacts, and a desire to move to the countryside. The result was that he bought a house on Dorval Island, nearer to the Polo Club and the Royal Montreal Golf Club, of which he was a charter member.

There was enough room for MacDougalls both at MacDougall Brothers and at Charles Meredith, where Hartland Brydges worked. One reason is that the period before the First World War saw huge increases in the volumes of trading in both stocks and bonds. And, despite the many frustrations shown by the leaders of the Toronto financial community, Montreal retained its position as the leading exchange in the country. One illustration of Montreal's still dominant position in the financial markets was the cost of an exchange seat. In Toronto, the price went from $300 in 1874 to $3,500 in 1883, $6,400 in 1901, and $16,000 in 1913; in Montreal, a seat cost $500 in 1874, $4,500 in 1883, $12,850 in 1901, and $30,000 in 1913. Every year from 1901 to 1913, Montreal exceeded Toronto's volume of business, both mining and industrial. Montreal's share of the total business was steadily ahead of Toronto's in the same period. In 1901 Montreal accounted for 60 per cent of the total business in Canada; in 1901, 70 per cent; and in 1913, 79 per cent. Montreal also dominated the bond market up to the First World War. It consistently turned over 60 to 75 per cent of the bond business annually between 1901 and 1913.

But technology was breaking down barriers and increasing competition. In 1914 F.G. Osler, president of the Toronto Stock Exchange, reported that, until then, most stock transactions had been carried out through the mail, but now one-third of them were being done by wire. Communications had improved so much that traders in London, New York, and Paris – even Montreal and Toronto – used one or other of the exchanges, depending on the price. J.H. Dunn and Company reportedly told their associates in London in 1906 to make use of both Montreal and Toronto in order to obtain the best price. The two exchanges were also losing business to New York, where it was cheaper to trade some stocks, and to London, where most of the Canadian stocks were also listed. Before 1900, in fact, the securities market in Canada was not a major factor in the Canadian economy, especially in generating capital. It wasn't until after 1900 that an indigenous Canadian capital market started to develop.

As a consequence, to prosper in Montreal or Toronto in the financial business, you needed first-class contacts in New York, London, and Canada among banks and governments and private businesses. If there is anything the MacDougall clan understood by 1900, after sixty years in the business, was that a broadly based network of contacts was as valuable a tool for brokers as a steering column to an automobile.

SEVEN

A New Century

The bulls and bears are organized bodies
of men who play with loaded dice.
Monetary Times

After a short spell with his uncle and cousins at MacDougall Brothers, from 1900 Hartland found a home at Charles Meredith, a
financially sound firm whose owner's background was as a banker.
Charles and Hartland had a lot in common. Charles started with the
Merchant's Bank and rose to head its western branches in Regina
and Brandon before moving in 1887 to Montreal, where he bought
a seat on the Stock Exchange. He was a keen sportsman, a good
rower and boxer, and he hunted and fished for salmon whenever
he could. Like him, Hartland could call himself a banker, having
started in the financial business at the Bank of Montreal, and he
too was widely recognized as a superb sportsman, which Meredith
no doubt noticed. The MacDougall name was also silver-plated,
through Hartland's late Uncle Lorn; his late father, Campbell; and
his still active Uncle St Clair. And they both married daughters of
eminent businessmen – in 1893, six years before the MacDougall-
Reford marriage, Charles married Elspeth Hudson, daughter of
R.B. Angus, president of the Bank of Montreal between 1910 and
1913.

Hartland moved quickly up in the company, obviously gaining
the confidence of Charles, and became a partner before he was
thirty-two. As time went on, they developed more mutual interests, even out of the office. Hartland established a country home at
Saraguay off the west end of the island where Charles had a house.
They were half-a-generation apart in age, Hartland being twenty-

five in 1901 and Charles thirty-seven. But their relationship was like that of father and son.

There was lots of action in Montreal at the time and Hartland jumped right into it. He became a member of the Montreal Stock Exchange in 1906; he was elected governor in 1909 and president in 1914. In 1912 he became a director of Penman's, the largest woolen clothing manufacturer in Canada, owned by Dominion Textile but run separately. It was best known for its hosiery, underwear, sweaters, and blankets, outdoing the indomitable Stanfield's. He was put there by Charles to represent the Bank of Montreal's interests.

Montreal was changing as Hartland was launching himself. The industrialization of the city began in the 1890s, pushed by the replacement of coal and steam by electricity, and proceeded at a dramatic pace during the first part of the twentieth century. For example, the net value of the production of electric light and power in 1900 was $1,960,000, rising to $12,892,000 in 1910 and $67,500,000 in 1925. The best estimate of the net value of production of all manufacturers in 1900 is $214,526,000; in 1910 it hit $564,467,000 and in 1925 $1,304,557,000. Industrialization on this scale kept Quebecers, mainly French-speaking Quebecers, home because there was plenty of work. Between 1881 and 1891, 132,000 Quebecers had left the province. But, in the period from 1901 to 1911, the number dived to 29,000.

In 1909 Montreal was a city of 450,000, very much among the leading urban centres in North America. It was shedding its Victorian cloak for some Edwardian grandeur, represented by the jolly, easy-going, and stylish monarch, Edward VII. The face of Sherbrooke Street was taking on a new look. In rapid succession, the University Club was built on Mansfield Street; the staid and sheltered Mount Royal Club was erected at Stanley and Sherbrooke; a new marble-faced entrance for the Montreal Museum of Fine Arts was being contemplated (finally completed in 1912); and the nine-storey, gingerbread-like Linton Apartments at Simpson and Sherbrooke opened for rentals in 1908.

But there was something missing for a city that aspired to world status: a world-class hotel. That is what inspired a group of Montreal investors including Herbert Samuel Holt, Charles Blair Gordon, Hugh Montagu Allan, and Charles Rudolph Hosmer, along with Lionel Guest and Harry Higgins, to meet on Christmas Eve 1909 to form the Carlton Hotel Company of Montreal, with a mandate to "erect and operate a first class residential hotel." The estimated cost was $2 million (about $45 million today), to be financed by selling 20,000 shares at $100 each. The financing was made easier because the directors were backed by their companies, which included Montreal Light, Heat and Power, the Royal Bank of Canada, Dominion Textile, Molson's Bank, Allan Steamship Line, Canadian Pacific Telegrams, and Montreal Gas.

Land at the corner of Drummond and Sherbrooke was sold to the group by the financial house of Charles Meredith & Company, of which Sir Charles Gordon was a director. Gordon "served there with another of the Ritz-Carlton's first major shareholders, the eminent Montreal banker, Hartland Brydges MacDougall ... who had become one of Meredith's senior partners and was there to serve both the company and the new hotel."[1] One of the duties of the thirty-four-year-old banker, who found himself in the company of some of Montreal's leading businessmen, was to sell the shares.

It helped that the land at the corner of Drummond and Sherbrooke was owned by Meredith. The price of the lot was "one dollar, but with good and valuable considerations," which is what they were. Meredith received $787,500 in preferred shares (worth $17.3 million in today's money) in the Carlton Hotel Company, for which it paid $314,404 in cash, the balance of $469,096 to be covered by "goodwill, benefits and advantages." These were never fully explained, but it is clear that Meredith was an important shareholder and would become a major influence on how the hotel was run and its future. Cesar Ritz allowed his name to be used for a fee of $25,000, with the added provision that the "Ritz Plan" standards would be adhered to. Built at its original cost of $2 million, the hotel was officially opened on 31 December 1912, the occasion marked by a gala ball celebrating the "first class residential hotel" dreamed of by its investors. People who lived there permanently paid $29 a month (about $661.44 today), although a single room with a bath was $3 a night and a suite of rooms with a bath was $8 (about $182 today). Lunch in the Oak Room was $1.50 (about $34 today), dinner in the Oval Room was $2.50, and tea in the Palm court was thirty cents.

A few blocks away, the MacDougalls lived graciously with their five children. According to the 1911 census form, the household also included four servants in their twenties, a governess named Jane Robertson, twenty-four, a coachman named Allan Frank, thirty, and a groom to look after the horses. It was the last era when having multiple servants and attendants on this scale was possible. Soon, the war, the coming of the automobile, more and more women working, and the faster pace of life led to fewer servants in households like the MacDougalls, especially in the cities. And the first jobs that became redundant were those of coachmen and grooms.

From the time the brokerage business began in Montreal in the 1840s, there were critics in Parliament and the press and in the general population. They complained that the brokers held all the cards. They could manipulate prices if they were so inclined, to the detriment of the traders. No one seemed to control the interest rates they charged. The world of brokers was, to many, nothing less than a gambling den, and in Victorian times, even more than now, there were powerful religious and secular groups loudly opposed to gambling.

Lorn, St Clair, and Campbell MacDougall were well aware of the reputation of brokers. So, from the beginning, Lorn had made sure that the Board of Trade provided an umbrella to oversee the business. Later, by virtue of Lorn's role in founding the Montreal Stock Exchange, and acting as its first president, they themselves assumed partial responsibility for the MSE's reputation and signalled that MacDougall Brothers did not practice the "hundred kindred arts" (presumably slick, under-the-table deals) referred to in the *Times*. No doubt, there was a touch of high-mindedness in their thinking. It likely served as welcome reassurance for clients in Canada, London, and New York when they saw that one or other of the MacDougalls sat at the high table on the MSE.

Until about 1900, the number of MSE members was limited to forty, inviting the perjorative phrase "40 thieves" used widely by its detractors. But that number quickly expanded after 1900 to seventy-five and more as new joint stock companies were formed and the industrial growth exploded. While that countered the charge that the MSE, like its junior counterpart, the TSE, was creating a closed shop, it didn't automatically or instantly burnish the image of brokers. Manufacturing of all sorts, and especially the metal trades, was considered real work for real men. Brokers were tolerated as conduits of cash and dealers in stocks and bonds for the manufacturers. They raised funds that started new businesses that included railways and streetcars, insurance companies, bridge-building enterprises, iron and silver mines, toll roads – and that's not all.

Apart from the connection that brokers established with the Board of the Trade, they also cultivated friendships with the political class governing the cities, provinces, and country. Not all of them joined the political class – at least the MacDougalls shied away from any political involvement (save with some who did, most prominently, the Forgets. Louis-Joseph, who founded his own firm in 1876, and his nephew, Sir Rodolphe, who joined the firm a few years later, were spritely participants in politics, Louis-Joseph becoming a senator and Rodolphe running successfully three times for the federal Parliament, in 1904, 1908, and 1911.

Brokers supported worthwhile causes, usually anonymously and mainly through the churches. They also tied themselves to bankers, and indeed often viewed their own role as similar. The operational model for many brokers was closer to how trust companies operated in the first part of the twentieth century than investment houses of today. During these years, brokers, who also styled themselves as bankers, expanded their numbers and broadened their reach to help finance a growing industrial base. This took the spotlight away from attempts to regulate them. (The Investment Dealers Association [IDA] was formed in 1916.) In fact, the first tentative effort made to regulate the industry wasn't until the 1930s and it was only in the following decade that legislation began to appear, with Ontario setting the pattern. And, as the investment business has become more and more complex, governments and the stock exchanges have set tougher regulations. It shows no signs of stopping.

There was a whiff of military hostilities in the air in 1911–12 but Canadians still seemed surprised when they found themselves at war in the late summer of 1914 after Archduke Ferdinand was assassinated in Sarajevo. Surprised or not, the country rallied to the mother country's defence in an atmosphere of great excitement, its young and middle-aged men lining up to join the forces. But very little fighting took place in the first few months and, for a brief period, it felt as though no more troops would be needed. In fact, many countries continued to enjoy good relations with Germany or were indifferent to what was going on in Europe.

The mood changed quickly with the sinking of the *Lusitania* by German U-boats off the coast of Ireland on 7 May 1915. Some 1,198 persons perished, many of them Americans. It stirred up anti-German feeling across Europe, not to say in the United States. What few friends Germany could count on before the *Lusitania* sinking quickly deserted her afterwards. There was now no doubt in the minds of neutrals that Germany was bent on war.

Back in Montreal, whether the *Lusitania* sparked it or not, Hartland MacDougall volunteered for service overseas on 11 May. Two days later, Herbert Molson, describing himself as a "brewer," enlisted to join the fight overseas and was assigned to the 42nd Battalion, 5th Royal Highlanders of Canada, later known as the Black Watch. They had been first-class athletes in their younger years and now were business partners and friends. The pull to participate was obviously strong because Molson was then forty with four children and MacDougall was thirty-nine with five children.

At the time of his enlistment, Hartland was described as follows:

Apparent age 39 and 2 months
Height 5ft. 9 ¾ inches
Complexion: Dark
Eyes: Brown
Church of England
Distinctive marks, and marks indicating congenital peculiarities or previous disease.

The last statement didn't seem promising, but it was overturned by Hartland's medical-examination certification. It read:

I have examined the above-named Recruit and find that he does not present any of the causes of rejection specified in the Regulations of Army Medical Service.

He can see at the required distance with either eye; his heart and lungs are healthy; he has the free use of his joints and limbs, and he declares he is not subject to fits of any description.

I consider him FIT for the Canadian Overseas Expeditionary Force.

DATE 11th May, 1915

PLACE Montreal

Signed: A.A. Mackay, Medical Officer

Hartland's war service began with his appointment on 18 May as paymaster of the 42nd Battalion, 5th Royal Highlanders, with the rank of honorary captain. He served in France in that job for almost eighteen months before transferring to the 3rd Canadian Infantry Division in late 1916. At the end of 1916, he got word that he was being posted back to England. He left on New Year's Day, 1917, for England but was subsequently told to proceed to the United States to take up the post of deputy assistant adjutant general to the British military mission to Washington. He was now an acting major. While in Europe, his duties expanded far beyond those of paymaster. The official history of the 42nd Battalion explained that he had been with the battalion since its inception and his influence reached to every corner of the organization: "His skill as an advance agent and billeting office was known and envied throughout the Corps. His continued and expert interest in the Battalion transport has done much in raising it to the high pitch of efficiency it has attained. His personality and wide acquaintanceship has gained us many friends, so there is hardly an aspect of our life and work that has not felt his influence and help. We see him go with deep regret."[2]

In the new job in Washington, Hartland was involved in the procurement and supply of urgently needed arms and other equipment to boost the British and Canadian war effort. Even though the Americans had not yet entered the conflict – and would not do so officially until 6 April 1917 – the mission was also charged with advising and preparing the Americans for war. Because of his experience in France, Hartland had a ground-level perspective on what supplies were needed and how to transport them as well as how the average soldier could cope better in the muddy battlefields of Europe.

His posting in Washington in 1918–19 allowed him to keep closer watch over the home front in Montreal, his family as well as his business. By that time, his daughters, Grace and Lorna, were eighteen and sixteen, and his sons, Hartland Campbell (Tommy),[3] Robert, and Peter, were thirteen, nine, and five. He could visit Montreal from Washington every few months, which was not an option for him when in France. As for business, he kept his name in the public view by taking out an advertisement in the *Gazette* during the war years with an eye to jumping back into the banking and financial world just as soon as demobilization was declared. In January 1918 he was promoted to major and from then on, for the rest of his life, he would be known as "the Major" to friends and colleagues.

Meanwhile, he left two close friends in France with the 42nd Battalion. Herbert Molson served with distinction in the lines. He was wounded and for his leadership and gallantry was awarded a Military Cross (MC) and was made a Companion of the Order of Saint Michael and Saint George (CMG). When he returned to Montreal, he and Hartland resumed their friendship and their business ties. They also spent part of the summer together in Metis, which is where Hartland's eldest son Tommy wooed Herbert's daughter Dorothy.

Hartland's closest friend and best man at his wedding, Lieutenant-Colonel Bartlett McLennan, was killed on 8 August 1918 after winning the DSO on the battlefield. Their families had been close during the last part of the nineteenth century when the McLennans were heavily involved in a variety of profitable businesses from making sewing machines to textiles. McLennan, a bachelor, left an estate of $903,000 (about $12.2 million today) which he distributed widely among his family and friends, including Hartland MacDougall and his children. One of Bartlett's young friends before he went to war was Tommy MacDougall. Then aged thirteen, Tommy was devastated by the death of his older pal and his respect for McLennan carried through to the birth of Tommy's second son twenty years later, whom he named Bart.

One of McLennan's great loves was horses, an interest he shared with the MacDougalls. Part of his will read: "The deceased's stock in the Back River Polo Club is left to Bartlett Ogilvie and Hartland MacDougall ..."

MacDougall Brothers continued under St Clair's direction through the first decade of the twentieth century, helped by his son Leonard and E.R.D. Applegath, married to his daughter Geraldine. Noticeably missing was Hartland, who, then ensconced at Charles Meredith, was already showing his independence of mind and his ability to tackle challenges on his own.

In 1912 St Clair, then seventy-two, jumped at an opportunity to semi-retire from the financial business. It came when his friend Edward Rawlings, who was president of the Guarantee Insurance Company of Canada, founded by A.T. Galt and Lorn MacDougall decades before, died. The directors chose St Clair, then a vice-president and long-time director, to succeed him. The company was extremely successful. In 1909 it had an accumulated surplus of $1 million (today about $22.8 million) and it was putting up a ten-storey building it called "Montreal's first skyscraper" on land adjacent to its Beaver Hall office. It would cost over $200,000. The company's history describes it this way: "It was lavishly furnished in oak and marble with fire places in the executive offices and cuspidors beside the elevator cages."

Despite the move to Guarantee, St Clair was still listed with MacDougall Brothers through 1916 along with his son Leonard and Edward Applegath. It was clear he was still watching out for the company. But business was slow during the First World War because of a decree by the MSE shortly after war broke out that virtually closed down the exchange. The rule of 28 July 1914 stated that "no trades were to be permitted at prices under the closing prices of July 28." The same action was taken at other financial centres. When business opened, minimum prices and other restrictions were applied. Roughly the same rules remained in place until 15 April 1915, when minimums in some stocks were removed. The minimum price of bonds was removed in February 1918 but it wasn't until 23 June 1919 – eight months after the Armistice – that all minimum prices and other restrictions were finally lifted. Such restrictions caused much frustration among brokers.

St Clair enjoyed his home on Dorval Island, built by the Montreal architects W. and E.S. Maxwell, who became famous for public and private buildings around the city. The location of his house allowed him not only to indulge his love of horses, one of his great passions from the time of his arrival in the country, but also to play golf at the Royal Montreal, then located in Dorval. He was a director of the Montreal Hunt and the Montreal Jockey Club. He was one of the founders of the Mount Royal Club, an ex-president of the Forest and Stream Club, and a member of the Royal Montreal Golf Club and the St James Club.

St Clair knew the insurance business almost as well as he knew the brokerage business and there was likely more action at Guarantee during the war years than there was at MacDougall Brothers. While stocks and bonds were not highly sought after, the country and the city continued to manufacture shells and an enormous amount of weapons and vehicles for the war effort, as well as textiles, shoes, sewing machines, and dozens of other goods. The need for surety bonds never stopped and Guarantee continued to prosper.

Then, on 10 April 1917, readers of *the Gazette* opened their newspapers to read this announcement: "Hartland St. Clair MacDougall, senior member of the firm of MacDougall Bros., stock brokers, an ex-president and honorary member of the Montreal Stock Exchange, died this morning at 'Ashburton,' Dorval, in his seventy-seventh year. Death came to him suddenly as he had been seriously ill but two weeks. He was honoured for his business achievements and also for his character." "Exceedingly popular and held in high respect by everybody," said the *Star*. "No country has produced a finer type of gentleman," said the *Metropolitian*.

Long before his death, St Clair had become a well-known figure on St James Street, often seen striding between his office and the exchange, dressed in a tweed suit and a homburg hat, and carrying under an arm a book that recorded every one of the market transactions taken at the exchange. He helped keep the family business up-to-date and prosperous, first by working with his older brothers, Lorn and Leigh, and later, beginning in the late 1860s, with his younger brother, Campbell. His partnership with Campbell had been happy and profitable, as they dealt in stocks and bonds, as agents for insurance companies, and as investment advisers to those same companies.

St Clair had carried the MacDougall financial house from the early 1860s through to the first decade of the twentieth century, surviving the deaths of his oldest brother, Lorn, in 1885 and his younger brother, Campbell, seven years later, a period of fifty years. He served longer in the financial business than anyone in his generation, and, in the last twenty years of his life, he became a highly respected consultant on financial affairs to businesses and industrialists.

St Clair saw many changes in the time he lived and worked in Canada. By 1916, New York had replaced London as a source of the federal government's external borrowing because of the war, just as it had earlier for the country's provinces and cities. Within Canada itself, when St Clair arrived in the mid-1850s, the population of Montreal was about 60,000; when he died it was 600,000. The population mix had changed greatly, too. The Scots no longer dominated the business and financial field as they once did, although the English language still held a paramount position. Another marked change was the increase in the Jewish population, from 1,115 in Canada in 1871 to more than 100,000 by 1914, three-quarters of them in Toronto and Montreal. Textiles and textile products, an industry that Jews were often associated with, produced an estimated $32,800,000 worth of goods in 1900 and $160,000,000 in 1923. But Jews were also in tobacco, other businesses and industries, and the law.

By the middle of 1918, exhaustion had set in on the Western front in Europe and an Armistice was signed on 11 November to end the war. But those in the field and at home found little to cheer about. Canada had lost 67,000 killed and about 153,000 had been wounded, some very seriously. It was a promising generation wiped away. They came from small towns and big cities, from notable families and from more modest backgrounds: farmers, fishermen, brewers, butlers, stevedores, surgeons, professors, policemen, bricklayers, bar boys, trainmen, tailors – every occupation imaginable. The vast majority died in the ground war. It was a sad, sobering way for a country to grow up, as Canada did in that war.

And, even as the ships sailed home, yet another and different war was being fought against Spanish influenza, which started in the United States and spread over oceans and through continents. There was hardly a corner in the world that wasn't hit by the killer pandemic between March 1918 and June 1920. The number of deaths was staggering, perhaps as many as sixty million. It is estimated that 7,000,000 died in India; the United States lost between 500,000 and 650,000; Britain about 250,000; and Canada about 50,000. More died with the flu than in the war. It was a horrific aftermath to what many called "the war to end all wars."

The war, almost by accident, transformed public perceptions of the financial world. Prior to the First World War, bonds were slowly emerging as a significant, new trading opportunity for dealers and investors but it took some innovative marketing towards the end of the war to introduce millions of Canadians to this form of investing for the first time – in fact, to the varied world of investing itself which few knew much about. Canada was so fervently committed to participating in the war that little thought was given to how to finance it. When the first two war loans were planned, the Department of Finance in Ottawa didn't bother to consult the Bond Dealers' Association. By the time the ever more desperate government started thinking about the third and fourth loans, the government finally turned to the association for advice.

The result was an elaborate country-wide campaign to sell the bonds through the dealer network, insurance agents, and every other type of financial institution. The time, care, and enthusiasm paid off. The $150-million issue attracted $419 million and 820,000 subscribers. The fifth loan in 1918 was set for $300 million but attracted $690 million in subscriptions and 1,080,000 subscribers; the sixth war loan in 1919, also for $300 million, fetched $678 million and 830,000 subscribers.

The success of these war loans brought a much wider group of Canadians to dabble in investing. It hastened the time when individual Canadians would buy and own bonds and it promoted more active trading in bonds. Within a few years, bonds no longer traded on the stock exchange but through bond dealers. Quickly, brokerage houses specializing in bonds developed within regular brokerage houses. Before the First World War, a sophisticated bond and stock underwriting business had developed. However, it took the necessity of financing the war effort to develop a robust selling organization for both stocks and bonds. And this, in turn, was one factor why the 1920s became the most notorious decade in stock market history.

The mood by 1920 was one of exuberance. Why else would two men, already successful brokers, well known in the community through their hockey prowess and their families, with wide contacts and, in the case of Hartland MacDougall, holding a partnership in Charles Meredith & Company, want to cut their ties and begin again?

EIGHT

Boom and Bust

As judges of polo ponies and hunters, men like Mr. MacDougall and
the Messrs. Ogilvie, of Montreal, are hard to beat ...
Iris Clendenning, *The History of the
Montreal Polo Club, 1900–1940*

Most of the soldiers who fought in Europe or were stationed in
England returned in 1919 to put their lives back together. Every few
weeks there was another parade through the streets of Montreal.
One of the most colourful was on 19 May when the Royal 22nd
Regiment, the "Van Doos," made up mostly of French Canadians,
marched from Place Viger Station to Fletcher's Field. A contemporary account described the scene: "They were welcomed by all
classes of citizens and at the parade there were at least 4,000 troops
... the scene was a riot of noise and color. Never was there a greater
ovation or outburst in the history of French Canadian Montreal. It
was a veritable pageant."[1]

The returnees could sense a scare about "Bolshevism" in the air,
a reaction to the Russian Revolution that was taking place half-a-
world away. They saw the effect of unionization through the war
years in strikes at the Montreal waterworks and then, the monster
of them all, the Winnipeg General Strike in the spring of 1919.
Union membership nationwide had grown from 143,000 in 1915 to
378,000 in 1919.

The returning soldiers also encountered a moral crusade against
alcohol that had swept through the United States and now was seep-
ing into Canada, especially Ontario. Quebec more or less ignored
the temperance movement. In fact, Montreal benefited from Prohibition. It became the city where thirsty Americans visited most
often to live it up. A headline in the New York *Tribune* on 9 August

1920 read: "Montreal is now a great Convention City – This quaint town profits from prohibition – Unprecedented crowds from the States have filled hotels of the Quebec Metropolis."[2]

When Major MacDougall returned from Washington in 1919 to pick up his business career, he found a changed situation on two fronts. His uncle Hartland St Clair, after whom he was named, had died two years before. While MacDougall Brothers remained open and was still advertising in 1920, it was being run in a reduced scale because of the war by Edward Applegath, St Clair's son-in-law. Hartland Leonard, St Clair's son and the Major's cousin, had left the business a year or two earlier. He died in 1923 in his mid-forties.

The other development was that, earlier in 1919, Charles Meredith, with whom the Major was a partner, had created the United Financial Corporation, which included some prominent names on its board and advertised offices in Toronto and Montreal. Sir Charles Gordon, president of Dominion Textiles and vice-president of the Bank of Montreal, headed the board. It was not long before Hartland Brydges became involved with the new enterprise: the name Major H.B. MacDougall, vice-president of Charles Meredith & Company, was given a prominent place in United Financial's advertisement in the *Globe* on 31 July 1919. The company then listed offices in Winnipeg and London, England, and its stated aim was to "purchase entire Issues of Bonds, and deal in Government, Municipal, Railway and other Investment Securities." Meredith, now in his late fifties, was easing out of the business.

There were still valuable contacts and accounts at MacDougall Brothers which the Major could use and grow. And those, along with his experience before the war operating within the upper tier of the city's business community, gave him confidence to open a MacDougall & MacDougall partnership, taking over from MacDougall Brothers, with his old friend Robert E. MacDougall on 1 January 1921. He remained a director of United Financial but the new partnership provided a wider territory for him to operate in. The partnership, known as "Mac & Mac," proved a lasting and fruitful union.

The year 1921 was not a good one for business anywhere in the country but by 1922 the economy was picking up. Later in his career, H.C. "Tommy" MacDougall, Hartland's eldest son, would write that the "newly formed company" of Mac & Mac "experienced rapid profit growth throughout the 20s; from a taxable income of $105,000 (about $1.26 million today) in 1925 to $304,000 ($4.1 million today) in 1928." Obviously, with business piling in, Hartland and Robert needed reinforcements. In 1927 Tommy MacDougall joined the firm at age twenty-two, along with Norman Root. Less than two years later, Victor A.B. LeDain was brought in as general manager.

Tommy had spent the war years at Bishop's College School, where Hartland had gone in the 1890s, and become an accomplished tennis and football player. The tennis prowess acquired at BCS proved valuable in a key stage in his later life. But tennis was just one of many sports he excelled in; the others included racquets, polo, and hockey. Tommy then took his athletic abilities to Royal Military College, Kingston, Ontario, which had first opened its doors in 1876, the same year the Major was born. RMC, although it offered a four-year course, was not a university in the 1920s, but a student graduating from there could move on and earn a degree with one more year at McGill or another university. Immediately after the war, it retained its cachet for young people of ambition. It produced an officer corps for the services but much more besides. Lawyers, doctors, even priests and ministers were proud to say that they were RMC grads. And, of course, education beyond high school was still a rarity in the 1920s.

Tommy was well suited to the life at RMC, where he was able to play his racquet games, football, and hockey. Horses continued to occupy an important place in RMC training in the 1920s, and riding or minding horses was nothing new to Tommy. His generation at RMC was one of the last to train with horses, which, of course, became redundant to the military after the 1914–18 war. In later life, though, Tommy got immense pleasure from horses, whether it was riding in a rough-and-tumble polo match or watching them jump the fences at Cheltenham in England, known for its annual spring festival showing off the best racing jumpers of the year.

Tommy moved quickly from the military life to the floor of the stock exchange when he joined Mac & Mac in 1926. By then, the 1920s were "roaring." The stock market was flying so high and there was so much demand to be listed that the Montreal Curb Market was created for unlisted securities, companies that could not meet the requirements of the Montreal Stock Exchange. At the beginning, 100 members signed up for the Curb Market; the majority were also members of the MSE. In its first year, the Curb Market (later to become the Canadian Stock Exchange) included 37 public utility and miscellaneous shares along with 37 mining shares. By the late 1930s, more than 100 mining shares were listed, along with 157 utility and industrial shares and 32 oil stocks. The number of shares traded on the MSE from May 1926 to May 1927 was 6,887,908. Between May 1928 and May 1929, it hit a then record 19,513,217 shares.

The 1920s was breaking new ground in other ways. The dial telephone became an everyday household tool. About one quarter of Canadian households owned a telephone in 1920, compared with three-quarters of the households by 1930. It helped bind the country together. So did the automobile, which moved from being a rich man's toy to something within the price range of Mr Everyman. And the new fashion for women signalled the new role they would play in Canadian society. It was called the "flapper" style. The women who leaped to join the crowd were seen as strong and free. The signs of the new freedom were hemlines dangling just above the knee and the waist almost disappearing. The effect was the "boyish look" and, despite the name, the new style was a joy and revelation to the men of the era, more used to dresses that covered the ankles.

The music of the era was lively, matching the new fashion for women's clothing, and the most famous of the new dances was the "Charleston," which required an agility and suppleness never seen at tea dances before. The "Charleston," along with the telephone and the car, transformed the way North Americans lived beyond what anyone could have imagined twenty years before. These heady days led to a wild spree of gambling that, in turn, led to frothy markets. There was no better illustration of this exuberance

than the cost of a seat on the Montreal Stock Exchange, which shot
up from $36,000 in 1920 to $225,000 in 1929.

Market excitement was generated partially by a resource boom
in Canada led by a race to develop hydroelectric power, the discovery of significant mineral deposits, especially in Quebec, Ontario,
Manitoba, and British Columbia, and a huge demand from the
United States for paper, and especially newsprint, for a growing
newspaper market. Searching for precious metals opened up new
areas in the four provinces. Between 1921 and 1929, silver production doubled and gold production tripled. Zinc, lead, and nickel
production increased by four times and copper production by
seven times. There had been mining stock booms before, but nothing like what was happening in Canada during the 1920s. It would
continue for decades.

The paper industry was the leader. At its peak in 1929, 33,000
people were directly employed by pulp and paper companies and
another 180,000 people were indirectly dependent on it. There
were 108 mills spread over six provinces, with Quebec accounting
for about half the production and Ontario one-third. The demand
came from increasingly literate Americans who, in 1919, read sixty-
one million newspapers; by 1930, the number had jumped to ninety-
one million newspapers. By the mid-1920s, Quebec-based Price
Brothers was one of the largest paper companies on the continent.
Established in 1817 as the W. John Price Joint Stock Company, it
was run by Sir William Price until his death in October 1924. He
was succeeded by his son, John Herbert "Jack" Price, then only
twenty-six and married ten days before to Lorna MacDougall,
one of the daughters of the Major and Edith Reford and sister to
Tommy.

The families knew each other and Jack, while born and brought
up in Quebec City, was schooled at BCS, seven years ahead of
Tommy, and then enrolled in RMC. He fought in the First World
War with the Royal Field Artillery, won the Military Cross for gallantry, and ended the war as a lieutenant-colonel, a very high rank
for someone in his early twenties. Within two years of taking over
the family company, he cemented the family relationship further
by appointing three new directors to his board. One of them was
his father-in-law.

The Major was more than Jack Price's father-in-law. Whether on the golf course, the tennis courts, or the polo field, in the many clubs he belonged to, or on St James Street, the Major was a consummate connector of people and often the key person in business deals. He was a highly popular and astute businessman who, at fifty, counted as friends most of the senior members of the Montreal business community, as well as a few powerful members of the New York and London financial community. His connections reached to the top of major companies like Molsons and the Bank of Montreal. The head of the Bank of Montreal in 1926 was Sir Vincent Meredith, brother of Charles Meredith, the Major's partner at Charles Meredith & Company, and he was succeeded in 1927 by Sir Charles Gordon, who also worked with Charles Meredith and was active in the consortium, along with the Major, that built the Ritz Hotel in 1912. Clearly, Jack Price, relatively young and in a big job, needed people of experience around him, and no one had more experience than the Major.

In the mid-1920s, the Major again found himself involved in hockey, this time as an owner, builder, and enthusiastic spectator. In 1924 he, along with others, created the Montreal Maroons, hoping that there was enough room for two teams in the hockey-mad city. (The first American team, the Boston Bruins, also joined the National Hockey League that year.) The Maroons were organized to attract a mainly English-speaking crowd while Les Canadiens, formed in 1909, were backed by French Canadians. Leo Dandurand, Joseph Cattarinch, and Louis A. Letourneau had bought Les Canadiens in 1921 for $11,500 (about $120,000 today).

Despite the rivalry, both teams realized that a new arena with artificial ice and more seats was needed. They persuaded Senator Donat Raymond and the president of the Canadian Pacific Railway, Sir Edward Beatty, to put together a consortium to build the Montreal Forum called the Canadian Arena Company. The Major, along with one of his closest friends, Herbert Molson, was quick to hit the phones and sell the company's shares. The new rink would cost $1.2 million (about $15 million in today's dollars), and, when completed, would accommodate 10,000 spectators (9,300 of them seated). As for the Maroons, they flashed across the hockey screen briefly. They played for fourteen years before financial constraints, and the realization that French Canadians were more supportive of their team than the English-speaking population was of theirs, led to their demise. The team's glory days were in 1926 and 1935 – their third-to-last year – when they won the Stanley Cup.

In rapid succession, Les Canadiens were sold to the Canadian Arena Company, then controlled by Senator Raymond, which also owned the Maroons. In 1940 Dandurand took over the presidency of Les Canadiens and a man the Major helped recruit, William Northey, became vice-president and the chief operating officer. There were many more twists to the saga of Les Canadiens, in which the Major and his son Tommy, as well as Tommy's brother-in-law, Hartland Molson, were involved, but those came after the Second World War.

It wasn't hockey, however, that preoccupied the Major, his friends, and later his children. It was polo, which, strangely enough, began in Canada in High River, Alberta, thanks to the efforts of English expatriates. The oldest polo club in Canada dates from 1883 in Calgary. By 1909, Alberta had fourteen strong teams. It took until 1899 for the Montreal Polo Club to get organized. By 1905, the Back River Club had been put together by Hartland MacDougall, Bartlett McLennan, A.E. and G.L. Ogilvie, George Hooper, and Hamilton Gault at Saraguay. The Montreal Polo Club then moved from its grounds in Saint-Lambert, on the south shore, to the west end of the island. The Montreal club disbanded in 1910 and the Back River Club officially became the Montreal Polo Club in 1920.

Polo was a sport more for the classes than the masses because it required a superior type of horsemanship that came only after years of riding and a sharp eye for good horses, which were expensive. But, even by the turn of the century, the Montreal Club had travelled to Saratoga, New York, for matches, and a cup was given for competition between Toronto and Montreal. Travelling to places like Saratoga and Toronto, even to Aiken, South Carolina, then and still a place famed for its polo, was not unusual, and while sport was the main object of a long weekend or a week away (even a month in the south), the social activities drew crowds as well.

By 1910, it was time to establish another cup, known as the Grenfell Cup, to be played every year for the Canadian championship.

Except during the First World War, polo was played every year until 1940. Most years from 1910 to the late 1920s, the Montreal team was led by the Major, usually with two Ogilvies. In 1926 Tommy MacDougall made his debut on the team along with his father and two Ogilvies. The Major had to drop out because of a stroke he suffered in 1929, but from 1926 until 1939, the last year of competition, Tommy played in every Grenfell Cup match and was joined in two separate years by his brothers Robert R. (Bobs) and Peter.

A history of the game played in Montreal states that the club members rarely reached above twenty and sometimes numbered as few as twelve. Montreal polo was largely "a family affair, one reason being that a family is better able to support the expense of maintaining polo ponies than is an individual. Often two generations of a family played polo; brothers played together; non-polo playing fathers and even grandfathers helped finance and support younger players. Thus, the lists of the players for Montreal show two generations of Ogilvies and MacDougall and the Gordon brothers dominating the line-ups."[3] Through polo, the Major was "almost as well known in the States as he is in the northern country," said a short biography of him in the American magazine *Town & Country* in October 1927, which added that he and others from Montreal had made it a practice to spend part of the winter months in Aiken. "As judges of polo ponies and hunters, men like Mr. MacDougall and the Messrs. Ogilvie, of Montreal, are hard to beat, and their services as judges are eagerly sought for important shows such as that of Bryn Mawr."

There was no polo at Metis Beach because it was as far north and east of Montreal as New York was south. Rather, Metis Beach was well known for its sea air, said to be laced with healthy amounts of ozone. It was also where the young MacDougalls spent their summer holidays. Then as now, it was not unusual for Metisites to spend part of both the first year and the last year of their lives among their friends and relatives taking in the Metis air. During those idyllic summers, young people learned how to play tennis and golf around the modestly built, shingled club house. While the niceties of playing these traditional games were observed – as necessary to learn as good manners – Metisites knew from an early age that competition was also encouraged.

MacDougall family lore tells of a tennis match one day in the summer of 1919. Tommy, then in his early teens and still at BCS, encountered an old friend from Toronto on the street in Metis. When Tommy asked the friend what he was up to, the friend said he was on his way to ask Dorothy Molson, daughter of the Major's good friend Herbert Molson, to play in the mixed doubles. "Too bad," replied Tommy brazenly. "I already asked her." Disappointed, but resigned, his friend departed. Tommy then hurriedly sought out Dorothy, whose family rented a house near where the MacDougalls were staying. Luckily, Dorothy was found; happily, she said "yes" to Tommy; and gloriously they won the tournament.

Of course, the teenage courtship of Tommy MacDougall and Dorothy (known most of her life as Dosh) Molson in Metis got more serious and ended with their marriage in Montreal. This marriage, which took place on 25 April 1928, was an elaborate celebration that Montrealers saw rarely.[4] It matched in style and colour the wedding four years earlier between Tommy's older sister, Lorna, and John Herbert "Jack" Price.

The Price-MacDougall wedding, held at the Anglican Church of St James the Apostle, was described by the Montreal *Daily Star* as "one of the fashionable events of the season." The newspaper's description of the wedding, to which 500 invitations were sent out, ran for a full column and included this depiction of the bride's dress: "The bride ... wore a gown of ivory satin draped to one side under a cluster and fall of orange blossoms. Her train, draped from the shoulders, was of silver sprayed brocade, lined with satin. And her tulle veil falling over her face was held with clusters of many orange blossom buds forming a coronet around the head."

On 2 April 1929 Lorna, the eldest child of Tommy and Dosh, was born in the Montreal Maternity Hospital, now the Royal Victoria. While visiting his new granddaughter, the Major suffered the first of several strokes which resulted in a paralysed left side. He was only fifty-three. His father had died thirty-seven years before at the age of forty-nine, something the Major no doubt mulled over. But if he thought about it, he didn't do so for long.

He knew he could no longer play the games he loved – polo, golf, and tennis. Nor could he ride a horse, something he had done since he was a child. He was told that he would never get out of a wheelchair. His reaction was not to get in one. As one of his grandchildren remembers him, he kept his open, charming personality but his frustration showed through often in his crustiness. He never really accepted his paralytic condition, which may be one reason why he continued to live a productive life in business, both in the financial world and in the world of sport, and as part of his extended family for another seventeen years. He attended more hockey games in the 1930s and 1940s at the Montreal Forum than most coaches. And he was lucky that one of the youngest and brightest neurosurgeons ever to settle in Montreal, Wilder Penfield, was his attentive doctor.

The major event of 1929, one that devastated the lives of hundreds of millions of people in the capitalist world, began in the fall when there were flashing signals that the economy in the United States was faltering. Few believed that the stock market would collapse. A *Saturday Evening Post* poem caught the feelings of the naysayers:

Oh, hush thee, my babe, granny's bought some more shares
Daddy's gone out to play with bulls and bears
Mother's buying on tips, and she simply can't lose
And baby will have some expensive new shoes!

The Canadian markets mirrored the New York market. On Black Tuesday, 29 October, more than 800,000 shares were dumped at sharply lower prices on the Montreal and Toronto exchanges, including the best-known Canadian stocks: Ford, International Nickel, and Noranda Mines. As in the United States, probably less than 3 per cent of the Canadian population held brokerage accounts. But the depression that followed those late October days of 1929 had only started. By the winter of 1933, "Black Tuesday" had become a "Black Pit," as one writer put it. In 1929 it was estimated that Canadian stocks lost a total of $50 billion on paper. And, by mid-1930, the value of stocks of the fifty leading Canadian companies had fallen by 50 per cent from their peaks in 1929.

The contrast between the 1920s and 1930s was stark. Farmers bought 17,000 tractors in 1929 and only 892 in 1932. Some 250,000 vehicles came off the assembly lines in Windsor and Oshawa in 1929 and by 1932 the number had plunged to 32,000. Steel production had dropped by three-quarters in those three years. The devastation slowly spread, throwing once thriving communities into despair. With no work in sight and little food to eat, the federal and provincial governments set up food stations. The army was commandeered to run camps for homeless and the unemployed. Political leaders talked about unemployment insurance and other measures to create what we would later call the "welfare state." Simultaneously, one million Canadians emigrated to the United States between 1921 and 1931, many of them doctors and engineers. The exodus was especially noticeable in smaller provinces like Nova Scotia. In conversation today, Nova Scotians still half-jokingly refer to "the Boston states," a recognition that tens of thousands of their neighbours and friends have taken a boat to New England.

Yet, at both ends of the country, governments, led by the federal government, were barring entry to immigrants, even stripping those who had already come of their rights. Chinese and Asians were banned on the west coast from coming to Canada. And, on the European side, Ukrainians and Germans, many of them Jews, also found their entry barred. The fear was that Canada would be overrun with Bolsheviks. Underneath, there was a barely disguised strain of anti-Semitism at work in the land, from Prime Minister Mackenzie King through the top levels of government in Ottawa and the provinces, especially Quebec. It infected many institutions – hospitals, government services, schools, clubs, and universities. Jews could get only menial jobs when they could get any.

Two figures tell the lamentable story. Between 1900 and 1930, five million immigrants arrived in Canada. Between 1930 and 1940, barely 140,000 were admitted, usually the number taken in one year in the first thirty years of the century. And Canada's response to 800,000 Jewish refugees trapped in Europe in the 1930s as they tried to escape the Nazis was to accept 4,000 in the peak period between 1933 and 1939, far fewer than any other country. The United States took 240,000 and Britain 83,000. Argentina took 22,000. It was 1947 before the government in Ottawa began to open the immigration gates. And it was well into the 1950s before open discrimination against Jews and others, including Asians, began to recede.

Not long after the "Black Tuesday," it became obvious that an earthquake had struck the capitalist system and there was a threat that the American and Canadian economies could collapse. The MacDougall family tells the story that the Major came home from the office one evening and collapsed in a chair. "The bad news is we are virtually broke," he said to the assembled family. "The good news is that we have no debts and owe nobody." But the company remained shaky financially as it negotiated through the next few years. "At some point in the 1930s the partners, having invested as much of their own funds as possible to save the business, had to approach business friends to assist them," a family member recalled. "Fortunately, certain relationships were strong enough to see them through these difficult times."

Historians of the period point out that a large number of the small and medium-sized financial institutions were in "technical" bankruptcy for part of the late 1930s and were saved only by the patience of their bankers. The Bank of Montreal, no doubt, was asked to indulge Mac & Mac. From the earliest times, it had been the bank of the MacDougalls. It also propped up many other institutions in that period, including the Montreal *Gazette*.

And there is the story about the time disaster was avoided in the 1930s. It involved another brokerage firm that called Mac & Mac one day requesting more time to settle an outstanding transaction. In those days, each share transaction was settled directly between buyer and seller. If a firm defaulted on a major transaction, the other firm could be dragged into insolvency. When the call came to the partner in charge at Mac & Mac requesting the postponement, even though the two firms were friendly, the caller was told to settle or be forced to settle. The instinct leading to a rebuff by the Mac & Mac partner was right. The next day the second firm went bankrupt.

The Great Depression did not hit Canada as hard as it did the United States. One reason was Canada's consolidated banking sector. In 1875 there were fifty-one chartered banks, but, with mergers, failures, and a conservative philosophy towards banking inherited from the Scots, the number was reduced to eleven in 1925. It was a different story in the United States. In 1929, 659 banks failed there. But that was slightly below the annual average of the previous decade. In 1930 the number doubled to 1,352 and in 1932, the worst year of the Depression, 2,293 banks failed. The most damaging single failure was the Bank of the United States, based in New York, which had 450,000 depositors including many small merchants and working-class Jews.

The worst years in Canada were 1932 to 1938, illustrated by the taxable profits at Mac & Mac from the late 1920s to the end of the Second World War. These bounced up and down like a rubber ball on a string. In 1928–29 profits hit $330,000 but by 1930 they had dropped to $80,000 and by 1932 to minus $10,000. In 1937 and 1938 they rose again to $60,000 but during the war they dipped to deficits in the range of $5,000 to $10,000, picking up again only in 1944.

The profits at Mac & Mac in those years, and very likely those of other firms, mirrored the volume of trading on the Montreal Stock Exchange. For example, in 1929 volume on the MSE totalled thirty-three million shares but by 1932 it was only four million shares; by 1938, it was back up to sixteen million shares, and, for the first few years of the war, it was down again to two million shares.

In the late 1930s, Canada, like other countries, began to realize that Hitler was determined on war and started to rearm. Old industries were fired up and new ones cobbled together to make, tanks, ships, airplanes, and ammunition. The military started recruiting again, and, twenty years after the end of the First World War, there were veterans of that war ready to sail off to war again, leaving families and businesses behind.

For new recruits living in Canada, where one-third of a million people were still unemployed, survival was assured with one, or better two, square meals a day and a weekly pay check. And when they signed up for the military, it was often their first job, their first pair of boots, and their first suit. It was a dangerous job to be sure. This war would test much new technology, particularly in the airplanes and ships, which had created new and devastating ways to kill people. Yet science had also produced more and better ways to save lives. Many of the 60,000 Canadian deaths in the First World War were the result of diseases which were preventable by 1940. Medical advances alone saved thousands of lives of young soldiers, sailors, and airmen in the 1939–45 war.

Looking back, Canada found itself on a roller-coaster ride in the 1920s and 1930s. There was a boom to beat all booms until October 1929 and then a bust to beat all busts until 1938. Thousands enriched themselves and just as many, or more, lost fortunes. Millions found themselves on the dole after the crash, their jobs gone and their savings washed away.

Almost unnoticed, during the 1920s and 1930s, were new trends that emerged in the financial business. First, the United States replaced Britain as the major foreign investor in Canada in the early 1920s. U.S. investment in Canada amounted to 14 per cent in 1900, 23 per cent in 1914, 50 per cent by 1922, and 60 per cent by 1939. (It eventually hit 81 per cent in 1967.) Second, and a cause of the first trend, interest rates rose in the United Kingdom, making it less attractive to borrow there and signalling to Canadians that the United States was a more congenial and profitable place to borrow money because it was closer than Britain and cheaper. Third, Canadians greatly increased their purchases of new bond issues of companies and governments that were issued almost every week.

These three trends would accelerate, and intensify, in the decades ahead. And it would all take place in the context of a fundamental shift in power. When the war started, Greater Montreal had a population of 1,023,158 and Toronto 900,491. It would not be long, however, before Toronto caught up in size and importance to Montreal and then surpassed it. The dominance of Montreal in the country's financial life was to be a thing of the past – much to the regret of the MacDougalls, among others.

NINE

War and Peace

He is the greatest example of the human spirit I have ever known.
Wilder Penfield on Hartland MacDougall

In December 1939, within a few months of the outbreak of the Second World War, Tommy, aged thirty-four, was dispatched to Britain with the 5th Light Anti-Aircraft Battery, a regiment in which he had been a reserve officer since he graduated from RMC in 1926. He was stationed in southern England to guard the country from German air attacks and he served there for nearly four years, returning to Canada in October 1943.

Britain was familiar territory. Dosh had been partly educated in Britain and never lost her love for the country. Before he married, Tommy's father took the family to Britain several times; no doubt, the Reford connections in the shipping world helped to get them there both when he was young and when Tommy and Dosh as a couple visited England in the 1930s and later. There were multiple attractions for Tommy in Britain, beginning with hunting, polo, and horse racing. There were also old contacts to re-establish that the Major had made over the years and new ones to use in growing the business back home, especially after the war ended.

In the 1940s and 1950s, his children recall, Tommy travelled to England, Scotland, Paris, and Lucerne every year to maintain contacts and keep business coming in. "He kept the names of all his contacts in a little black book and always appeared to know every head waiter, doorman, driver or CEO ... he brought all his clothes with him for hunting and steeple chasing. And he kept his bowler hat at the Connaught Hotel," says one of his children who was taken along on a trip.

Horseracing was a special attraction. Both on the flat and over hurdles and fences, horseracing is a blue-ribbon sport in Britain but also extremely popular with working-class men and women. The daily papers take up enormous amounts of space printing programs and results from across the country. There can be as many as two or three meets at different locations in Britain on a given day. And then there are racetracks that attract special audiences, like Ascot, near Windsor just outside London, with its special "Royal" week in June. Noteworthy, too, are Aintree in northern England, where the Grand National Steeple Chase is held every spring, and Cheltenham in Gloucestershire, where the grand celebration of the end of the jumping season in March is held. One of the late summer meets, where the ladies sprout colourful hats and frocks, is Goodwood, in south-central England. It is one of the more picturesque racecourses in the country and no doubt Tommy attended a Goodwood meeting more than once. It was such a favourite of his godfather, Bart McLennan, that he named his house in Saraguay "Goodwood."

Saraguay is one of several communities on the "Back River," as Montrealers call it, the stretch of water that borders Montreal on the northeast side. Until 1918, it was at least an hour to Montreal by road but that year a rail tunnel was built under Mount Royal to Central Station, making Montreal accessible by train via a station near Saraguay called Cartierville. The first family member to move to Saraguay was the Major, about 1910, who bought a country house there, named Ashantee, following his then boss, Charles Meredith. Ashantee, first the country house and then, after the mid-1930s, the main residence of the Major, was next to Bart McLennan's Goodwood. Not long after his marriage to Dosh, Tommy acquired Goodwood as a summer residence. He and Dosh eventually rebuilt it and it became their principal residence in the late 1930s.

On his return to Canada in late 1943, Tommy attended Canadian Staff College in Kingston and he was joined there by Dosh and the family, Lorna, then fifteen, Hartland, then twelve,[1] and the two younger ones, Bart, seven, and Marian, four. In the spring of 1944, he was promoted to lieutenant-colonel and moved to Canadian Army Headquarters in Ottawa, again joined by Dosh and the family.

By coincidence, his friend and brother-in-law, Hartland Molson, was stationed in Ottawa at the same time. He had joined the Royal

Canadian Air Force (RCAF) in 1939 and served in Britain with
the No. 1 Fighter Squadron. In 1940 he flew on sixty-two missions
during the Battle of Britain. After being wounded in action, he was
returned to Canada and served in increasingly important admin-
istrative positions, the last of them in Ottawa. Just after D-Day in
June 1944, he was promoted to group captain. The Molson and
MacDougall families were close before Tommy married Dosh, and
that was the reason why Hartland Molson, born two years after
Tommy, was named after Hartland Brydges MacDougall, Tommy's
father.

In Ottawa, the brothers-in-law found spare time to discuss and
debate and tell stories as only "tour expired" officers can. We can
only speculate what they talked about but hockey was likely a
major topic. Their fathers were keen hockey fans and key members
of the syndicate that built the Montreal Forum. Although Hartland Molson and Dosh MacDougall's father, Herbert, died in 1938
while still head of Molson's, the Major kept up his intense interest
in hockey through the Second World War. Also as a result of their
time in Ottawa, the two men found themselves with a new interest
a few years later, in 1948. That was an Olympic year, and it looked
as if Canada had a medal hopeful in skater Barbara Ann Scott,
who had trained at the Minto Skating Club in Ottawa during the
final years of war. Her star qualities were undoubtedly known to
Tommy and Hartland during their time in the capital.

The Olympics was truly an amateur sporting event in the 1940s
and nothing could taint the image of Barbara Ann Scott; however,
the brothers-in-law found a way to help without compromising her
amateur status. They quietly financed her trip to Switzerland. There
she won the Gold Medal, securing a place of honour for herself and
Canada, as well as building a solid foundation of support for figure
skating right across the country that lasts to this day.

Once back in Montreal in 1945, Tommy and his brother-in-law
Hartland found that rationing was slowly lifting on everything
from sugar to gasoline. But the signal that hard times were truly
over came when nylon stockings, known simply as "nylons," hit the
stores. What a celebration those first sales caused! For Tommy and
Hartland, though, it wasn't long before the reality of work in their

hometown set in. Hartland went back to the brewery and its associated businesses, and Tommy turned his attention to MacDougall & MacDougall and a growing family.

The stock market that Tommy encountered in 1945 had, for the last few years, experienced ups and downs in response to the shifting military fortunes of the Allies, but the post-war picture would be better. In 1942 the Dow Jones Industrial average hit its lowest point, registering 92.92; then, as the war news got better, it began to perk up and by early 1946 it would reach 212.50, finishing the 1940s about 161. Volume on the Montreal exchange followed the same pattern. The MSE traded about 2 million shares in 1941 and 1942 and hit 10 million shares in 1950. Taxable earnings for MacDougall & MacDougall told a similar story. During the war, they ranged from a $10,000 profit to a $10,000 deficit. But by 1945, profits had begun to rise slowly, and, from then until 1948, they touched between $50,000 and $80,000 (about $900,000 in today's money) annually. Financial houses like Mac & Mac relied almost entirely on commissions from transactions, which is why the volume of trading, at that time, was so important.

While Tommy had been away, the Major, Victor LeDain, Norman Root, and R.E. MacDougall ran the business. The war was preoccupying investors to such an extent that it was difficult to round up new business. But there were Victory Bonds to sell and the country was humming with new industrial activity. Canada had little choice but to power-up by building planes, ships, and other material needed in the war and for the economy at home. As an example of how quickly the country readied for war, the Canadian gross domestic product (GDP) rose by 47 per cent from 1939 to 1941.

But it wasn't until the end of the 1940s that Canadians began to see the results of the new industrialization. The expected depression after the war never happened. Employment kept increasing and immigration began to pick up to the rate of about 80,000 annually. Canada's steel-making capacity improved by 50 per cent compared with pre-war totals and for the first time the country was producing synthetic rubber, electronic equipment, diesel engines, and plastics. At the same time, although it was not evident right away in the stock market volume, the industrialization was providing new companies to invest in, which meant new opportunities for investors and investment dealers. While the metal industries were reaching a crescendo, new sources of oil and gas – especially the Leduc fields, thirteen miles southeast of Edmonton, discovered on 13 February 1947 – and the successful Canadian production of nuclear energy would prolong the boom for the next few decades. Again, oil and gas became virgin territory for new and old investors, providing healthy profits for investment houses, including small ones like MacDougall & MacDougall.

Goodwood was now the full-time home of Tommy and his family, next door to Ashantee, where the Major and Edith presided. Neither family was short of friends and relatives. On the MacDougall side, Tommy's sister Grace Pitfield[2] and her seven children lived down the road, along with his brothers Robert and Peter, plus the Patersons, a family headed by Hartland MacDougall Paterson. There was lots of room at Saraguay for the children to roam, swim, sail, play tennis, and, of course, ride in the summer and skate in the winter. Both before the war and after, Tommy and Dosh revelled in skating parties at night with their friends. It was a novel way to entertain but one of the advantages of living at Saraguay was that there was lots of land and assorted retainers to keep horses, skating rinks, and dogs as pets. But there were changes from the pre-war years. Polo had become too expensive and it was abandoned. To replace it, Tommy set about reviving the Montreal Hunt, which he did so successfully that, through the late 1940s and 1950s, it became a family affair to which friends were invited from all over the island. They even came from as far away as the Eastern Townships. The younger MacDougalls and Pitfields rode with the pack beginning as teenagers, and Tommy was master of the hunt for twenty-seven years.[3]

Back at the office, Tommy had two years more with his father to soak up the Major's collective wisdom and experience. The Major had proved a good deal maker, occasionally crafting his deals publicly, as in the cases of the Ritz and the Canadian Arena Company that built the Forum in the mid-1930s, but usually discreetly behind the scenes. During his career, he was a board member of Penmans, Price Brothers, and the Ritz. Neither he nor his father or uncles was ever a bank director. Nonetheless, they worked closely with banks and held shares in many of them for themselves and their clients. Even if they had been asked to become bank directors, the conflict was too obvious. Most of Mac & Mac's clients conducted business with a bank and wanted to separate their affairs between a brokerage house and a bank, and have them seen to be separate. Tommy had inherited the Major's affability and ability to get along with people, whether British or American, whether from Ontario or British Columbia. He also inherited the Major's near-obsession with never revealing a client's name. The Major and his partner, Bob MacDougall, were likely full of ideas for Tommy about possible new deals and new ways to attract investors. But what MacDougall & MacDougall and its predecessor, MacDougall Brothers, did well and would continue to do well was "manage wealth," long before that term came into common use. Their asset mix might include investing in a cargo of timber or ashes or grain heading for Europe or the Middle East as well as Bank of Montreal and Commerce Bank shares and city of Montreal bonds. It is not a mix you would find today but it kept the clients happy.

On 28 April 1947 the Major died of a heart attack in the back seat of his car on his way to work. He was watching over MacDougall & MacDougall to the end. He spent the winter of 1946–47, as he did all winters after his stroke in 1929, driving to the Montreal Forum to watch hockey, whether it was the Canadiens or the Montreal Royals or the Junior Canadiens. He was not only a fan but a strategist. He either stood or sat behind the bench or, at times, was seen watching from a place near to the goal judge at one end of the arena.

If you were a hockey fan in the late 1940s and 1950s, the Forum on Saturdays and Sundays was a piece of heaven. The Canadiens played Saturday nights to a capacity crowd, including standing room; the Montreal Royals played on Sunday afternoon and the Junior Canadiens on Sunday night. The careers of goalie Jacques Plante, without the mask but wearing a colorful, homemade toque, were just beginning and by the mid-1950s Maurice "The Rocket" Richard had built his reputation as a superstar. (One of the authors remembers as a teenager lining up with a friend outside the Forum at 6 a.m. to buy a standing-room ticket for a Saturday night game. The cost was $2 but the experience of seeing "The Rocket" was priceless to us. When we returned at night, there were scalpers everywhere on the sidewalk selling seats for double the face value. For important games, they even sold standing room!) Ward Pitfield II remembers accompanying the Major to a Maroons game at the Forum in the late 1930s when he was a teenager. Even more of a thrill for him, though, was to go to his grandfather's house on Mountain Street, get into his pajamas, and come down to the living room before going to bed to say "goodnight" to the Maroons hockey players who had been invited home by the Major for a beer.

After the war, Tommy, who was a friend of Senator Donat Raymond, became a director of the Canadian Arena Company, which owned the Canadiens. The passion for hockey continued to the next generation. Tommy and Dosh's children, Hartland, Bart, and Marian, remember with fondness those evenings and afternoon when, as teenagers, they accompanied the Major to hockey games. The toughest test for the young people was surviving in the car while they drove back and forth from Saraguay. "As he was a pipe smoker, the car was always filled with smoke, which on more than one occasion made me ill at the end of the drive home," says Bart. "We always sat behind the bench and the players regularly spoke to us." Of course, the Major knew them all, players like Kenny Reardon, Gerry MacNeil, and Cliff Malone.

Young Hartland was especially close to the Major. "I was privileged to be the only person apart from his valet and chauffeur who was permitted to put his bad arm into his pocket," he says. He also notes that the Major "was an avid bridge player who refused to let anyone shuffle or deal for him ... he invented or found (we're not sure which) a machine to do it with one hand." And he was about to give in to a new fangled contraption just before he died. Hartland relates: "Some time after he died, Dad (Tommy) got a notice from the customs that an electric car had arrived that his father had ordered so that he wouldn't always have to depend on others to get around."

The Major loved old cars, especially fast ones of which he had several. According to his grandson Hartland, he aspired to a Rolls Royce and eventually got one. "Therein lies a story ... after several periods of overtime he apparently walked into the locker room and told one of his players – believed to be Hooley Smith – to go out and get the winning goal and he would get the Major's Rolls Royce. The very person got the goal and the Major reportedly walked into the dressing room and tossed him the keys." He liked to be known as someone who paid his debts.

He went to the office in the Aldred Building, which stands between Notre Dame Church and the Bank of Montreal headquarters on Place d'Armes, nearly every day by car. Tommy went by commuter train from Cartierville. Their office was at the hub of the financial district at that time, about a block away from the Montreal Stock Exchange. From there they could operate on the phones and by telegraph to points east and west, and across oceans.

The Major had a highly developed sense of humour along with a touch of the rascal which came out in his antics from time to time. For instance, before being driven home at night, he often directed his driver to the Montreal Neurological Institute so that he could pay a visit to the nurses he had come to know from his many stays and visits there. ('There were no male nurses then!) And he had a red cross painted on his car's roof so that he could see from his office window when it had arrived. It also served as a deterrent to the police if they were tempted to ticket him.

For twenty-seven years, he led MacDougall & MacDougall through highs and lows in the market, through times when profits were high to times when bankruptcy seemed to loom every week. He may not have been universally liked but he was respected and loved by people who were important to him – his family, his friends, and his clients. He was a distinguished presence in what was then still a small financial community in Montreal and Toronto. But there was a wider community both in Quebec and Canada where he was better known, the sporting community. It is fitting that the best of the eulogies was delivered in 1976 when he was posthumously inducted into Canada's Sports Hall of Fame:

CITATION – CANADA'S SPORTS HALL OF FAME
Induction Ceremonies August 28, 1976
HARTLAND MACDOUGALL

Hartland MacDougall, like the famed Lionel Conacher, was one of those select athletes who excel in many sports. He played nationally and internationally, hockey, football, polo, tennis, squash and golf, and in the later years of his life, contributed much to the development of sport.

As a hockey player, MacDougall was a member of the famous Montreal Victorias which won the Stanley Cup ... as a football player, with the well-known teams of the Montreal Amateur Athletic Association, he was regarded as a great fullback. Newspapermen at the time commented that it would be hard to improve upon his running. Descriptions of the game note a neat pass back gave MacDougall a chance for one of those brilliant runs which characterized his play during the rest of the afternoon.

He was a very enthusiastic polo player and still is regarded as one of the greatest this country has ever produced. He was a keen and highly skilled horseman.

He was an active member of the Montreal Racquet Club and played regularly in the Canadian and United States Championships.

One hot summer day in 1928 [sic], following a strenuous polo match, a swim and three sets of tennis, Hartland MacDougall suffered a massive stroke which ended his career as an athlete.[4] He was 53 years old at the time.

He never gave up interest in sport, however, and turned his attention to hockey. He was a director of the Montreal Maroons and a member of the group that financed the construction of the Montreal Forum. Until his death on April 28, 1947, he was highly regarded for his sports knowledge and expertise.

In the late 1940s, both the volume on the Montreal exchange and the profits of Mac & Mac began to brighten. By 1950, volume on the MSE, which stood at nearly 10 million shares in 1944, had jumping to 20 million. The volume stayed in the range of 12 million and 24 million for the rest of the 1950s. Taxable profits also began to pick up by the late 1940s. In 1945 they hit $50,000 (about $430,000 in today's dollars) and by 1951, $120,000 (about $1,000,000 in today's money).

At the beginning of the 1950s, the volume on the Montreal Stock Exchange increased considerably, from 20 million shares in 1950 to figures in the range of 12 to 24 million for the rest of the decade. The story at Mac & Mac was much the same, the firm's taxable profits hitting a high of $120,000 (about $1,000,000 in today's money) in 1951 and staying between $50,000 and $120,000 during the remainder of the 1950s. And, while the profits picked up, so did the number of dealers. In 1945 there were 102 members of the Investment Dealers Association of Canada and by 1955 the number had risen to 208.

In the 1950s, the Dow Jones Industrial Average also began to rise with the sparkling economy, touching 521.05 in 1956 and 660 by the end of the decade. And the value of stock trades on the American exchanges was nearly $42 billion in 1955, compared with the nearly $4 billion total of the Canadian exchanges. This was humbling enough for the Canadian business community, but the statistic that likely produced the most alarm in Montreal involved events closer to home. It was clear by 1948 that the MSE was losing out to the TSE in volume of industrial shares. Montreal had earlier fallen behind Toronto in the value of stock traded annually on the two exchanges. In 1939 the value of the TSE trading represented 56.3 per cent of the Canadian total, and by 1955 it was 68.6 per cent; Montreal's percentages in those two years were 41.5 and 29.4. It was part of a long-term trend that saw Toronto replace Montreal as Canada's financial capital. There were many reasons for this shift in power. One was that Quebec was much slower to develop an industrial economy compared with Ontario. Another was that, as a consequence of its slower pace of industrialization, Quebec's population growth was not keeping pace with Ontario's. From 1951 to 1956, Quebec's population grew from four million to 4.6 million while Ontario's increased from 4.6 million to 5.4 million.

Some of the economic growth in the 1950s stemmed from the Korean War (1950–53). Canada played its part in this United Nations–sponsored war, sending nearly 27,000 armed-forces personnel to fight. More than 500 Canadians died. During this time, Canada was building and equipping its warships, which played a major role offshore in support of its ground forces. But there were other factors boosting the economy, particularly in Ontario and western Canada. This was the decade when a dramatic increase in direct U.S. investment in Canada became visible and, to some extent, controversial. In the five years between 1945 and 1950, foreign capital investment in Canada hit $1.5 billion, 50 per cent more than the total between 1926 to 1945, a nineteen-year period. The highest proportion of that investment was ploughed into petroleum and natural gas, and the United States was the largest investor. As an example, U.S. direct investment in petroleum and natural gas was $141 million in 1945 and $636 million in 1951.

The 1950s are often called "The Eisenhower years" after the modest, decorated American general who was a hero of the Second World War and was elected to the first of his two four-year terms as president in 1952. Those years were celebrated by those who lived through them as a peaceful, joyful period. While Europe was furiously rebuilding its devastated cities, North America was building automobiles, new houses, and television sets at record rates. "What is good for General Motors, is good for America," the saying went. The young were playing and dancing to "Rock Around the Clock" and "Blue Suede Shoes," sung by the gyrating Elvis Presley from Memphis. There were few cares in the world. TV was beginning to produce hugely popular sitcoms like "I Love Lucy," "The Honeymooners," and "The Ozzie and Harriet Show," which reflected the cheerful, even goofy mood of the times.

And, while Americans were enjoying the laid-back style of "Ike," Canadians re-elected Louis St Laurent as head of the Liberal Party and prime minister in 1953. It mattered little that he was seventy-one years old or that the Liberal Party had been in power for the last eighteen years. "Uncle Louis" served as prime minister until he was seventy-five and the Liberals extended their winning streak to twenty-two years.

Eisenhower and St Laurent became friends and the picture that could sum up the decade in Canadian-American relations was of the two leaders perched in a new-fangled machine called a golf cart, riding around Eisenhower's farm at Gettysburg. Those who followed them reported that they were keen golfers but not up to professional standards!

Canada as a whole saw its population jump 4.5 million, or 40 per cent, between 1941 and 1956, to a total of 14 million. Much of this group later became known as "Baby Boomers," who would exert determining influence on the social, political, cultural, economic, and educational institutions of the country well into the twenty-first century. The tranquil, almost self-satisfied world into which these Canadians were born masked rumblings on the economic, political, and cultural fronts that would dominate the next few decades. The two biggest provinces, Ontario and Quebec, were undergoing transformations that would not end until Ontario became the most industrialized and richest province, in effect, the economic leader of the country. Quebec, after years of trying to live in its own cocoon, suddenly felt the thin skin holding its society together crack and then unravel. And, finally, western Canada, especially Alberta, was bent on rivalling Texas as the oil and gas capital of North America.

Ontario was exploding with huge investments in the steel, car, and mining industries. Its centre-right governments were leaders, not followers, spending massive amounts on education (including universities), roads, hydro, and nuclear power. Quebec was far behind. Its education system, at least for francophones, was still dominated by cassocks and habits – priests and nuns. The church hierarchy determined what would be taught at school and university. It also dictated what days the retail stores would open. The stores were forbidden, incredibly, to open on days like the Feast of the Immaculate Conception. And the provincial and municipal governments bowed to the clerical dictates.

There was no education ministry in Quebec. The bachelor premier, Maurice Duplessis, approaching seventy and in power for eighteen years, had no wish to confront the church hierarchy. His industrialization policy was based on head-to-head meetings with American or Canadian industrialists and investors, a process that saw him making a deal and then telling his ministers what he had done and instructing them to make it work. Supplicants who wanted a school built or a road diverted found that the most expedient way to get what they wanted was to visit "le Chef," as he was known, while he ate lunch at the Ritz Carleton in Montreal on the weekends.

Few in government were aware that Montreal had lost the competition with Toronto over financial domination in Canada. But in the business community there was one prescient voice, that of

Eric Kierans, an entrepreneur-turned-economist who took over as president of the Montreal Stock Exchange in 1960 and would later serve in the provincial cabinet. Understanding the need to awaken Quebec to mid-twentieth-century realities, Kierans wrote in later years: "To begin to retake our place in the sun, it was necessary to convince Quebecers, and the French Canadian population in particular, that investing in equities instead of merely sticking the money in municipal bonds, was not always hazardous ... the French press had little more in the way of financial reporting than the stock prices that were furnished by the exchanges. They had scant commentary and no analysis."[5]

Quebec's closed political system, narrow education opportunities, and church-dictated cultural life (the film *Martin Luther* was shown in Protestant church basements in the 1950s because it was barred from public cinemas by the Roman Catholic hierarchy) were together creating an angry class of educated francophones who wanted to turn the system upside down. As for the country as a whole, in 1957 it experienced a political upheaval in the form of a Progressive Conservative Party minority government under John Diefenbaker that defeated the federal Liberals under St Laurent. Diefenbaker quickly turned his minority into a majority in 1958, at the expense of the Liberals and their new leader, Lester Pearson. A noisy and, at times, raucous political era had begun in federal politics.

By the end of the 1950s, Ontario was in full expansion. Quebec was shifting through its past and grappling with its future. Western Canada was demanding attention from the central provinces and the federal government as a region that, because of its large deposits of oil and natural gas, was increasingly wealthy. And, just as the last messages were being sent across the world telegraph system in Morse code,[6] both the advent of the space age and the computer's invasion of business and private life compounded the political and economic forces already in play.

By 1960, MacDougall & MacDougall was beginning to rethink its future. Tommy MacDougall noted: "Parker Reid joined H.C.

MacDougall, Victor LeDain, and Larry Mather, who had married Betty Molson, Dosh's sister, to form a very successful partnership throughout the decade. Profits in the fifties generally fluctuated between $50,000 ($380,000 in today's currency) and $120,000 (about $900,000 today) per year." Tommy turned fifty in 1955, a milestone that, considering the stroke that hit his father at the age of fifty-three, probably prodded him to think about succession, especially inside the family. He turned first to his nephew, Tom Price, the fourth child and third son of his sister, Lorna, and her husband, Jack Price. Tom was a strikingly handsome young man and a natural salesman. And, like his older sister Joan (who would be a very successful consul general for Canada in Los Angeles in the late 1980s and early 1990s), he was genial and outgoing. He enjoyed nothing more than a golf game with his buddies and a room full of attractive women. They also enjoyed him, of course.

Tom had followed his father and many uncles, as well as his grandfather, at Bishop's College School in the Eastern Townships, where he became a star athlete and got his first taste of the military in the cadet corps. After school, he crossed the river to Bishop's University where he quickly became a school leader in sports and on campus. The plaque in the lobby of the Sport's Centre tells part of the story:

Thomas E. Price

BA 1951

HOCKEY, FOOTBALL, TENNIS

Tom Price was an exceptional all-around athlete at Bishop's University. He excelled at hockey, football and tennis for three years. During that time Tom was chosen twice as "The Best All-around Athlete at the University."

The Price family had supported Bishop's University through the nineteenth and twentieth centuries. While at university, Tom was elected to the Student's Council, and subsequently he became a member of the Corporation, where he served an apprenticeship canvassing for the university's various capital campaigns. The experience later served him well in his prodigious volunteer work in Montreal.

After Bishop's, Tom was persuaded to begin work in the insurance business, where he lasted only a few years. It lacked the camaraderie he enjoyed so much at school and university and at the Black Watch, which he joined in 1950. So, at his Uncle Tommy's behest, he joined "Tomacs," as Mac & Mac was also known, this being their cable address. In May of that same year, 1956, he married Merne Perry. In his first few years in the firm, he served the obligatory time in the cage (the secure area where cash and securities were handled) and then transferred to the stock exchange floor. This was much more to his taste, and he especially enjoyed the pranks the floor people pulled on each other.

Six years younger than Tom, Bart MacDougall, Tommy's youngest son, was sent off to BCS like his grandfather and his father. He moved on from there to Royal Military College and, taking a leaf from his great-grandfather, Campbell, in the 1860s and his grandfather, Hartland Brydges, in the 1890s, joined the Bank of Montreal. After a few years training in that venerable institution, he joined Tomacs in 1959 as "a very junior clerk." He was so junior, as he put it, that he "took a cut in pay to $2,400 from the lucrative BMO bond trading job that paid $2,800." He, like the rest of the firm, was heading into the 1960s, a decade that would prove a test for everyone in the financial business.

TEN

The Genesis of 3 Macs

Yesterday, all my troubles seemed so far away …
The Beatles

If you can remember the 1960s, you weren't there. So say yesterday's flower children when they reach back into their addled memory banks. But the 1960s were very important years in the history of MacDougall & MacDougall, setting the stage for the direction the company was to take over many decades.

In early January 1960 the board appointed Tom E. Price and George Deveney to partnership, thus acknowledging the contribution that both gentlemen had made to the company. Then, on 20 January 1960, MacDougall & MacDougall merged their business interests with MacTier & Company. The resulting MacDougall, MacDougall & MacTier was the progenitor of the "3 Macs" nickname that has withstood the test of time.

The merger of these two Montreal companies was beneficial for the partners and employees of both entities. MacTier & Company was deemed to be almost exclusively a bond house and the investment patterns of the prior period underscored the need to have a broader resource in this key investment area. MacDougall was a stock brokerage firm and thus the two parts contributed to each other, creating larger, more reliable sources of revenue for all.

MacTier was headed by a decorated war veteran, Colonel W. Stuart MacTier, MC, who had been wounded in the Great War and still carried the discomfort of his injuries. He was well regarded by his clients and the industry and, although he could be impatient and difficult, it was always understood that his somewhat unsettled temperament was the result of the physical pain he endured daily. He was well known in the bond business and he and his partners derived most of their business from the fixed-income area of the marketplace. MacTier was a director of the Imperial Bank of Canada, an honorary lieutenant-colonel of the Black Watch (Royal Highland Regiment) of Canada, and a significant fundraiser for the 1950 campaign to build new facilities for the Montreal General Hospital, the Children's Memorial Hospital, and the Royal Laurentien. The campaign raised $18 million and was chaired by Hartland de Montarville Molson.

On 1 November 1960 letters patent were granted creating the incorporated company MacDougall, MacDougall & MacTier, with the common and preferred shares held by the directors at that time: Chair W.S.M. MacTier, President H.C. MacDougall, Vice-Presidents Joe A. Leddy and Parker B. (Banty) Reid, and Directors A.M. (Alf) Dobell,[1] Thomas E. Price, John M. Baird, and George A. Deveney. It was felt that a sum of $250,000 would be an adequate capital base to continue to carry out business. Accordingly, the shares were distributed in proportion to the capital already invested and to the contribution of the individuals to the profits of the prior years. One hundred common shares were issued, with H.C. MacDougall and Colonel MacTier controlling sixty-nine and the balance, in smaller amounts, being held by the other six shareholder/directors. Additionally, there were issued 240,000 $1.00 par value preferred shares in the same relative proportions. Although the company was now incorporated, it was essentially a partnership and continued to operate as a collegial group of friends and business associates.

The bond market in Canada was then very much dominated by the trading houses in Montreal; about fifty dealers maintained an active interest in the daily interchange of verbal called markets and one of the measurements of success was the ability to call markets of a significant magnitude. Size mattered in the bond business. John Baird, at 6'6" and about 220 pounds, was known as the "Biggest Trader on the Street." MacTier & Company had size, so its merger with MacDougall created a firm that was well positioned to take advantage of an expanding and enthusiastic financial environ-ment that was a continuation of the robust years of the late 1950s. Shortly after the merger, 3 Macs moved from the Aldred Build-ing, across Place D'Armes, to the newly constructed modern office tower of the Bank of Montreal at 129 St James Street.

In 1960 the public's focus was on elections that were held in Quebec and Montreal, as well as the United States. The government of Jean Lesage swept to power in Quebec, bringing with it a sense of renewal after many years of Union Nationale politics. The hope was that a new and vibrant Quebec would find its way in the form of a "Quiet Revolution." The populace felt ready for a change and was eager to throw off some of the restrictions that the more paro-chial Union Nationale government had contrived over the many years it was in power. In Montreal Jean Drapeau was re-elected mayor and he carried that triumph to city hall with a panoply of grand schemes that would become his hallmark and the joy of the city, at least until the wondrous achievements had to be paid for in later years by the taxpayer.

While Montreal was enjoying a traditional slow summer in the markets, the presidential election campaign in the United States attracted considerable interest in Canada, with most Canadians hoping for the election of Senator John F. Kennedy. Young, hand-some, wealthy, and likable, Canadians were drawn to his charisma and hoped that the new Camelot would include our country as a valued friend and neighbour. In November, Kennedy won his elec-tion and a sense of goodwill was felt across North America.

Montreal was still very much a busy financial hub for Canada, the site of many head offices and senior decision makers of lead-ing companies. The Montreal Stock Exchange was an active trad-ing centre and daily volumes were good if not growing. The shares listed were almost entirely the well-known blue-chip corporations of Quebec and Canada, with traditional support for their trad-ing values from a broad base of retail clients and private pools of money. The exchange boasted a membership of almost one hun-dred investment dealers and regarded itself as the older, more respectable trading floor compared to the three other exchanges in Canada.

This aloof attitude was a comfortable pew for the elders of the stock brokerage community but in Toronto a newer and brasher attitude was creating a distinctly more vibrant exchange. The catalyst for this new dimension of volumes and value was the mining industry in Ontario and its need for capital. The Toronto Stock Exchange recognized the value of creating a robust facility for the heavier volumes of trade and allowed less restrictive rules for the acceptance of companies onto its board. The TSE also encouraged junior oil companies to list their shares as the burgeoning oil and gas industry emerged in the west. The daily quote sheets separated the junior mines and the junior oils into their own selected areas and the apportioning of these securities was supposed to reflect the attendant risks that less seasoned issues carried for investors.

The TSE was indeed the mining market, and while volumes were dramatically enhanced as speculative activity was drawn to the promise of new and profitable ventures, there was a certain wild west feeling about the frenzy surrounding this brokerage business. A well-repeated, tongue-in-cheek anecdote was about the salesman from a minor broker-dealer leaning out his office window overlooking the cacophonous excavation of the new subway and yelling down his phone: "I am right at the drill site and you should see the fabulous gold they are pulling out of the ground."

An increasingly prosperous Canada looked ahead to several years of dynamic growth and counted on a continuation of its strong alliance with the United States. To be sure, the economy was still quite small and Canada was cautious by nature and careful with its balance sheet. In mid-1960 the chartered banking system showed the following major areas of operation: personal savings accounts, $7,086 million; loans outstanding, $6,154 million; National Housing Agency (NHA) mortgages, $983 million. The Gross National Product of the economy was calculated at $39,646 million, or approximately $2,214 per person for the entire country.

Conservative asset allocation was partially dictated by the inability of the chartered banks to lend money at rates higher than 6 per cent, or to offer mortgages not guaranteed by the federal government through the NHA. These constraints were chafing at the

banks and a revision in the Bank Act would be needed to transform the financial system in Canada. Yet, despite the restrictions
under which they operated, the banks were the fundamental cornerstone of the financial system and their integrity and cautious
lending practices would stand them in good stead as times became
more turbulent.

More than ever, prosperity was within reach of a broader range
of the working population and this expanding wealth created new
opportunities for managers of money for individual clients. When
American Growth Fund announced with pride in the fall of 1960
that its banner mutual fund had accumulated a total of $10 mil-
lion of investors' money, it became clear that the nascent mutual
fund industry was indeed a growing force to be reckoned with.
The "mutual" concept was fairly new to Canada and replaced the
closed-end funds that had prospered after the Second World War.
These new funds were a boon to the investment industry because of
the very large commissions attached to the purchasoo and the sales
appeal of having the client's money managed professionally. The
fund business fed the brokers and the brokers returned the favour
with increasing sales for years to come.

In the meantime, the Canadian markets were attracting attention
from foreign investors as well as indigenous traders, and the action
in the mining shares in Toronto had seriously skewed trading volumes away from the Montreal exchange. The average volumes in
July 1960 on a daily basis tell the story: Toronto, 2,500,000 shares;
Montreal, 260,000 shares; New York, 3,280,000 shares.

The more conservative nature of the Montreal market provided
a comfortable niche for 3 Macs and helped create a very special
relationship with clients that continued in subsequent years. The
investment opportunities that were being recognized by a more
prosperous community resulted in a requirement for financial
advice, and the traditional repository of sensible guidance was
the banks. But, since the banks were not prepared to undertake
this advisory role on their own, they forged correspondent links
with trusted investment dealers. In Montreal the Bank of Montreal
established contacts with two such dealers and funnelled requests

for advice to them. MacDougall, MacDougall & MacTier was one of the selected advisers.

Any request for investment advice was routed to 3 Macs from a Bank of Montreal branch, with client anonymity. The firm's letters of advice were written under the supervision of Banty Reid and, if the advice was taken, the Bank introduced 3 Macs to a variety of new clients. The letters themselves were worded so cautiously that even Canada Savings Bonds were noted as carrying risk should Canada not be able to pay its debts. The investments recommended always contained top-rated bond issues and a carefully chosen list of quality common and preferred shares. Usually, the list included a recommendation for exposure to transportation (CPR), the steel industry (Steel Company of Canada), the senior mining sector (International Nickel), and a chartered bank ... like the Bank of Montreal! Some suggested that the weight of the advice was only barely matched by the heavy grade of paper it was written on, which was compared to a premium brand of linoleum. In any case, 3 Macs considered the service and the physical appearance of the advice to be an indication of its stability and strength.

Conservative investment advice was prominent at that time in Montreal and the newspapers carried weekly advertisements by the leading dealers suggesting suitable selections. A typical ad in July 1960 from A.E. Ames and Company recommended a list of sixteen bonds and eight common shares of leading companies. The bias was a reflection of the importance of the bond market for not only Ames but the Street in general. The selection of the common shares was a nod in the direction of the growing confidence Canadians were feeling about their own level of financial risk.

Concurrent with the growth of interest in common shares was the attraction to stocks listed on American exchanges. In the fall of 1960 three offices of U.S. dealers were opened in Montreal: Merrill Lynch, Bache, and Dean Witter. These three leading investment houses brought with them a direct access to the New York and American stock exchanges while also boosting access by Americans to the Canadian markets. The Montreal Stock Exchange undertook discussions with the Boston Stock Exchange to develop a link that would allow Canadian investors and traders easy access to the shares dually listed in Boston and New York.

The Montreal marketplace was profitable for 3 Macs and the firm was able to pay its employees and shareholders year-end distributions that were the result of two overriding business principles: low overhead and generous partners. Accordingly, the company declared a bonus for all employees of $36,500 in 1961 and a dividend on the common shares of $85 and a preferred dividend of 5 per cent. The common share payout represented an 85 per cent rate of return on the initial purchase price.

Accompanying the more dynamic investment climate for retail investors was the growing importance of the pooled or institutional money flows that were finding their way into the markets. Traditionally, pension funds and insurance companies had limited their portfolios to an almost insignificant percentage of common shares, with the huge majority of the funds in bonds and guaranteed mortgages. As portfolio managers began to see the possibility of creating excellent long-term values from a more balanced selection of bonds and stocks, trading activity in shares began to grow more rapidly. In 1960 pension plans reported that their combined asset mix was 95 per cent fixed income and 5 per cent stocks. By 1968, that distribution became 65 per cent bonds, 20 per cent stocks, and 15 per cent real estate, or mortgages.

In 1961 the government of Canada had created by order-in-council the Royal Commission on Banking and Finance, under the chairmanship of the Honourable Dana Porter, chief justice of Ontario. The resultant report filed in 1964, a remarkably readable document and the most comprehensive analysis of its kind to date, set the groundwork for significant changes. The staff of the commission was headed by Montrealer H.A. (Tony) Hampson and included a young recent graduate of the London School of Economics, Jacques Parizeau.

The Porter Commission (as it was commonly known) recommended several key changes for the banking business in Canada, and although it was several years before the Bank Act was revised, the impetus for the amendments that eventually were made came from the report. The major recommendation was to revisit the restriction placed on the chartered banking system by way of the ceiling on loan rates, a regulation first introduced in 1867 at a maximum level of 7 per cent and reduced to 6 per cent in 1944. The commission recommended a floating rate and endorsed a more competitive marketplace for the banking system and for monetary policy. Hitherto, the Bank of Canada had influenced the degree to which banks could lend by issuing directives to expand or curtail their asset base dependent upon the central bank's view of the economy.

Alongside this almost casual approach to regulation was the chartered banks' understanding that during periods of tight lending they would not use any influence to win a client away from a rival. Thus, they operated in a fairly controlled environment that encouraged a similar schedule for all elements of business charges. It was not unusual for this same rigid but very profitable attitude to find its way into the brokerage business, and indeed fixed rates of commission were the key to making a successful living for most investment houses.

In 1963 Bartlett H. MacDougall was made a shareholder, becoming the first non-director to be thus rewarded. Bart had held the position of assistant secretary for several years and was an active and increasingly important contributor to the retail volumes as a salesperson. At about the same time, Colonel MacTier began a divestiture of shares as his day-to-day activities wound down.

The passing of shares from one person to another was done within the confines of a loosely worded arrangement that satisfied the notion of maintaining a partnership approach to the incorporated company. The minutes reported that "the foregoing proposed transfers, being to other shareholders or a son of the transferor, were exempt from the requirement of approval or authorization by resolution of the directors."

Around this time, Robert G. Ross left the employ of a seasoned local dealer, Collier, Norris & Quinlan and, after joining 3 Macs as sales representative, moved quickly to the role of sales manager in Montreal. Bob was another graduate of Bishop's College School and thus joined other members of this fraternity that is one of the enduring links for employees of the company. He brought with him valuable clients and soon established himself as a respected portfolio manager with a growing asset base.

With the economy growing steadily and 3 Macs' traditional business continuing to support its ambitions, the company prospered for several years. In 1962 the firm's common shares paid a dividend of $95 and in 1963 they paid $100. By then, all the original shareholders had recouped their investment and were also enjoying a 5 per cent return on the preferred shares.

By 1963, despite volumes having not increased by much, profits were still adequate and comforting. In October the Dow Jones Industrial Average was then 732, while the average daily share volumes were almost 20 per cent higher than the levels of 1960. Volatility was not yet a factor in the markets and so the gain in three years provided a significant incentive for the public to remain invested and in fact increase its shareholdings at the expense of the more traditional bond portfolio.

In 1964 3 Macs declared a bonus for the staff of $95,158.80, indicating a very successful year and an attention to making every penny count! In addition, the shareholders received a $100 dividend. Prosperity was a reality on the "Street" – as St James Street, the heart of the financial district was known – and in 1965 the MSE moved to new quarters in the Stock Exchange Tower adjacent to Victoria Square. The membership included brokerage houses that traded on either the Montreal or the Canadian stock exchanges (or both) and numbered 110 dealers. The new facilities were billed as the most modern in the world and included new technology for increasing trading speeds and facilitating information distribution.

Amid this new enthusiasm for commerce and risk taking, however, arrived the usual leavening factor in the form of Atlantic Acceptance. A creation of the fertile mind of C. Powell Morgan and the beneficiary of the unlevel playing field between chartered banks and other lenders (acceptance companies were not bound by the constraints that applied to the banks), Atlantic Acceptance grew to be a $150-million asset-based company specializing in commercial loans and equipment leasing, but in the summer of 1965 its banker failed to renew a $5-million short-term note and the company imploded. A royal commission reporting on its demise found it to be a fraudulent operation with no merits. Its founder escaped from Canada and its debtors were unable to recover any substantial worth to cover their holdings of its hitherto well-regarded debt.

The failure was a severe shock to the investment fraternity and caused a serious downturn in daily business for the majority of those houses involved in the money market and underwriting areas. Royal Securities, a well-financed investment dealer, was saddled with an inventory position of Atlantic's short-term paper and faced a serious write-down of its capital base. The concern by the Bank of Canada and the federal government was real and their reaction was helpful. The introduction in due course of deposit insurance for the banking system was a direct result of the meltdown triggered by Atlantic Acceptance.

During the summer of 1965, the *Financial Post*, in its column of advice from members of the brokerage business, printed a report written by Ian Black of W.C. Pifield & Company, Winnipeg office, that selected a list of conservative companies worthy of consideration; they included such well-regarded Canadian companies as Massey Ferguson, Moore Corporation, Imperial Tobacco, and Rothmans.

Back at 3 Macs, at the end of the 1965 fiscal year, Tommy Price became executive vice-president and Bart MacDougall was elected to the Board of Directors. As well, the company declared a bonus of $83,703.25 and another $100 dividend for the common shares. Thus, since the incorporation of 3 Macs, the common shareholder had received a total of $480 in dividends against a $100 purchase price. If public information for investment dealers' return on equity had been available, 3 Macs would have been near the top of the list.

During these five years from incorporation, the company expanded its revenue base by adding sales staff and encouraging additional business from institutional accounts. Alf Dobell turned his hand at being a sales manager and reported regularly on the efforts of his charges; unfortunately, several were found lacking and decided that their fortunes could be made elsewhere. However, with Reid McKiee, who joined the sales force in these years, there was promise, and he would be instrumental in organizing plans to expand the company's operations.

During the early months of 1966, the markets lived up to their promise of earlier years and the New York market, as measured by the Dow Jones, reached the remarkable level of 1,000 on an intra-day basis. This cresting action brought with it wonderful hopes of a long and continuing prosperity, proving once again that it is always brightest just before sunset.

By now, the war in Vietnam was beginning to attract headlines. In 1965, with its policy of lending "technical advisers" to South Vietnam not yielding the expected results, the United States launched major bombing raids. Continuing for almost nine more years, this undeclared war was a serious distraction for the political and financial establishment, and markets became increasingly wary of an administration headed by President Lyndon Baines Johnson that was committed to both "guns and butter."

In early 1966, 3 Macs hired Hugh A. (Buster) Jones away from MacDonald Currie (chartered accountants) and installed him as secretary treasurer, a move that was welcomed by all since Jones had performed the annual audit for years and was well known by the company. He acted as a de facto chief operating officer for the company for many years and also developed a very large and successful "book" of retail and semi-institutional clients based on his skill as an accountant and shrewd interpreter of the Income Tax Act.

The defining characteristic of the business being done within the company at this time fell into the category of wealth management. The firm handled its client base in much the same manner as the well-regarded trust companies of the day. Not only was investment advice dispensed, but a personal service was added that grew into the trademark of the company. Clients could count on their sales representative not only to invest their money shrewdly and conservatively but also to advise them on charitable donations, tax preparation, estate planning, and such other matters demanded by the growing wealth of the individual investor. In the area of tax preparation, Buster Jones was key; he had brought with him the skill and aptitude for the completion of tax returns for clients, and at 3 Macs he began fulfilling this task for a small fee. The service was welcomed by many clients who had paid for this service from accounting firms at much higher expense, and, as most of their financial records were already based at MacDougall, it was a natural extension.

The investment industry was under pressure to upgrade its research of individual companies and the industry category they competed within, both in Canada and globally. MacDougall had relied for years on the individual salesperson to have a familiarity with the stocks it recommended and produced simple single-page summaries of its principal recommendations. Although adequate for most retail investors, these were not considered to be much more than reminders by the more demanding institutional client. Accordingly, the research department was beefed up and some talented individuals were attracted to the company.

Within the research department was a most extraordinary analyst who worked for years with little fuss and no bother. Orvald Gratias, a native of Saskatchewan, a Rhodes Scholar (1930) with a doctorate in physics, past president of an asbestos company, and a diligent acquirer of knowledge, was happiest when doing research of almost any kind. He joined 3 Macs in 1966, eventually retiring shortly before his eighty-seventh birthday. A gentle man, he was loved by all and his work as an analyst was outstanding and persuasive. The sales force embraced his ideas, which stood the test of time as the solid, well-financed companies that he recommended produced steadily increasing earnings, dividends, and share prices. His presence within the company was a testimony to the conservative nature of its investment advice and the belief that diverse talents made good companions.

While revenues were almost entirely derived from brokerage commissions, the company was also involved to some degree in bond trading and syndicate participations. The role traditionally played by 3 Macs was as a member of bond-underwriting syndicates that provided a steady source of revenue and product. The positions were never very large but from time to time would create a sales opportunity to earn revenue with little risk.

By 1967, Montreal was set for a summer party unlike any celebration seen before in Canada. Expo '67 opened in April and continued to hold the city in thrall until the late summer. It was a monumental undertaking for the city and created a legendary festive attitude that reflected Canadians' joy over their country's increasingly important role in the world. Although the Cold War was still unsettling and Russia's imperial ambitions had not all fully played out, the community of nations that came to Expo contributed to an inspiring event and Montreal threw a party that was talked about for years. Everyone has a story from that summer, and some of them do not bear repeating even from the safe distance of four decades later!

The company took an opportunity presented at that time to acquire a small but well-respected brokerage firm, Burnett & Company, and asked H.S. Bogert, a senior partner, to join the board. Burnett was comfortable joining with 3 Macs since both firms had a long history of shared experiences. Its founder, James Burnett, had been on the initial board of the MSE and later served as its president. He started the company in 1868 and, at the time of its acquisition by 3 Macs, it was believed to be the oldest Canadian investment dealer operating under its original name. Burnett & Company was active as a bond underwriter in its early years and was an active correspondent for investment interests in Great Britain. The staff was reportedly happy to leave their seventy-year-old premises on Saint-Sacrement for 3 Macs' "ultra modern" space in the Bank of Montreal Building on St James Street.

Despite the buoyant mood in Montreal, the markets were absorbing new fears of inflation and interest rate increases. The Dow settled at 800 in January, which was a large correction from the euphoric height of twelve months previous. Although short-term interest rates were comfortable at 4 per cent, the outlook was for higher levels and concerns about the economy left investors more cautious. At the same time, institutional pools of money were growing with a rapidity that presaged a very dramatic shift in the drivers of the traditional stock business. Investors Group in Winnipeg surpassed $1.2 billion in assets and demonstrated that mutual funds were here to stay and would create serious competition for the retail investor's savings dollar.

Within the company, a growing awareness of new requirements for the continuing practice of client service created new positions and an embryonic department was to become one of the primary reasons for client retention. In 1967 William Cowen had joined the company from Royal Securities as a trader but, finding the posts overstaffed, he requested an opportunity to expand the client services department and the board responded enthusiastically. The business grew and became a considerable anchor for the mooring of clients' accounts within MacDougall.

Bruce Whitestone joined 3 Macs' research department in early 1967. He was well regarded by the buyers and was recognized by the Street as being a competent and accurate analyst; in fact, he was asked to be a guest speaker at a Wood Gundy investment seminar held in September 1970.

Also in 1967, with Buster Jones now on the board and acting as secretary, the minutes of the company became more informative and the annual declaration of bonuses for the staff and shareholders would henceforth be a more nuanced affair. Revenues remained solid. In that same year, the company produced gross revenues of $854,475 and a profit of $283,791, a margin of 33 per cent, which fell neatly into the Street's theoretical guideline of 33–33–33 per cent for annual allocations for sales/overhead/profit. The company was clearly enjoying good years and the future looked bright.

Discussions began about opening an office in Toronto to participate in the growing needs of the institutional money pools. Initially, sentiment leaned towards finding a suitable candidate already in Toronto to bring established business to the venture, but, after several unsuccessful conversations, it was agreed that Bart MacDougall would move and find space and begin hiring staff. Joined by Reid McKiee, MacDougall found space in the Bank of Montreal tower at King and Bay. The timing of the expansion was exquisite since Montreal was on the cusp of a new and dramatic era, one that many citizens found invigorating but others found uncomfortable and unsettling.

In 1968 Bruce Whitestone's considerable contribution in the area of research was recognized by his appointment to the board. Concurrently, J.L. Marler & Company's remaining partner, Leslie Marler, decided to give up his firm's seat on the MSE and move in with 3 Macs. The company was growing and as it did the realization came that a pension plan would be a valuable benefit for all employees. It was felt that an initial contribution would be made to kick-start the investment holdings and help fund the retirement of long-serving employees. Accordingly, Tommy MacDougall wrote a cheque for $25,000 from his own resources. It was a typical gesture by the chairman and showed again his concern for the well-being of the staff.

The pension fund was administered by Royal Trust and was guided in its investment strategy by an in-house committee of three directors. Over the next several years, the fund grew well ahead of actuarial requirements and the excess surpluses were used to increase the benefits of all the participants. The fund remained under the supervision of the directors until 2002, when its size was considered to be too large for casual supervision and was handed off to professional managers. But for the generosity of Tommy MacDougall it might not have had such a promising start.

Canada was also growing and the country was enjoying a very substantial pace of annual increments in its Gross National Product. A compound rate of almost 7 per cent per annum lifted the average wage and the simultaneous improvement in the standard of living produced a demand for more goods. Inflation was picking up and the country was not paying much attention to this deadly underlying trend; in fact, it was caught up in a love affair: the federal spring election was the focus and Pierre Elliott Trudeau was the captivating centre of attention. Swept to victory in 1968, on a wave of what was dubbed "Trudeaumania," he began a period in office that was to last longer than that of any other prime minister except for Sir John A. MacDonald and Mackenzie King.

In the summer of 1968 Russia invaded Czechoslovakia and world tensions increased as a consequence. This escalation of the territorial ambitions of the USSR was a reminder of the real threat of instability in many parts of the world. The Vietnam War was still raging in the Far East, and on the streets and campuses of the United States there were daily demonstrations to bring the troops home from what appeared to be a losing cause. The U.S. economy was struggling under the weight of the war effort and the domestic need to expand social security and medical benefits. President Johnson clung to his belief that the country could handle the war and his program of social reforms. The combined cost of the war and Johnson's "Great Society" agenda was to create a distorting inflationary bias in the North American economy and provide a springboard for the huge escalation in prices that would be the prevailing headwind throughout the 1970s.

In May 1968 the Toronto office was opened and Bart MacDougall, as resident director, went about hiring suitable staff for the sales department and operations areas. The intent was to focus as much as possible on the institutional sector of the investment arena and also service what retail business could be attracted to the office. As noted, the timing was perfect for this expansion since it provided a haven for residents of Quebec who found political events unsettling.

In 1967 a cabinet minister of the Lesage government, René Lévesque, had resigned from the Liberal Party and established the Mouvement souveraineté-association, which in October 1968 became the Parti Québécois. Lévesque was well known throughout the business community as the architect of the nationalization of the province's power companies. Considered to be bright, articulate, and likeable, he had brought together various factions professing a common belief in an autonomous Quebec. For business leaders, the precedent of removing the power companies from the private sector was a source of worry and the new political movement was deemed to be unruly and a bit too radical for comfort.

The daily newspapers were reporting on the growing importance of the huge hydroelectric power facilities within the province and the obvious drive to make Quebec self-sustaining in energy. Huge proposed dams on rivers never before considered accessible became subjects of detailed study and attracted a considerable amount of attention in the capital markets. Within the borders of Labrador rushed a series of grand rivers that converged at the historically named Churchill Falls, and a private company (Brinco) undertook to build a dam and went about raising the required funds from the New York bond market. Morgan Stanley was given the assignment and with skill and enthusiasm unmatched by any Canadian dealer raised a record $500 million, the largest single bond issue for a foreign corporate borrower in the history of the marketplace to that date. The transaction was assisted by the signing of a controversial agreement between the provinces of Quebec and Newfoundland

and Labrador, which allowed Quebec Hydro exclusive rights to the power generated at set rates in exchange for building the very expensive transmission lines in an exceedingly hostile environment and over very difficult terrain.

The Churchill bond issue was a major breakthrough for the Canadian economy and opened the way for a substantial increase in cross-border financings, particularly for the growing demands from governments as public spending grew at alarming rates. In Canada the growth of accumulated pension plan money was accelerating and had reached a total of almost $8 billion by 1968, with 65 per cent of this money invested in fixed income bonds. Quebec's Caisse de Dépôt et Placement reported that it had accumulated $670 million and had invested 15 per cent of the assets in Canadian common shares. The economy was strong but actual growth rates were being disguised by a steady and injurious increase in the rate of inflation. By now, the statistics were concealing a 6 per cent rate of inflation and the country still seemed oblivious to the pernicious nature of the threat.

In October 1968 Colonel MacTier resigned his position of chair and handed the title to Tommy MacDougall, who assumed the dual role of chairman and president. MacTier stayed closely associated with the company as an adviser and maintained an office for many years. The year had been very successful and a profit in excess of $500,000 was recorded. The staff and shareholders were well served by the company and the client base was expanding and happy.

In early 1969 the Montreal Stock Exchange was rocked by a bombing of its premises by the Front de Libération du Québec, an event that led to many injuries but thankfully no deaths. The blow to the nervous system of the financial community was severe and long-lasting. Faced with this new threat to the relatively peaceful relationship between the city's two founding language groups, business became wary. Investment dealers began to worry about the safety of securities held in local vaults and a transfer to other locations started as a slow exodus without any undue discussion.

ELEVEN

Turbulence and Opportunity

It's only rock and roll but I like it …
The Rolling Stones

To look back on the turbulent years of the 1970s and pick a defining event for the opening of the decade, it might be useful to revisit the movie *M.A.S.H.* Released in 1970, it was a seminal film in that it portrayed an unpopular war within a commentary that was outrageously humorous. It was the screenwriter and director's attempt to show that feigned insanity helps to withstand the mindless, numbing bureaucracy of government and the futility of waging incomprehensible wars in foreign lands. The United States was ready for such a film and its iconoclastic message was received by an enthusiastic audience. The film may not have been, by itself, an agent for change, but subsequent events indicated that the message had fallen on a welcoming public.

In May 1970 the world was shocked when a student protest against the bombing of Cambodia resulted in the shooting of four Kent State University students by the National Guard unit called out to monitor the unrest. The shock was compounded by the apparently callous attitude of the recently elected President Richard Nixon and his administration about both the student deaths and the public's real concern about the incursion into "neutral" Cambodia. The United States was beginning to lose faith in its elected leaders and the tide was turning against the savagery of their foreign policies.

The Vietnam War was grinding ahead with little success and Nixon had replaced Lyndon Johnson as president with the usual rhetoric about ending the conflict. His term coincided with sharp international tensions and concluded in a hasty resignation. It was also marked by several financial events that set in motion serial changes that played out for many years. Faced with a demand by the French government to convert billions of offshore dollars into gold reserves, Nixon removed the United States officially from the de facto convertibility of the currency and effectively devalued the dollar. The attendant inflationary bias to such an action propelled the already high annual deflator to a new and dangerously higher level.

Canada was growing and prospering but structural changes were occurring under the surface that would have unsettling effect on the markets and the population. The census numbers show that the country's population in 1970 was 21.3 million and that its Gross National Product was approaching $86 billion, or about $4,022 per head. This was up from $2,214 per person in 1960, a compound growth rate of almost 6.u per cent and a great testimony to the expansive nature of the world's requirements for Canada's natural resources. That rate of growth was accompanied by a serious increase in the rate of inflation and an attendant rise in interest rates. By 1970, the official Bank of Canada rate had increased to 8 per cent from 4 per cent in 1967. Still, a certain complacency was evident in the markets and business was good and trade was profitable.

Reprising earlier expansions, 3 Macs began discussions with another Montreal-based, well-regarded investment house, Kingstone & Mackenzie, with the intent to merge their businesses and capture more clients and market share. Kingstone & Mackenzie, originally started by Herbert Kingstone in 1919, had become a partnership when Philip Mackenzie joined in 1920. Frank L. Stuart, son-in-law to Kingstone, joined in 1945 and in 1957 John V. Kerrigan became a senior member of the firm. Kerrigan was an accomplished athlete and excelled throughout his life at golf, the particularly social game that was noted for developing client relationships. "Skank," as he was known, held the club champion's award both at the Royal Montreal Golf Club and at the Knowlton course in the Eastern Townships. A smooth swing and a competitive attitude made him a recognized player on many teams and probably won him many new accounts.

The fit of the two firms was a natural since once again the relatively small market for independent dealers was getting tighter and making it more expensive to operate as separate entities. The two companies also shared a similar client base and had social connections to a lot of the same people. The Kingstones had long been summer residents of Metis and therefore were well known to the MacDougall and Price families. Metis was and is a retreat for many wealthy families during the hot summer months and social gatherings included clients of both firms.

Stuart and Kerrigan were the senior partners and accompanying them to the merger in 1970 were associates James R. Ballantyne and Stewart Arbuckle, along with ten other employees. This additional workforce brought 3 Macs to a total of about seventy-five people, with a considerable overlap of jobs in some cases. However, the policy had always been one of consideration to long-term employees so few layoffs were expected and the forecast savings were not realized immediately.

In June, Tommy MacDougall and Joe Leddy sold shares of 3 Macs to Frank Stuart and John Kerrigan at book value. The merger was complete, but an agreement that bound 3 Macs to a number of contractual payments was appended to the closing documentation that illustrated the caution that had entered into the partnership method of doing business. The agreement placed a degree of separation into the status of Stuart and Kerrigan for a number of years that may have favoured these two directors over other partners.

That year, Montreal was enjoying warm and sunny summer, weather that lasted well into the fall, when suddenly the province was thrown into turmoil and confusion. The now well-known October Crisis confirmed the suspicions of many in the business community that a movement was afoot which made it unwise to confine operations within the borders of Quebec. The Parti Québécois had already broken into the ranks of elected members to the National Assembly, with seven candidates gaining seats in a provincial election, and its stated mandate to achieve sovereignty-association with the rest of Canada was disturbing.

MacDougall, MacDougall & MacTier viewed all of this with extreme caution and undertook to assure its clients in Montreal that it was not of the opinion that current political trends threatened their assets and income streams. Yet the firm's ability to offer clients a haven in Toronto if they so desired was a comfort for many of them, who asked that their physical securities be moved to the custodial vaults of Ontario branches of the Canadian banks and trust companies. Although headlines spoke of massive corporate defections and an exodus of anglophones, the core clientele of 3 Macs stayed home and patiently waited for more sensible times. They waited a long time.

The Toronto office of 3 Macs was prospering and a gradual but steady increase in revenues over the years endorsed the original decision to open the branch. Discussions were held about the practical matter of trading on the floor of the Toronto Stock Exchange with the company's own traders and it was decided that an offer should be made to a known trader who could undertake that duty. Hitherto, the trading had been done by local firms that acted on behalf of 3 Macs, but, as volumes grew, this practice became more expensive and the seat was activated. In due course, Ricky Craig joined as a floor trader, and subsequently Phil Barnoff moved to Toronto to undertake the job of institutional trader for the burgeoning business being done with the growing pools of pension and mutual fund assets. Barnoff had joined the company directly from high school in 1952 and by 2008 was the longest-serving employee still with the company. A hardworking natural salesman, he found fertile ground to plough and assisted Bart MacDougall and the research team to make inroads in this highly competitive area. Barnoff established his business by following the example of the partners and displaying an unusual capacity to execute large trades with complete confidentiality and integrity – a skill much valued and admired by his clients.

In 1971 Tommy MacDougall informed the board that he wished to reduce his role within the company and stepped down as president. As his successor, the board named Thomas E. Price, with Tommy as chairman. Tom Price was a natural choice, a leader both within the company and outside it in the world of the Black Watch and charitable organizations and his beloved Queen Elizabeth

Hospital. Warm and sociable, he made friends, and attracted clients, easily, all of them drawn to his trustworthiness and goodwill. His contributions to the company were significant and he was a major producer of the day-to-day brokerage revenue that drove the fortunes of the firm. Tom also enjoyed the privilege of commanding the honour guard for the Queen Mother when she made her various trips to Canada as the commander-in-chief of the Black Watch. A picture of Tom in full regimental dress towering over the Queen remains in his old office as a memento of these illustrious occasions.

H.S. Bogert retired and left the company, declaring that the years together had been happy and profitable and he was glad he had made the choice to merge the two partnerships. There was a mandatory retirement age of seventy for 3 Macs directors at that time, as well as an unofficial understanding that those who wished to remain active would be provided with a desk and, albeit on a much reduced basis, a secretary. Remuneration was still provided by commissions earned and thus a number of the older gentlemen chose to continue to "go to the office." This gave rise to the Morning Room, a shared facility for the retirees and a convenient facility for the firm. The name derived from the hours that the old guard appeared capable of enduring before retiring for lunch and the day.

At a board meeting in August 1971, the question arose about making non-directors eligible for share ownership. It was decided that H.A. Jones would consider the subject and make a recommendation sometime in the future. Until then, the only holders of the company's shares were directors and it was felt that, since the ranks of the employees were expanding and the size of the board was getting to be larger than required for the running of the firm, perhaps an old tradition could be shelved. Another argument for change was that some new and dynamic producers were not shareholders and thus did not fully benefit from their efforts. The matter remained unresolved until 1990. At the time, a concern was expressed that to open the shareholder's list to non-directors might create a dumping ground for unwanted shares. The attitude reflected the reality that owning shares of a small brokerage company was a risk and the liability should be borne by those best able to assume this responsibility. And, in fact, conditions were getting a lot riskier.

Things were not going well for the largest economy in the world. In 1973 it was reported that almost $80 billion U.S. dollars were in the hands of offshore investors who were getting very worried about the continuing slide of the greenback on the currency markets. With the dollar down almost 20 per cent against a basket of other currencies, the outlook was not good despite the continuing talk of the need for a strong dollar by Arthur Burns, chairman of the Federal Reserve, and George Shultz, secretary of state. The resulting price escalation in primary assets such as commodities began to unsettle the producing nations and the consuming countries began to fear that inflation would derail the apparent improvement in world trade.

The first dramatic reaction to the decline of the U.S. dollar was the rise in the price of gold from $70 to $120 in twelve months. This forewarned of more inflation and possible difficulties for financial markets. The next shoe to drop was considerably larger and had a much more significant impact. The Organization of Petroleum Exporting Countries (OPEC) held an emergency meeting and without an apology raised the previously agreed price of oil from $2.50 a barrel to $12.00. Welcome to a new age of price distortion set by monopolistic producers and not by demand from users.

The year 1974 would be remembered for a long time in the investment industry, as markets tumbled and volumes dried up and investors became aware that the world was not unfolding as it should. In no particular order, the markets were absorbing the reality that inflation was clearly running out of control, averaging 13 per cent in the developed world; an opinion was widespread that, with wheat trading at $6 a bushel, much of the undeveloped world was flirting with starvation. By summertime, a noted economist described the credit markets as being in "a period of terror because of the lack of availability of money to borrow." Lenders were not inclined to be generous when they were being paid back in dollars with purchasing power worth 10 to 20 per cent less than at the time of the initial transaction.

Accordingly, the stock markets collapsed and volumes became so light that sixty of the ninety members of the Toronto exchange reported losses in the year to June. In August 1974, the total weekly volume of the TSE was less than eight million shares, and the world had just witnessed Richard Nixon resign his office in the face of serious charges of illegal activities, the first U.S. president to do so. In October the Dow Jones recorded a low of 584, marking a bear market on the New York exchange that had run for 631 days. It was not pretty. That fall the Canada Savings Bond campaign attracted billions of dollars since the rate was set at a generous 9.75 per cent and carried the usual cash-on-demand obligation.

Yet 3 Macs suffered only mildly. Profits in 1972 and 1973 were $595,000 and $663,000 respectively and slumped to $410,000 in 1974. Clearly, the benefit of a captive, loyal clientele was never more evident. Part of the firm's success during this period can be attributed to the growth of revenues in the Toronto branch. A solid increment of business with both retail and institutional clientele allowed the unit to record increases in gross commissions from a base of $123,000 in 1970 to $650,000 in 1974. The emphasis on selected research and intense coverage of friendly accounts was spearheaded by the employment of salesmen who were allowed access to the large accounts with little internal competition.

The requirement to create more revenues from institutional accounts was met by a selection of young aggressive sales people who joined (and left) 3 Macs in the 1970s and 1980s. The effort was diverse and relied on a coterie of individuals who could do both research and sales and provide advice to the traditional sales force at the same time. The inclusion of Bruce Whitestone in the preceding decade had allowed the board to see the benefits of this new dimension to their business and in due course the Toronto office under the guidance of Bart MacDougall hired a succession of able employees. John Budden was the first true institutional sales representative and he was soon joined by Murray Pollitt, Peter Legault, Kim Kertland, Nigel Lees, and Michael Farrugia, all of whom had special talents in their chosen areas of expertise. Budden and Pollitt joined the Board of Directors in 1972, Legault in 1976, and Farrugia in 1980, but by 1985 they had all left to find greener pastures represented by a larger ownership share in their new locations. It should be noted that Pollitt and Legault went off to start their own company and took with them a talented and well-liked young salesperson in Montreal, Luc Bertrand, who went on to fame (and some reasonable fortune) as president of the Bourse de Montréal.

But the attraction of doing well-paid institutional business was gaining ground on the Street and the larger investment dealers were devoting more attention to their research and trading abilities. The exchanges also recognized the need to be slightly more competitive on their pricing structure and various reductions in trading costs were introduced, dependent upon the value of the trade. Over time, the commission rates developed a tapering schedule that lowered the rates for large trades and the initial steps were taken to introduce the much feared removal of fixed rates.

In Montreal, 3 Macs recruited new talent from the Street. Jawaid Khan came from Rothschild's in the fall of 1972, followed by Ian Black (from Pitfield) in the spring of 1973. Both brought their clientele with them and added valuable production during these unsettled times. Reflecting the directors' preference, the company retained a cautious and conciliatory attitude to decision making and continued a practice of deferring agenda items from meeting to meeting. A typical moment could be described as follows. Mr X appeared to be opposed to the idea presented by Mr Y, his opposition manifested by hand signals made to the chairman while Mr Y was speaking. The chairman finally stated that the matter would be discussed by the Management Committee at a later date.

Business was slow in 1974 and early 1975 and steps were taken to ensure that all staff was fully employed and busy. Several clerical staff retired and few were fully replaced. The Toronto and Montreal exchanges discussed the benefits of imposing surcharges on larger trades to help the member firms survive. With the boards of the exchanges composed entirely of members, the discussion must have been less than far-reaching. Certainly, 3 Macs was an interested party, since Kerrigan served on the Montreal board and carried with him the message that the increased tariffs were in keeping with the needs of the industry. All of these discussions were shelved when, on 1 May 1975 (May Day!), the New York Stock Exchange acceded to a ruling by the Securities and Exchange Commission and declared that, from that date forward, each commission charged must be set by negotiation with the client. Fixed commission rates were history and the industry had to respond with a new set of dynamics. The industry responded immediately by lowering all commissions for large orders and maintaining a "card rate" for retail clients. It was not a very fair shake for the smaller client and gave rise to the advent of the discount-brokerage facility now so readily available for all investors and traders.

At about that time, Tom Price informed the 3 Macs board that the remaining partner of the Quebec City firm Barry & McManamy, M. Gerard Delagrave, had died and the senior representative, Olivier Samson, wished to throw in his lot with their correspondent and good friends, 3 Macs. The relationship between the two firms was of such long standing that it is suspected that the first orders were placed on behalf of Barry & McManamy sometime around 1910, when the communication between the two trading desks was done by telegraphic Morse code and required an experienced operator at each end. (In fact, this method of communicating orders was still in use when Bart MacDougall joined the company in 1959.)

The deal was approved on the condition that a suitable candidate be found to bolster the branch and apprentice under Samson. It is maybe just as well that Samson made no condition to continue the name of his company within the acquisition. Three Macs and a Mc might have been too much for the predominantly francophone population of Quebec City. Even MacDougall, MacDougall & MacTier does not trip off tongues easily in most of Quebec. But Samson's reputation was well established and the acquisition was a boost for all involved. In short order, Olivier was asked to join the board, concurrent with the appointment in Montreal of Ian Black.

The news improved in mid-1975 and markets began a substantial recovery from the lows, and leading the way was the good news that Trans Canada Pipelines had signed a potential $500-million contract with Imperial Oil to bring the gas found in the Mackenzie River Delta to market. It was noted that the pipeline would not be in place until the mid-1980s and would require approval of the National Energy Board. It was also noted that maybe the energy policy of Canada might have to be revised to reflect world prices, as domestic crude oil was priced at $6.50 a barrel against the prevailing world price of $10.50. The federal government of the day watched with interest the growing strength of the petroleum industry in Canada, and when the Iranian revolution brought the next sharp increases to oil prices (1979), it turned away from the stated policy of merging the pricing structure into the prevailing world price. The pertinent fable of King Canute was not being retold in the parliamentary halls of Ottawa.

November 1975 marked the retirement of Tommy MacDougall from the chair and from his role as an officer of the company, but he remained an active participant in the handling of accounts. Joe Leddy also retired and vacated his chair at the bond desk. At the shareholders' meeting in January 1976, Tom Price was awarded the additional role of chairman, a title he held for over twenty years; Buster Jones and Bart MacDougall were named vice-presidents.

By 1976, the population of Canada was over twenty-one million and the Gross National Product was about $9,000 per head. The growth rate was high and general business conditions were good, but the underlying inflation rate was disconcerting and covered a multitude of business and financial weaknesses that would be discovered in subsequent years. Leading the cheering was the Dow Jones Industrial Average, which celebrated its return to the majestic height of 1,000 by June. The market received further comfort from the assurance of President Gerald Ford's chief economic adviser, Alan Greenspan, that the recent bout of inflation was abating and the future looked bright.

In Quebec, the election of 15 November 1976 provided a new and dramatic point of reference for Canada and for Montreal in particular. On that day, the Parti Québécois defeated the incumbent Liberal government of Robert Bourassa, giving a considerable boost to the notion of a separate Quebec. The country was plunged into uncertainty and the financial markets began marking down the price of the securities issued by the province and companies with large exposure there. The discounting was swift and expensive and was factored into the calculations of the analysts and economists who supplied the marketplace with valuations. House prices in Montreal were quickly lowered and "À Vendre" signs appeared on a lot of lawns in Westmount. In 1978 the wording on car licence plates changed from "La Belle Province" to "Je me souviens," which alarmed English speakers until they were reminded that this phrase was in fact the official motto of the province. But a more ominous note of concern was struck when the Sun Life Assurance Company voted at its annual meeting in April to move its head office from its storied building in Montreal to a location in Toronto. This decision of an emblem of tradition and financial stability became a lightning rod for all manner of uncomplimentary commentary in the press and symbolized the fears of the anglophone business community in Quebec.

During this period, 3 Macs continued to grow its business and added employees. One addition at that time was Athol Gordon, an old friend of Tom Price who had recently left the construction business. It was felt that Gordon's talents could be redirected into sales and he was soon placed on the board. He also added many of his broad list of contacts to the client base. An avid fisherman and an extensive traveller, Gordon brought an international outlook to his investment selections and his clients enjoyed the bull years of the Japanese market as well as the more familiar selections in the North American markets. The investing public was becoming more intrigued by stories of great wealth accumulating in foreign lands and looking for suggestions to participate in this growth.

Indeed, capital was accruing in several parts of the world and civilian demands on these new wealthy countries provoked a desire to have even more riches on hand to ensure that the populace remained compliant. Accordingly, as the decade grew to a close, the world was pummelled by another shock from OPEC, which raised the price of a barrel of oil to an astounding $40. This dramatic move created another volatile upward trend in the prices of almost all commodities, and the cost-of-living indices of most of the developed countries spiralled up to agonizing levels.

Canada was increasingly vulnerable to any economic downturn owing to the unprecedented annual deficits and staggering accumulated debt of governments at all levels. As inflation mounted, so did interest rates, and the attendant financing costs crippled Canada's ability to maintain the confidence of foreign lenders. Although viewed as a country rich in vast natural resources, debt levels began to shake the markets' confidence, and, as the world grappled with distorting rates of inflation and interest rates, Canada veered closer to the brink of disaster. The international community was growing sceptical of Canada's ability to repay its obligations, and the country was on the verge of losing a coveted AA rating on its foreign debt.

Economic imbalances were being felt all over the world and the political rhetoric of the time seemed to involve a great deal of bluster on the part of elected officials. Nowhere was this more evident than in the United States, where President Jimmy Carter, appalled by the rise in the price of gas at the pump to over $1.00 a gallon, called on the nation to "fight the moral equivalent of war" on energy waste and pledged to reduce the dependency of America on imported oil. This rousing call to arms in 1977 was subverted by the release that May of the blockbuster movie *Star Wars*, four years in the making at a cost of $11 million, which helped the public to forget its immediate troubles and revel in the imaginary world of space warfare created by special effects.

In 1976, 3 Macs had dispatched Peter Johnson to Quebec City to assist the office with its ability to attract institutional business and to help grow the retail side. Johnson, fluently bilingual, was successful in this mission. Enjoying the laid-back ambiance of the city, he stayed there for two years before returning to Montreal and handing the branch to Bill O'Connor. Marc Jobin joined the company, and, after a period of training in Montreal, moved to Quebec City and became the manager a few years later. Johnson's new mandate was to take charge of institutional trading and work with the sales people, who counted on these accounts to provide their livelihood.

Discussions were held at regular intervals about the need to create more shareholders and thus more directors, but the discussions seemed to end each time with no clear policy being formulated. Some of the more senior non-director staff were getting anxious about their inability to participate in the growth of the company's worth, and the pressure to do something to address this problem was increasing.

But a more important and consuming pressure was mounting in world markets as the annual rate of inflation caused distortions unseen for years and created difficult markets for both stock and bond buyers. The U.S. annual rate of inflation broke through 9 per cent in 1978 and the price of gold, long considered a safe haven to offset the damage, rose above $245, heralding the return of the gold bugs who cried about the end of the world as we knew it. The administered rates of interest rose and soon the world was looking at 10 per cent short-term rates that spoke of harsher conditions to follow. All this was, of course, very unsettling, and so 3 Macs was forced to review its traditional conservative capital structure and its modest payrolls. Profits indeed did drop in 1976 but by 1979 they were back on stream and the business was growing as the threat of more people and accounts going down Highway 401 to Toronto did not seem to materialize, at least not with the core client base. There was some movement of institutional funds, and the production unit concentrating on this business in the Toronto office added to the retail side and in combination produced over $800,000 in revenues – a very welcome source of profits and a reflection of the serious erosion of the city of Montreal's ranking among financial centres. In this world, Montreal was now relegated to a second-rung position.

One of the magnets that kept the existing clients on board was the growing dependence they felt on the services offered by the company. Bill Cowen and Buster Jones had expanded the client services department into a one-stop shopping facility for the wealthy. Tax preparation had become a key element of the bond between 3 Macs and the clients. A highly regarded knowledge of the tax rules, combined with complete record keeping of the security holdings and income therefrom, allowed the client freedom from the anxiety associated with increasingly complex annual filings.

In Rome an event that would help shake the world's political establishment took place on 16 October 1978 with the election of Cardinal Karol Wojtyla as the first non-Italian pope in 456 years. He took the name John Paul II and became a fast-moving, much travelled champion of freedom and a beacon of hope for Catholics around the world. His Polish background gave him a significant education in the brutality of nazism and communism and he worked overtly and behind the scenes to help break down the Soviet empire. His initial travels to Poland and South America, along with the new formal links forged between China and the United States, gave pause to the Russians, and the slow but inexorable pace of a new revolution started to have traction.

Unfortunately, the world economy was more focused on rising inflation, poor performance by corporations, painful interest rates, and escalating oil prices. By the end of 1979, the U.S. Congress had decided that one way to offset the cost of rising energy prices was to vote in favour of a tax on "windfall profits derived by the oil producing and refining industry." Shortly thereafter, Chrysler Corporation stunned the marketplace by announcing the largest loss recorded by an American company. It blamed the $1.1-billion debacle on the driving public, who had collectively decided to turn away from trucks and gas-guzzlers and look for smaller, fuel-efficient cars. Gasoline was heading for $1.50 a gallon.

Economic forecasts were speaking of credit defaults, energy shortages, and political unrest. Montreal was beginning to identify with that last concern in particular as the province prepared itself for a referendum on "sovereign association" and a restructuring of the old order. But 3 Macs, demonstrating its steady course in these perplexing times, recorded its first profit (before shareholder payouts) of $1 million and reiterated the need to be careful about escalating overhead costs.

In November 1979 Frank Stuart retired as a director and offered his 10 per cent of the company's shares for sale. They were redistributed to recently appointed new directors and he continued to be an associate servicing his old and related clients.

TWELVE

Inflation and
Volatility

Don't go breaking my heart ...
Elton John

"Look up, waaaay up." For years, these words welcomed a generation of children to the CBC's "Friendly Giant" program. Developed
and performed by an American with the help of a remarkable cast
of puppets and voices, the show portrayed a gentle, loving giant
who played the flute and told warm and entertaining stories with
his pals. Robert Homme (the Giant) and Rod Coneybeare (puppets and voices) became symbols of decency and reliability for millions of children, and the idea of meeting a giant helped to keep
their attention.

In 1979 the U.S. Federal Reserve, the dominant monetary manager in the world, was faced with the difficult task of wrestling to
the ground the twin dragons of the worst inflation and the slow-
est economic growth that had been experienced in years. President Jimmy Carter was displeased with the incumbent chairman,
William Miller, and so, instead of renewing his term in office, he
replaced Miller with the presiding chair of the New York Federal
Reserve, Paul Volcker. Volcker, who headed "the Fed" until 1987,
was a giant man, 6'7", but he was not friendly ... at least not to the
dreaded foes he was asked to defeat: inflation, stagflation, sinking
currency, labour unrest, and other assorted evils. He pulled up the
drawbridge and rounded up his supporters and went to work on
the task at hand. He was a formidable man and inspired a worldwide following as he began the unwinding of years of neglect by

his predecessors. The fire-breathing monsters were to be contained or slain, whichever came first.

Volcker began his task by raising the reserve requirements of banks, and shortly thereafter he moved the administered federal funds rate to 13 per cent. The message was received by the financial markets: Don't mess with Hopalong Cassidy! The big man with the big white hat was going to be the saviour of the nation; however, the road to salvation was going to be bumpy and the Dow Jones Industrial Average "plunged" 26 points and the volume traded reached an unprecedented 81 million shares on one day. Shock waves were felt throughout the investment community and serious steps were taken to reduce exposure to all manner of risk. The way ahead was dark and dreary and would remain a difficult path to follow for several years.

In early 1980, 3 Macs, still debating the need to open the share-holders' list to new entrants, elected Bill Cowen, Phil Barnoff, and Michael Farrugia to the board. The appointments represented recognition of the revenues that each had brought to the company and their contribution to the overall growth of profits. Unfortunately, their worth was not appreciated by all and Farrugia resigned shortly thereafter to pursue an independent future in the resource industry. His decision to leave was emulated by Nigel Lees a few months later, thus reducing the institutional sales force in Toronto by about 50 per cent and forcing the focus back to the retail business that the firm was dependent upon through good times and bad.

Business was good during the fiscal year 1980: revenues hit over $5 million for the first time and pre-bonus profits exceeded $2 million. The equity base remained small as the requirement for excess capital continued to grow, but, despite Buster Jones's best efforts to keep expenses bottled up, the firm was forced to issue shares to bolster the capital base. Accordingly, new common and preferred shares were issued and distributed among the shareholder/director ownership. It is of note that, while the larger firms were also finding capital requirements more onerous, 3 Macs was able to tap its existing shareholders without offering any undue financial or banking assistance. The Street was more dependent on helpful banks to assist individuals with share purchases despite the inherent very high risk in the security. By the mid-1980s, it was estimated that the banks owned about 70 per cent of the capital of the dealer fraternity through loans to the shareholders.

In April 1980 world tensions escalated when the United States announced that, in protest against the Russian invasion of Afghanistan, it would not participate in the Moscow Olympics. This boycott was, of course, a useless display of belligerence and did nothing to make the diplomatic process any easier. Russia was content to hold a reduced Games and revelled in its haul of medals, with more gold and silver than ever before. The Olympic movement was chagrined and annoyed but somehow managed to regroup and go on to become one of the largest business ventures in the world.

That spring also brought a sigh of relief to the collective psyche of Canada, as Quebec's first referendum on the Parti Québécois project of "sovereignty-association" resulted in a victory for the "No" side. It was thought that maybe this display of hostility towards the separatist movement would quell its appetite for disturbing the peace, but such hopes were short-lived and political turmoil surfaced again shortly thereafter.

In October 1980 the federal government unveiled a highly divisive National Energy Program that threatened to divide Canada at the Manitoba-Saskatchewan border. At best, the policy could be described as an attempt to ensure that Canada's oil and gas reserves would remain in Canadian hands; at worst, it was a misguided and highly destructive intrusion into provincial affairs and the marketplace. Its lasting effect was a deep and abiding fear and distrust of anything Ottawa proposed to the western provinces. So Canada was subjected to political unrest along regional lines that belied the image of a population not much stirred by anything but a Leafs/Canadiens hockey game.

To celebrate Christmas 1980, 3 Macs appointed more board members, bringing the total to nineteen, a very large proportion of the total staff. John Benson, Doug Reynolds, Jawaid Khan, and Rick Craig entered into the ranks of shareholders. Benson had for many years been assistant treasurer and ran the "cage." Reynolds and Khan had secured their client base and were an important part of the Montreal sales staff. Craig was an experienced trader on the floor of the Toronto Stock Exchange and oversaw the resident floor staff, emulating the position that John Baird had in Montreal. Concurrent with these appointments, Jim Kinnear joined the sales staff in Montreal.

The trading of stocks was still a two-exchange affair and required a dealer to have trading staff on the floor of each exchange as well as staff to handle the order flow. Wisely, 3 Macs invested considerable time, money, and energy in the training and care of the traders, secure in the knowledge that, despite higher volumes and speedier transaction times, the client was deserving of a good "fill" (considered to be a completed order at a price that is reasonable at the time) and the thoughtful execution of an order. This trading service was invaluable and continues to be a hands-on part of the activity of each order. The prevailing operating philosophy at 3 Macs is that a well-executed trade will compensate for the commissions charged for executing the order, and the firm is paid to provide that added benefit.

The 1981 New Year rang in with some very serious questions about the success of the actions taken so far by central banks to reel in the express train of inflation and its running-mate, interest rates. In Canada, a five-year guaranteed investment certificate (GIC) issued by a first-line trust company was available at over 13 per cent, and buyers would "shop" the rate with the hope of getting 25 basis points more. The pressures on the bond markets were substantial and economic activity was slowing at a frightening pace as lenders began to withdraw from the markets with realistic fears that corporations and maybe governments were not going to be able to repay any borrowings. The United States became hostage to the collapse of the savings and loan (S&L) business, as home owners walked away from their real estate, prices collapsed, and re-sale became impossible. A frantic federal government passed a very strange tax amendment that allowed these S&Ls to divest themselves of their primary portfolio of loans and re-purchase another basket of mortgages and apply their first loss against future earnings. This merry-go-round was a bonanza for investment bankers and fortunes were made at the expense of the public since eventual losses were absorbed by the taxpayer. The hubris and vanity of the leaders of Wall Street were well known and the annual bonuses handed out made headlines as the rest of the economy sank into a severe recession. There was talk of much needed reform of the investment industry, with a particular focus on its role in the collapse of the home-mortgage market.

By the fall of 1981, the U.S. Federal Reserve had raised interest rates to heights not believed possible before and the world stood in awe, and in shock, as Paul Volcker stood firm and faced down the tide of criticism, demonstrating why he had been chosen for the job in the first place. President Ronald Reagan, Carter's successor, had reappointed Volcker and embraced his harsh methods of returning the value of the currency to its proper level and disabusing the public of the notion that inflation was here to stay. The GIC rate rose in Canada to 18.75 per cent and the mortgage rate was set at over 21 per cent. Things were slowing down, fast. The ability to set a made-in-Canada interest rate was impossible because of the need to borrow from international lenders to help offset the huge deficits that were the order of the day. An apparent inability to restrict federal and provincial spending had led to a disproportionate burden of debt falling on Canadians, and total interest costs as a percentage of government revenues were clearly leading the country to a ranking beside those of emerging nations and even "banana republics."

Into these very unsettled times stepped 3 Macs' first two female investment advisers, Joan Neville in Toronto and Elizabeth Ballantyne in Montreal. Both required training, but the hiring of women to the role of sales was not unusual in the industry and indeed firms were then hiring college graduates and training them by exposing them to all areas of the business. Neville apprenticed with Bart MacDougall, while Ballantyne was given a desk and a phone and proceeded to learn her job much as all young recruits did at 3 Macs, by observing and listening to the other salespeople around them. It was not a structured environment and only those who had a considerable amount of self-assurance could survive. It hasn't changed much.

Despite all the disconcerting realities about the economy, the Dow Jones managed to regain the 1,000 level before retreating once more. By December 1981, it was down to 871 and volumes were low. As for 3 Macs, it recorded revenues in excess of $5.1 million and an excellent gross profit of $2.0 million, but the sun was ducking behind some very dark clouds and the next year showed a dramatic downturn in the level of revenues as the high interest rates proved to be too much competition to the traditional stock business. Investors were worried that inflation was not coming down fast enough and maybe another bout of escalating interest rates was required. The bargain rates presented to investors were without precedent and those who purchased long-term bonds would have one of the best-performing assets for the next fifteen years.

But the high rates were compounding interest payments on Canadian government debt at a breathtaking pace, and between 1979 and 1982 the interest paid annually on federal bonds more than doubled, from $7 billion to over $15 billion. The amount of debt outstanding rose by about 23 per cent at the same time, but the cost of rolling over low-interest bonds into the new rate structure was punitive and Canada was forced to face the reality of being too heavily dependent upon foreign lenders. Sequential annual deficits were the culprit and no elected leader seemed to have the courage to rein in runaway government spending.

A review of the economic data of the years 1981 to 1984 gives some measure of the effect that inflation had at that time and the draconian measures that were undertaken to wind it down. Unemployment in the United States and Canada surged to new highs, breaching 10 per cent, while inflation climbed above 12 per cent, creating a "misery index" of 22 per cent, a level considered just below "a-riot-in-the-streets" condition. But, by 1982, the world was using less oil and its price started to slide below the $30 level; it continued to sink for four years. Canadian energy demands had been growing at a rate in excess of 5 per cent for most of the 1970s and now started to shrink, being down a full 5 per cent in 1982. These numbers were equalled in most of the developed countries and recessionary factors bit into the economies. The dramatic slowdown allowed the central banks to start lowering rates and, by October 1982, the U.S. rate was lowered to 9.5 per cent and Canada followed the path to lower rates as well.

Montreal was still buffeted by political uncertainty, and when René Lévesque led a huge parade through the streets to signify disgust with the formal transfer of constitutional power from Britain to Canada through the patriation of the British North America Act, tensions rose. The significance of these outbursts was beginning to show in the slow but steady diminution in the creation of wealth in the city. An abridged table from Statistics Canada shows the trends:

INCOME ASSESSED PER TAXPAYER		
	1981	1984
Montreal	$19,043	$22,500
Toronto	$21,561	$26,052
Calgary	$24,216	$27,465
Vancouver	$22,807	$25,151
Quebec City	$20,394	$25,657

The surprise is, of course, the relative strength of Quebec City. One recipient of the wealth creation there was 3 Macs, whose little office in the old part of the city was housed in a building noted for its metal ceilings, thick stone walls, and high windows overlooking a neighbourhood not yet discovered by the urge to renovate. The office was slowly gaining traction with the assistance of Marc Jobin, and in 1984 Michel Bergeron joined as a salesman. A wonderful combination of Old World charm and the mouldy underpinnings of tradition, it was a favourite meeting place for older retired gentlemen who argued, dozed, enjoyed coffee, and generally added little to the commercial intent of the branch. Yet it prospered by being a very established, well-regarded member of the community, with an annual bonspiel competing for a trophy presented by the company under the sponsorship of Olivier Samson.

The clear falling away of Montreal's influence in the business community in Canada was taking its toll on the fortunes of the regional dealers in Montreal, and many of the smaller old-line firms either merged or disappeared. At one point there were about forty local dealers who serviced the retail business in the province and performed a valued function for their clients. Never hugely profitable but able to make a decent return on their invested capital for many years, they now found that the profit margins were being squeezed by internal costs, regulatory compliance, and a vanishing client base. The result was a sequence of takeovers by more profitable and larger companies that did a more national business and were less reliant on the retail public. Approached regularly to see if it would care to merge or be taken over, 3 Macs was comfortably profitable and content with its operating margins and returns. In fact, it continued to follow a policy of rewarding both staff and shareholders annually, but only after all costs had been covered and capital adequacy had been met. Tom Price and Buster Jones ran a tight ship; however, the staff knew that they would be protected and thus did not demand the highest wages on the Street.

The Toronto office was able to expand its business and, under the guidance of Bart MacDougall, continued to look for recruits to a business model that was clearly working and appealed to a certain type of salesperson who was able to supply good basic service without the pressure of following a corporate philosophy that usually put the house ahead of the client. This feature attracted Charles Kennedy and Nicol McNicol to the office and thus added substantial heft to the operation. Kennedy, at 6'5", and McNicol, well over 6', assumed roles of importance immediately. Kennedy (known in his neighbourhood as Chuckles the Clown for his role in the annual park fundraiser) came from a background of Bank of Montreal, Jones Heward, and McLeod Young Weir and had a burgeoning clientele. McNicol had also worked at McLeod but had additional experience as a corporate president. Their arrival was important since the office had lost both Pollitt and Legault and their institutional business. The competition for this type of business was getting intense and the commissions earned were under severe pressure as the comfort of fixed rates was removed from the market and lower commissions prevailed. The retail business continued to be the main source of revenue and Toronto's bias sided with the individual client, and away from the pools of capital.

As is so often the case in Canada, events far from our shores had been taking place that would affect the markets and the attitudes of investors. In 1979 the United Kingdom had elected Margaret

Thatcher as prime minister and her government had gone about the task of turning Britain back into an industrial powerhouse and financial centre. Thatcher's primary platform was to reduce the role of government in the economy and also to curtail the power of the labour unions. The country was thrown into a dismal recession but emerged fitter and leaner than it had been for almost fifty years. A substantial program of privatizing the many government agencies provided a huge boost to the economy and created a new broader base of shareholders across the nation. Beginning with British Telecom, proceeding through various water companies, steel mills, and coal mines, and culminating in the disposal of government's 40 per cent interest in British Petroleum (BP), the program reaped huge opportunities for the investment community both within Britain and on Wall Street, with a modest spinoff to Canada's underwriters.

The success (mostly) of the privatizations gave other countries an incentive to examine their own portfolios of possible candidates and, as these divestments occurred, it became obvious to the investing public that some excellent possibilities for market appreciation were finally available for their investment selections. This broadening of ownership created a new dynamic in the markets as volumes increased and profits were distributed to a broad audience through increased dividends and stock splits. A new age of confidence dawned. The market, as represented by the Dow Jones, recovered from its low point in 1981 and by 1985 was up almost 80 per cent (at 1,542) and heading for higher ground. The wealth creation was substantial and investors were settling into a happy frame of mind.

Kennedy and McNicol were appointed to the board of 3 Macs and were joined shortly thereafter by Marc Jobin and Ron Campbell, bringing the total number of director/shareholders to twenty-two. Campbell (known by the conventional sobriquet "Soupy") had joined the company from Greenshields as an institutional sales/trader and had developed a close relationship with many Montreal accounts that provided revenues without adding fixed overhead. The system of paying the director/shareholders of 3 Macs had not changed over the years; profits were accumulated during the year and distributed on a semi-annual basis (or sooner if conditions warranted it) but did not necessarily reflect a direct relationship to the individual's contribution. The Street had moved almost universally to an "eat what you kill" method of compensation and not many producers were willing to rely upon the formulaic method of payment considered appropriate for 3 Macs. The slow, steady approach to financial risk was almost an anachronism in the turbulent environment, but it served the company well. The markets continued to enjoy activity and the Toronto Stock Exchange recorded its first day of over twenty million shares traded.

This activity was broadly based and allowed the company to redeem preferred shares twice during 1986, thus returning capital to the shareholder and indicating a well-managed balance sheet. Interest rates continued to decline and a five-year GIC was available at less than 10 per cent although mortgage rates remained well above 12 per cent. Investors were comfortable with the outlook and subsided into an almost cruise-control attitude. The Plaza Accord of late 1985 had realigned world currencies and the fundamental devaluation of the United States dollar and its side car currency the loonie had spurred new industrial activity and demand for machinery, autos, forest products, minerals, and energy that brought Canada new-found wealth.

The world was also helped by the almost total collapse of the control OPEC had tried to exercise over the price of oil. By 1986, oil was back down to $10 a barrel and this low price spurred demand for industrial growth to satisfy the need for more autos, houses, household goods, and just about anything that the public could dream of owning. It was a dramatic relief after the serious war against inflation that had bottled up the consumer for many years. Big cars gave way to even bigger cars, and the public demanded more.

The summer of 1987 brought troubling developments to the markets and by the fall the spectre of higher interest rates and lower profits had some market forecasters warning of an impending correction. At the same time, the United Kingdom was requesting bids on its shares of BP and a consortium of dealers had entered into what could be described as a bought deal, allowing the government to sell its shares despite a change in markets. The dealers were confident that they could unwind their positions and bravely struck a deal. The timing was not good. And timing is everything in financial markets. But the markets were buoyed by the knowledge that, from the bottom of the dips in August 1982 to the highs of August 1987, the nineteen largest markets in the world had appreciated an average of almost 300 per cent and the Dow had cleared 2,700. Clearly a new paradigm was evident. Then the Federal Reserve raised interest rates.

On 14 October 1987 the Dow sold off 3.8 per cent, and on the 16th it sold off 4.6 per cent before closing for the weekend. By the time the New York market opened on Monday, it was aware that world markets starting in Japan and moving to Europe were in full retreat. The Dow responded by selling off 22.6 per cent, or 508 points, creating Black Monday. This climatic event shook the money markets and overwhelmed the systems designed to effect the settlement procedures. On the fateful Monday, the NASDAQ market was unable to handle the volume of orders and its market makers retreated for hours on end. The highly valued shares of Microsoft traded for a brief forty-five minutes that day and illustrated the collapse of the comfortable attitude of the "most liquid markets in the world."

Oddly, the market responded to this chaos by rising sharply over the next few days, and much credit was given to Volcker's successor as chairman of the Federal Reserve, Alan Greenspan. Only on the job for a few months, Greenspan informed the marketplace that the Fed stood ready to supply all the money the banking system needed to sustain liquidity. Thus began the legendary Greenspan Put. This underwriting of the financial risks taken by banks and dealers would be tested over the subsequent years, causing pundits to declare that markets were now insulated from mistakes as long as you were "too big to fail."

The sharp sell-off presented the investing public with a new dimension of risk: the reality that volatility had reached new levels and that the actions of short-term traders were now capable of moving markets. The post-mortem on this particular sell-off was inconclusive as to cause but did make the authorities introduce so-called circuit breakers in the event of unusual movement up or down in the major indices.

While investors stood in shock and watched the meltdown, senior staff at many leading investment firms were horrified at the reality of seeing their capital base eroded by the destruction of values. The unsold portion of the BP secondary offering that remained on their books was the single largest cause of despair and the lead Canadian dealer had to seek help from a chartered bank to avoid bankruptcy. Funds were made available and the firm remained in business and recovered, but oddly remained curiously prone to excessive risk for many more years.

Although the market recovered its lost ground by the end of 1987, the damage was severe and many dealers, their staff, and clients paid a price in the form of physical exhaustion and mounting concern about the future of owning and trading in equity investments. Volumes were reduced again and business slowed down for smaller firms which did not have a wide range of products and services. The continuing decline in interest rates made bond dealers substantial profits and these carried the firms for several years. Skank Kerrigan chose the end of 1987 to retire and put the last of his shares up for sale. Although he was always welcome, he rarely dropped by the Montreal office and preferred to stay out in the country, playing golf and enjoying his retirement. Shortly thereafter, McNicol resigned to pursue another career.

Although 3 Macs was active in supplying bonds as an agent, it missed out on the profits accorded the firms that maintained substantial inventories. This was a direct reflection of the policy of avoiding risk and the inherent restriction imposed by a small capital base. Nevertheless, 1987 was a difficult year for the company and, to make matters worse, the partnership was imposing strains on itself by indulging in some second-guessing. The result was a slight schism between the very conservative Montreal partners and the more aggressive and younger Toronto contingent, including Norman Ayoub, then vice-president of sales.

In the midst of this, the question of shareholder value was popping up in the business community as several investment dealers filed prospectuses and issued shares to the public at substantial premiums over book value, thus providing benchmarks for the privately held companies. The apparent creation of wealth was instant and appealing. The chartered banks were acquiring the lead dealers in response to the removal of the some of the restrictions imposed under a "four-pillar" philosophy that had guided the financial scene for almost a century. The process of bulking up was evident within the industry and mergers were prevalent for several years. The attraction to enhance shareholder value was substantial and persuasive.

In the summer of 1988 Tom Price was appointed vice-chairman of the Investment Dealers Association. It was a natural choice, reflecting Price's stature among his peers and the enviable position the company held within the industry. Almost concurrent with this appointment, Price informed the board that he wished to step down as president of 3 Macs but remain as an active chairman. It was an informal meeting and Price's announcement was not much discussed outside the firm since the partners were not sure of finding a suitable replacement. On top of this, the year's financial results were a great disappointment for all and created concern about the company's ability to continue as an independent dealer. The fiscal year ending 31 October 1988 produced a revenue total of $6.3 million and a profit of $509,000, compared to the prior year's $8.6 million and $2.8 million respectively.

The idea of hiring an outsider to replace Price was not easily entertained and so the search was restricted to personal referrals. It culminated in a private client suggesting her brother for the role, whereupon Tom Price contacted the person in question, Michael Harrison, then resident in Toronto. Harrison was known to Price and to Bart MacDougall and was a native Montrealer with a background of work with the Bank of Montreal and many years' experience in all areas of the business with what was then Walwyn Stodgell Cochran Murray. After a brief review process, Harrison joined the company in the fall of 1988 and assumed the position of president and chief operating officer. He recalls the interview with Tom Price that led to his acceptance of the position: "Tom asked me if I wished to be paid at the same level as all the other director/ shareholders and thus would receive a monthly draw against a final profit distribution. I enquired as to whether or not the distribution was related to the financial risk of owning the shares and thus be a proportionate share. Tom replied 'Maybe.' I asked what the monthly draw was, and he replied $3,000. I explained that my personal obligations were more than that. It was at that point I began to understand why 3 Macs had been so profitable."

The process of keeping overhead low and profit distributions to the director/producers a matter of discretion was an enduring template that ensured the company's longevity. Yet it was not in keeping with the competition on the Street and the hiring of talent from other firms was clearly getting difficult. The practice of paying salespeople on a direct-drive basis was emphatically illustrated by the remarkable payment made to Michael Milken, of the U.S. firm Drexel Burnham Lambert. Milken had developed the junk-bond market and had struck a deal to be paid 40 per cent of his gross revenues. He took home $500 million in 1989, making himself the "poster boy" of the wretched excess that had become barely enough for the financial geniuses of the day. But the real lesson of the deal was that huge sums could be earned by participating directly in one's own production while still being a shareholder of a dealer.

In November 1988 the company was shocked by the news that Tom Price, while travelling with the IDA, had suffered a heart attack in Edmonton. The news was felt as a devastating blow since Harrison was an unknown and the firm had counted on Tom to be there to guide the company. Fortunately, Tom recovered and the company continued to do what it had always done, offer service and advice to its clients in a period when once again the world was undergoing huge political and economic change. The IDA, recognizing that Tom was not going to be able to fill the role of incoming chairman, offered the position to Harrison. He was familiar with the duties involved, having served as chair of the Ontario District and on the Executive Committee of the National Board.

In 1987 U.S. President Ronald Reagan had given a famous speech at the Brandenburg Gate in Berlin challenging the USSR's Mikhail Gorbachev to "tear down this wall." The Berlin Wall had long been used by the West to illustrate the tyranny of the communist rulers, and by October 1989 stirrings of unrest that started in Hungary, Austria, and Poland culminated in the breaching of the border-crossing barriers and the emergence of a huge peaceful uprising that finally brought down the Wall and most of the traditional communist leaders. Later that year, an unprecedented meeting between Gorbachev and Pope John Paul II at the Vatican revealed the important role the Catholic Church had played in the events of the past decade.

The dramatic release of Cold War tensions was emphatic and confusing for both markets and analysts. No one was able to agree on the immediate effects of this "peace dividend," and in fact, as the bias then was towards reduced government expenditures on armaments, there were good reasons for believing that it might have a negative effect on commodity prices. The other remarkable event of the late 1980s was the signing of the North American Free Trade Agreement. Championed by the Conservative government of Brian Mulroney, it sparked much discussion about the future of Canada and its association with the United States. The views of the population were split between sell-out and survival. The debate still has currency.

During the 1980s, 3 Macs added many employees who would have a very long history with the company and play an important part in its future. Not all became directors but as the firm grew their contributions grew with it. Debbie Cartier had joined 3 Macs on the floor of the Montreal Exchange and handled orders with sufficient skill that she remained a trader on the Montreal desk for years. Another recruit, Bruce Macaulay, has almost thirty years' experience in the complicated area of retirement savings plans. Fedi Vega and Debbie Cartier in Montreal and David Dotzko and Colin O'Handley on the Toronto stock trading desk have always acted as a team, and in their years with 3 Macs they have witnessed the transition from floor traders to the automated trading systems now in use. Judy Cochrane joined the company from Greenshields, assuring John Benson that she knew how to type when in fact she couldn't. Cricky Brodhead, Donna Whalen, Carmen Jankey, and Sheila Lipari continued to manage the directors they worked with, ensuring compliance with the burgeoning rulebooks enforced by the industry. Tim Price joined from Rowe and Pitman and bolstered the accounting side. The operations area was augmented by Donny Weston, Toni Colabella, Sue Giroux, Charlene Clahane, Shelagh Groves, Luc Allaire, Cathy Anderson, Tracey Bishop, Denise DeGrandpré, and the ever popular paymaster Janice Squires. In the sales/research area, the additions included Paul Hebert, Anne Dixon Grossman, Suzanne Mathers, John Gallop, Laird Grantham, and Marco Ouellet.

It is incumbent on a new member of an investment dealer to reach back to his old employer and try and hire as many good people as he/she can. This is done for two reasons: to reinforce what a good decision it was to go to the new location, and to have a few friendly faces with you in case the natives turn out to be restless and hostile. Harrison did just that and was soon joined in Toronto by salesman Peter Holland (known as Fly Rod for his long, thin physique) and Laird Grantham. Grantham, a talented analyst, was exactly what was needed to augment a diminishing group of researchers. Bruce Whitestone had left the company in the fall of 1988 and retired, leaving Orvald Gratias and a junior analyst, Jennifer Grunner, doing most of the heavy lifting.

At the annual shareholders meeting in early 1989, the shareholders approved the appointment of Tom Price as chairman, Bart Mac-Dougall as deputy chairman and chair of the Executive Committee, Michael Harrison as president and chief operating officer, and Hugh A. Jones as treasurer and secretary. A new Executive Committee was also approved consisting of the four officers and Robert G. Ross. This established a formal reporting basis for the company although all final decisions were to be approved by the board.

One feature of 3 Macs that Harrison found to be a bit disturbing was the random selection of portfolio purchases made by the sales staff on behalf of their clients. His concern was the possibility of two clients of the firm discovering completely different financial results from their portfolios even though they had the same investment objectives. He felt that a commonality of investment opinions would be the best course to follow, thus relieving the sales force of the responsibility of making stock selections and doing their own research. The method employed by Harrison is, of course, fraught with problems and must be handled with care because of one certainty: a good sales person has a healthy ego. The creation of better and more portfolio-specific research would become a guiding factor in the company's development.

The company was growing and the client base was expanding, but the need to augment the operations area with new technology and to become more competitive with pay scales and ownership distributions weighed on the traditional operating profit ratio. The next decade would see changes that had been on the company's agenda for years and that, once made, would allow 3 Macs to move ahead to new challenges.

THIRTEEN

Irrational Exuberance and the Bubble Economy

Fly me to the moon …
Bart Howard

As the 1990s opened, the markets were not helping the pursuit of riches by clients heavily weighted with common shares in either the U.S. or Canadian markets. The collapse of the Japanese real estate bubble was the beginning of a serious worldwide re-evaluation of property values and by mid-1990 the North American economy was deemed to be in recession and markets stalled. The Dow retreated from its post-1987 recovery high of over 3,000 and settled around 2,600, with interest rates again ticking up. Not a welcome environment to attempt changes within any dealer, and with news that the investment house of Drexel Burnham Lambert had become insolvent, dealers were cutting back as the leveraged buyout market subsided to the sidelines and credit became more difficult to obtain. The excess of the prior years had clearly come to an end. A book published late in 1989 had told of life at Salomon Brothers, one of the kingpin dealers on Wall Street. *Liar's Poker* should be required reading every few years as the economic cycle replays itself and restores glittering riches to the canyons of Wall and Bay streets.

In the summer of 1990, Iraq invaded Kuwait, and shortly thereafter the price of oil shot up again and the United States (with full authority from the United Nations) put together a coalition of forces that, by February 1991, had sent the Iraqi troops back over the border in full retreat. President George H.W. Bush, advised by his defense secretary, Richard Cheney, was restrained in his approach and essentially halted the war after the defeated army dispersed and withdrew in confusion. However, long-term constraints were imposed on Iraq and the country was kept under close observation. The brief war helped pull the United States out of a recession and prosperity returned in due course.

On 1 December 1990, at Dorval Airport, several thieves decided that the way to fast wealth was to steal a large shipment of securities bound from Toronto to the Montreal offices of the Central Depository System. The clearing and settlement of securities in Canada was still heavily dependent upon the physical movement of paper certificates and the shipment happened to contain some securities being transferred to 3 Macs' Montreal head office. The amount missing was large and the board was concerned about the information getting into public hands. Luckily, the shipment contained substantially more securities belonging to a much larger firm, and it was that information that made the headlines. Of course, the shipment was entirely insured and Herman Murray, a senior manager in the cage, replaced the main items (treasury bills) within forty-eight hours and was able eventually to get all the missing certificates replaced as well, but not without a huge amount of paperwork and hours of testimony in hearings. Herman, who joined 3 Macs in 1963, is still with the company today, making sure the settlement system works smoothly.

As always, 3 Macs' guiding principal in this case was the absolute importance of assuring clients that their securities and cash were safe within the company's custodial vaults. The quick action by the operations area allowed the public to be unaware of the drama and the company's reputation remained unsullied. In subsequent years, certificates for stocks, bonds, treasury bills, bankers acceptances, and just about all tradable securities were replaced by an electronic system, which allows transfers to be made by keystrokes in place of the legions of messengers who, in earlier days, transported billions of dollars of paper around in leather briefcases.

In early 1990 Tom Law left Nesbitt Thomson and joined 3 Macs as a versatile analyst with the intention of creating, with Grantham, a solid portfolio approach to the research and setting up a model portfolio that would contain the selections of the analysts and be measured against the traditional benchmarks. The idea was an extension of what Harrison had thought might be the best way to steer the sales force in a collegial direction. Simultaneously, the Executive Committee recommended to the board that remuneration for sales people be tied directly to their own production even if they were shareholders and directors. This idea was not entirely understood by or acceptable immediately to all directors, but, as in any sales organization, there is usually one leader who can see through the short-term adjustments and will view the future with prescient judgment. Such was the case with Ian Black, who championed the proposal, and the high regard accorded him by all helped sell the idea to the reluctant few. The result was a new and dedicated remuneration system untied from the partnership concept.

At the annual meeting in January 1990, the company welcomed numerous new shareholders to its ranks, and the process of distributing shares was finally able to break out of the stringent conditions of prior years. The move to broaden the share holdings was a difficult decision at that time because the outlook was not very promising for taking the risk inherent in the ownership. The staff responded with a solid vote of confidence and purchased a small tranche of newly issued shares from treasury with little hesitation and without any banking assistance. The obvious conclusion was that there was a substantial interest among the staff in owning the company, and in subsequent years the list expanded to include a significant number of employees.

In the spring of 1990, Marc Jobin announced his intention to leave the company, which presented an opportunity for younger staff members to step forward and assume greater responsibility. In Quebec City, the by now remarkably capable salesman Michel Bergeron assumed the role of branch manager and proceeded, with Marco Ouellet, to build a profitable business even though both were much younger than their client base. At the same time, John Baird requested that his retirement from day-to-day duties be honoured, and he stepped aside while maintaining a few retail accounts. The summer brought the resignation of Doug Reynolds, followed shortly thereafter by the departure of Bill Cowen and Ron Campbell. At that point Harrison was beginning to feel he was doing something wrong, so he made another suggestion to the board.

It was clear to Harrison that 3 Macs' best asset was the long-standing relationship it enjoyed with all of the clients. This was not like a normal client/broker understanding; it was rather like a trust company relationship whereby the clients relied upon 3 Macs to provide services well beyond stock selection and order execution. They expected (and received) individual attention unmatched by any of the competition. From portfolio management to safekeeping to tax-return filing to paying bills and even finding hotel rooms, clients enjoyed a very special feeling of comfort and service. Harrison, encouraged by several senior directors, suggested that the sales force should persuade their clients to pay a set fee and get generous discounted commissions on their trading.

This practice was then the preserve of trust companies and investment counsellors, but it was clearly a path that would do a few things: it would establish with the client the idea that only if they prospered would they pay more; it would relieve the salesperson of the burden of creating transactions to generate income; and it would establish, if all went according to plan, a revenue stream that would stabilize 3 Macs and provide a base for expanded services. Once more the idea met with some resistance but again Ian Black embraced it and the process was started. The transition from earning commissions only to combining fees and smaller commissions was slow but steady, as clients began to recognize the partial removal of the conflict inherent in the commission-only source of remuneration for the sales force. This conflict has always been a source of debate within the financial industry, with some investment counsellors and mutual fund companies obliquely suggesting that the client is at risk to nefarious schemes meant to generate commissions without regard to his/her well-being. The brokerage industry regulates itself and the number of complaints about this malpractice is insignificant in relation to the number of clients served and the huge number of transactions carried out each year. But the stigma remains.

Wilf Dinnick joined the Toronto office in 1990 and brought a great deal of experience within the industry to his post. A graduate of Wood Gundy and Dean Witter Canada as well as serving as chairman of the Writer's Trust of Canada, he was a welcome addition. Dinnick was persuaded to join the company by the realization that he could be involved in serving his clients without the pressure of responding to the wishes of a major dealer's own agenda. Shortly thereafter, Peter Sears joined in Montreal and established a very sizable retail clientele in short order. A mining specialist, he added a distinctive flair for fashion and hairstyle and brought with him his personal assistant, Danielle Viger.

By 1992, the company was truly embracing the portfolio approach to managing clients' assets, and as the economic picture improved, so did the markets. This improved the firm's financial results, but the upturn was sluggish and was not helped by the bankruptcy of Olympia & York, Canada's premier real estate and investment holding company. The demise of this icon and the savage dismantling of the Reichmann empire have been well documented and remain one of the textbook lessons of what leverage can do to a balance sheet.

The run-up in the price of oil after Gulf War I caused another spasm among the major auto companies and all reported losses of varying degrees for their 1991 year end. The restive American population decided that the main issue was the economy and elected Democrat Bill Clinton as president, with the hope that his policies would help them keep up their standard of living. He arrived in office on a platform of more spending and fewer taxes, but in short order the persuasive power of the bond market buyers forced him to restrain his earlier promises and embark upon a long-term policy of balancing the budget and reducing the debt. It was a successful plan, as the next years proved.

The great Art Carney (portraying Ed Norton in the television program "The Honeymooners") once said, in character, "You can take the man out of the sewer, but you can't take the sewer out of the man." This was a valid statement for Michael Harrison. Harking back to his days as the head bond trader at the Bank of Montreal, he determined, after receiving John Baird's retirement notice, to enlarge the scope of the company's bond business. The imminent decline in interest rates in the United States and a decided pattern of fiscal restraint within Canada suggested to him that bonds might just have a nice future for investors. He selected Judy Cochrane from the stock trading area to be his co-worker on the bond desk and gave her the assignment of learning all about bonds, particularly those issued by corporations. She dutifully completed a major study of all prominent issuers and handed her substantial report to Harrison, who put it in his drawer and thanked her for it.

The bond business grew by leaps and bounds, aided by a bull market and some extraordinary client connections that attracted huge trades and the attention of the other bond dealers. Never acting as principals, only as agents, 3 Macs was able to become a well-respected bond-trading entity and remains a highly regarded source for all bond clients. The company took the unusual step of resigning from all underwriting syndicates, including the Bank of Canada's government bond issues. In doing so, it ensured that there would be no conflict between the client and the company's position as a portfolio manager.

In Canada a significant piece of news changed the landscape within which 3 Macs operated: it was revealed that by 1992 Royal Trust was technically bankrupt. In fact, it was rescued from bankruptcy by the Royal Bank in 1993 for next to nothing and became an operating arm of the bank. Prior to its rescue, the shares of the company had traded for minimal amounts and clients watched while the bluest chip in the financial history of the nation was bled of its earnings by its voracious owners. It was a low point for the trust company industry but a wake-up call to clients, who had always presumed that they were in the safest hands. The trust companies' special status was diminished, and the playing field became much more level with firms such as 3 Macs securing a greater respectability and an enhanced reputation for safety.

The annual general meeting of shareholders in March 1991 was attended by an enlarged shareholder group and at that meeting new directors were appointed: Laird Grantham and Tom Law from the research/portfolio department and John Gallop and Joan Neville from sales. Neville, the first female director, had joined the company as a sales assistant to Bart MacDougall in Toronto. She had quickly shown an aptitude for sales and client relationships and had developed a broad client base. Gallop, who had come into the firm in 1987 from the consulting arm of Coopers & Lybrand, felt that he could use his many contacts to form a profitable business. His appointment as a director was in recognition not only of his achievements in this regard but also of the continuing interest he had in making things better for all salespeople. His inquisitive mind assisted in many ways and his innovations and ideas have been a strength for the company for many years. These appointments brought the board back to seventeen directors.

In early 1991 David Cobbett joined from RBC Dominion in Montreal, and David Stevenson from the same dealer joined in Toronto. Stevenson was no stranger to the company, being a relative of the MacDougall family and a descendant of the Molson clan. Eric Rappaport entered the company that summer and took immediate responsibility for the client services department. A chartered accountant, he was able to expand the client base and was instrumental in developing the estate-settlement adjunct of the service.

Summer brought the opportunity to open an office in London, Ontario. Harrison knew a dynamic salesman in that city who convinced him and other directors that the demographics were ideal and the service offered by 3 Macs was needed. Accordingly, a branch was opened and the manager hired a sales staff including Bob Ketchabaw and Paul Skinner. The branch was located in modest premises and was slow to start but showed promise. London is a conservative city and getting clients to move their accounts to 3 Macs was difficult, but a persistent team did make inroads and the branch received recognition within the community.

In 1992 Ken Mitchell, who had worked as comptroller and had been instrumental in presenting a financial reporting system that was more detailed and informative than the one that preceded it, decided that his fortunes lay out west and resigned. A quick search turned up an accountant who had experience in several companies, not the least of which was Molson Breweries. References were given and Tom Aiken was hired as Mitchell's replacement. The role of chief financial officer at 3 Macs defied description, encompassing everything from accounting to human resources to premises and information technology, a challenging mixture that required an individual who could juggle a daily agenda of mixed tasks. Buster Jones had held the job for many years and it was felt that he had done more than enough service and was asked to relinquish the title to Aiken in 1993. Far and away the only CFO on the Street who also enjoyed a very loyal and profitable retail clientele, Jones agreed, and he retained the role of secretary and concentrated on his client base. A successful transition was accomplished and the company was grateful for his complete cooperation. At much the same time, Tim Price was elected to the board. Tim, the elder son of Tom Price, was following in his father's footsteps and had left the accounting department to concentrate on sales. Working together, Tim and Tom Price devised a split of business that encouraged Tim to develop his own client base while sharing in Tom's revenue stream. This duality was, of course, ideal for the company since it did not require a large commitment in salary to the junior member of the team and thus kept overheads low. It was a useful template for future arrangements and allowed the steady and seamless transfer of accounts within the company.

The Toronto office was growing as Grantham attracted his former colleague, Jim Perrone, to the company. Perrone was well known as an analyst in the mining sector with emphasis on junior gold companies. His arrival coincided with an uptick in the price of the commodity and he was immediately successful in arranging financings for companies. These placements were made exclusively to institutional investors and therefore did not impinge on the "no underwritings to retail clients" in-house rule.

The Clinton years delivered a remarkable period of growth and stability and proved to be an excellent time for the appreciation of assets. A steady diet of employment growth, increased taxable profits, low inflation, and reasonably steady commodity prices allowed the North American markets to produce significant gains. In the case of 3 Macs, it used this period to add sales and research staff and to resume a high level of profit and return on shareholder equity.

The early 1990s brought the realization that information technology was a fact of life and 3 Macs was going to have to spend substantial sums on bringing its technology up-to-date. When Harrison arrived he brought with him an eighteen-pound "portable" Compaq computer with some software built in. He was surprised to find that he was the only senior person with a computer on his desk, able to write his own letters and keep his own records. Working with John Benson and a young, boisterous Tony Zirpollo, Harrison had all the office systems upgraded, and soon computers replaced typewriters and the "paperless office" was pumping out oceans of reports from a multitude of printers. In concert with this shift to technology, Benson found and installed the initial computerized portfolio system for keeping clients records and publishing accurate quarterly valuation reports. The evolution of the electronic databank and supporting facilities continues to this day, as more computing power becomes available and Internet-based communication becomes more intense. The pace of innovation is remarkable and the costs associated with it have become a major contributor to essential but expensive overhead.

Just as technology was changing the office procedures, it was also replacing the traditional marketplace on the floors of the Montreal and Toronto exchanges. Electronic transformation required the member firms to remove their staff from the physical arena of the exchange and bring them to the office where the trading was now done by entering orders into electronic trading systems and not by calling out their trading intentions on the floor of the exchange. The colourful jackets and casual atmosphere of the floor traders are now a thing of the past, and nothing can replace the close and lifelong friendships that the traders developed with their competition on that rough-and-tumble playing field. David Dotzko, Colin O'Handley, and Ricky Craig came up from the Toronto floor and Debbie Cartier and Fedi Vega moved up from the Montreal floor. In their hearts they remain floor traders and have no fear of a demanding execution, a difficult multi-market order, a complicated option trade, or a bad-tempered, self-important salesperson.

In the fall of 1993, the Liberal Party swept to power in Ottawa and commenced thirteen years of stringent budget control that saw the once debilitating annual deficits replaced by large and welcome surpluses. The pain involved in arriving at this massive shift in fiscal policy was shared across Canada by reducing the support given to the provinces and thus downloading the problem onto the next lower level. The policy was grumbled about, but the country responded by settling into a prolonged period of prosperity. In no small way, this was a reflection of the unparalleled expansion of world trade and the relative calmness of international politics. The subsequent years are best measured by the Dow Jones Industrial Average, which closed the year 1993 at 3,764 and exited 1999 at 11,497. There were bumps along the way but these were mostly contained by quick and decisive action by central banks around the world.

The Toronto office, always on the lookout for talent, was embraced by an American banker, Tim McNicholas, who desired to have his future in the business and joined with few clients but an engaging style. A compendium of trivia, he began by sharing some of the business done by Bart MacDougall but quickly built his own book. In London, Troy Nazarewicz joined as a rookie salesperson and, with a determined mind and a sensible attitude to risk and reward, began the long process of building his business. During this time, Olivier Samson retired, having completed sixty-five years of service to his work and to his community. He had been preceded into retirement by an exceptional clerk, Richard Trottier, who had opened the Quebec City office of Barry & McManamy or 3 Macs every day since 1929.

The operations area in the Montreal office was beefed up by the addition of Cathy Watson, an experienced and organized individual who immediately brought needed assistance to John Benson and attention to the growing volume of business. The industry was changing and required a much greater recognition of the compliance regulations that were becoming operating standards. Layered on the industry rules were new federal and international requirements for the detection of such crimes as money laundering. The casual "know your client" rule that had served the industry was replaced by stringent fact gathering, identification documentation, insider confirmation, and numerous other procedures that have become a huge, almost disproportionate, expense overriding the basic trust that all clients place in those handling their financial affairs.

Tom Law introduced Bob McKenzie to the firm in the fall of 1994 and convinced him that he would be happier working within a smaller, more flexible environment than he was experiencing at his major dealer location. His arrival coincided with that of Ben

Ball. They brought with them a client base and knowledge of some of the electronic services available to the industry. Harrison and Cochrane remember their introduction to the ubiquitous Bloomberg information system and its ability to price, among other things, international and domestic bonds. Swallowing hard, they agreed to install the system at an outrageous monthly cost. As it turned out, the service was so user-friendly and valuable that the bond business alone generated from this service repaid the cost in about three months. The hesitation to install the machines was, of course, a reflection of the ingrained cost-control philosophy that prevails within the company.

Markets improved and so did the financial results of the firm. From a low point of $7.2 million in 1990, the revenues improved annually and by the end of 1994 were at $16.2 million and throwing off a profit before distributions of about $2.5 million. In 1995 Canada was again bracing for a second referendum about Quebec and the summer brought the possibility that this time the "Yes" vote just might carry the day. Investors grew nervous once more and the press was filled with differing opinions about what separation would mean. It was clearly felt by some, on the eve of the vote, that if the result were a vote for separation the impact would be experienced overnight. The fear was palpable but, fortunately, groundless, because the "No" side won by the slimmest of margins and life went on with little subsequent distraction.

After the discomfort of the referendum, Denham Mitchell rejoined the company to head up the operations area. Mitchell had worked for 3 Macs prior to his departure to the Central Depository System and his return provided the firm with an experienced operator as the whole settlement system became "book-based" and free of the cumbersome physical certificates representing ownership that had prevailed since time immemorial. The change to these procedures was the single most important step in the advancement of the industry's ability to handle huge increases in the volume and speed of transactions. The changes in the back office were essential preparation for the next phase of market growth and the impact of worldwide events upon volumes and volatility.

Of interest to world economics, the price of oil, as quoted on the futures market, was up and down during the decade, with some direct consequences for the world powers. Oil was priced about

$25 when the Soviet Union collapsed. It settled to $13 when Russia invaded its unruly neighbour Chechnya, and finally bottomed out around $10 in 1999. By 1997, the world was witness to the remarkable default by Russia on its debt and the devaluation of the ruble, sparking a political crisis and concerns that the country was bankrupt. In due course, Vladimir Putin was elected president of Russia and a rebuilding process quickly got under way based on the country's absolute need to sell oil and gas at much higher prices, a move that would create enormous wealth for oil-rich nations of which Russia was one of the biggest.

Arriving during these turbulent times in the oil and gas industry, Eleanor Barker joined the Toronto office and promptly displayed her unusual talent for researching and financing smaller emerging companies. Barker was well known on the Street and had a certain notoriety as the only woman on the institutional desk of Gordon Capital, the famously aggressive dealer. She was instrumental, along with Jim Perrone, in completing various private financings that allowed the year ending 1996 to be a high-water mark for profits and return on equity.

The research department was fortunate to be able to add to its numbers, with Chris Sears, Rob Mark, Brian Weber, and Christina Barbeau forming a solid nucleus of new talent. Research remains one of those areas of the business that is difficult to measure in terms of effectiveness, because, no matter how right the analysis might be, the markets will sometimes ignore all practical measurements and dismiss the opinion of the analyst. The marketplace is home to cycles of extremes and, in the decade under review, the remarkable period of exceptional growth for the overall economy of the world led to forecasts of unimaginable levels of market measurement. The job of the research department was to make sound, comprehensive suggestions while watching a scene of "irrational exuberance." This term is credited to Alan Greenspan in the mid-1990s, and it became a piece of folklore as the markets rose in a parabolic curve to the beginning of the new millennium.

Beside the growth in the research department, there were a number of additions to the sales staff: Anna Young, Ian Clarke, Robert Corneil, Mark Gallop, Jean Ethier, Marc-André Plourde, and John Bridgman (and Maria Spanakis) all came from other investment dealers or bank-related entities and were able to establish their business quickly. Two other arrivals, Bassam Kadi and Bob Coulter, came from an investment-counselling/portfolio-management background and their style was a natural fit for the company. Douglas Berry came from a small house but was valued as a preferred share specialist, an area of the market that is remarkably overlooked by most investors. His skill became an important adjunct to the research-portfolio recommendations. In Quebec City the branch was greatly helped by the addition of Josée Cantin and Julie Aubin, both providing very capable support for the whole office.

In Quebec City, André Jutras joined with no prior experience, and in Toronto, Derek Rennie and Jennifer Peters arrived with the same qualifications. Somehow they survived the rigorous training program they were subjected to as new entrants and emerged at the end of that day unscathed and determined to make it on their own. In Montreal a graduate of the financial planners certification program arrived to add a new dimension to the services. Diane Perry (now Stoneman) was introduced by her cousin Lynn Perry, but after several attempts to communicate her skills to the sales force, she decided that her future rested with her own ambitions and transferred to Toronto and a successful sales career.

In May 1996 Tom Price died while playing a round of golf at his beloved Royal Montreal Golf Club. His death was a shock and a source of grief for all who knew the man. The huge attendance at his memorial service was testimony to the respect and love he was accorded. Tom was a man who carried with him many traditions and responsibilities and probably only after his death were people completely aware of the influence he had on so many important charitable and community projects. His success in persuading his clients to be generous donors to his many fundraising interests demonstrated not only the worth of the projects but also the high regard his own commitment engendered. Tom exemplified within the company the spirit of an earlier age when personal relationships were the backbone of a successful partnership, and his bonhomie extended to each member of the staff with a special regard to the distaff side. His position as chairman was a natural role for him since he had tired of the more contentious tasks of chief executive officer, and he enjoyed his last years without undue stress from his partners and the changing business environment. His ability to attract clients and his sense of pride about the company were an inspiration for all who worked with him for over forty years. His legacy was such that everyone knew they could not fill his office, and so the corner space became the Price Room. Bart MacDougall was immediately appointed chairman and continued to chair the Executive Committee meetings. It was a natural evolution and was warmly welcomed by the staff and clients.

The system of portfolio management was now becoming a strategy followed by more members of the investment community. This shift away from relying on commissions was as advantageous to the client as it was to the dealer and the years ahead provided a sound endorsement of the path chosen by 3 Macs. The downside was, of course, increased supervision by the regulatory bodies, which brought their full attention to bear on the format and dictated changes. The path to becoming a "portfolio manager" was now to be governed by formal educational qualifications, and those salespeople not grandfathered by experience would henceforth be required to prove their competence by passing industry-standard benchmarks.

In February 1997 Tommy MacDougall died, five years after his wife, and his passing was a reminder of the many attributes he had brought to the company. An athlete, a military officer, a community leader, a friend of hundreds, and a loving father and husband, he embodied the qualities of a gentleman and a business builder. His insistence on confidentiality and discretion acts as a guidepost for the company to this day. The same is true of his belief that respectful relationships with staff and clients were the keystone of a successful operation. The partnership concept was the determining influence for most of his business life and he chose his associates with care and with the understanding that a common commitment to values was paramount to success. He chose his clients with the same criteria and they in turn relied upon his services completely, trusting his ethics and business skills.

There are many threads in the history of the company and many of them can be found in the alumni lists of Bishop's College School and the Montreal Racket Club. The presidency of the Racket Club has been held by Tommy MacDougall, Tom Price, Tim Price, John Kerrigan, Peter Johnson, and Doug Reynolds. The membership has included many staff members and continues to be an important meeting spot for those Montreal gentlemen who like to play a ridiculously fast game of rackets and cool off with a nice lunch. Bishop's College School also has provided a series of valued employees over the years, and again the relationship within those fraternal surroundings has helped maintain a partnership attitude to the running of the company.

In the summer of 1997, a biannual actuarial report brought news that the accounting rules governing the pension plan placed a serious provision against the total equity of the company. Guided by Tom Aiken, the board moved to have the historical plan replaced by a defined contribution system, thus relieving the requirement to make large adjustments to the share value of the firm. The idea was endorsed by all of the staff and special arrangements were made for several members with long service records. Thus, the pension plan started by Tommy MacDougall was converted and an up-to-date retirement plan was introduced.

The board was enlarged during this period with the appointments of Eric Rappaport and David Stevenson. Both had achieved success in their respective areas, David as the branch manager in Toronto and Eric in charge of not only tax work but the fast-growing registered accounts as well.

By 1999, the markets were in full flight and stocks were creating wealth on a scale of such magnitude that anyone who wasn't a holder of a NASDAQ-listed technology stock was considered to be a Neanderthal, and definitely to be pitied. The NASDAQ was first established as an all-electronic market in 1971 and the index of its constituent listings was given a value of 100. By 1974, the index had suffered in the bear markets and recorded a bottom of about 54, and it remained an overlooked marketplace for almost ten years. Then, in July 1995, it hit 1,000 for the first time and investors began to look again at its listed companies. Focusing on companies that did not have a long history of profits, the NASDAQ marketplace became the nurturing parent of some remarkably dominant new-technology firms that were driving investor hopes. These few solid investment choices set an example for thousands of small high-risk ventures who aspired to greatness. The traditional measurements of profits, dividends, sales, book value, and balance-sheet ratios were forgotten or maybe forgiven as money poured into the new paradigm of investing. The NASDAQ became a frenzy of misplaced enthusiasms and ascended to prodigious heights. Warnings of vertigo went unheeded and cautious investors were relegated to the sidelines while the party carried on.

Contemporaneous with this reordering of the marketplace, the Montreal Stock Exchange struck a deal with the Toronto Stock Exchange and gave up listing stocks, becoming instead the single trading market for options and derivatives in Canada. The role of these two exchanges had been a muddle of confusions for years. Owned by essentially the same members and dependent for their business upon those same owners, they competed with each other for market share while watching their respective ratios decline because of foreign listings on the New York and London exchanges. The division of duties was a sensible conclusion and put a stop to the declining values of the memberships. As far as 3 Macs was concerned, it was required to note on its balance sheet the approximate market value of the seats it held on both exchanges. In 1990 the seats were accorded a value of $270,000 and by 1991 they had dropped to $90,000. They continued to have nominal value for years.

As the world headed for the celebration of the millennium, the buzzword was Y2K. This stands out in the lesson book as a "Madness of Crowds" event that summarizes what was happening in the markets. The conventional wisdom focused on the belief that, at the stroke of midnight, 31 December 1999, the traditional computer systems would fail and the world would experience collateral damages of biblical proportions. The investment industry spent millions of dollars on preventative measures and assured the public that it was ready for the doomsday scenario. For its part, 3 Macs felt a little exposed because the main IT man had quit and a new replacement had just joined the company. Further, Harrison as CEO had signed a form accepting full responsibility for any failures that might occur within the company, which was a great relief to the outside experts who had provided stunningly expensive advice. On

New Year's Eve, Glenn LeFrançois and Harrison sat in the Price Room and enjoyed the huge fireworks display on Mount Royal, and a few minutes after midnight Glenn said, "Well, I better test a few computers." Everything worked. It was a quiet moment and a relief, but it should have been taken as a harbinger of the future course of events in the markets. Just as the "madness" was revealed as accepted wisdom gone wrong, so was the coming unwinding of massive bets on stories and hopes with little or no fealty to sane investment practices or realistic financial measurements.

FOURTEEN

The New Millennium

You can't always get what you want …
The Rolling Stones

In February 2000 Charles M. Schultz, the creator of the "Peanuts" comic strip, died and his last original panels were printed. One of Schultz's signature lines, "Good Grief, Charlie Brown," could describe the first eight years of the new millennium. Over the course of fifty years, Schultz's protagonist was subjected to setbacks as part of his daily life. Be it kicking a football or trying to field a baseball team, he was the persistent kid who just wouldn't quit. His recurring battles with kites that surrendered to the highest branches were testimony to the resiliency of man and his attempts to outwit or, at least live with, factors beyond his control.

The financial markets of the world are always indicators of emotional attitudes and from time to time they are subjected to forces that go beyond the normal boundaries of intelligence and extend their parameters to extremes. Markets can travel through broad swings at all times and the underlying momentum is similar to a moving pendulum. The danger is when the arc becomes overextended in either direction, up or down. The opening year of the new century was such a case.

For 3 Macs, the year began with the publication of the first issue of *Info Mac*, an internal magazine providing information to the staff on events to follow, staff changes, babies born, and assorted trivia. The first issue carried a short summary of the stance taken by the research department on the market outlook. While expressing caution, it identified the Canadian stock market as the place to be – the world was finally going to recognize our incredible riches. Shortly afterwards, 3 Macs held a forecast seminar to describe the investment outlook and offer individual clients a chance to meet their investment adviser and the research staff.

Started a few years previously, these seminars had elicited very good client response. The forecasts were usually conservative by nature and any mistakes were kindly overlooked by the returning audience. At the seminar in February 2000, a speaker from a leading New York-based dealer enchanted the audience with bullish forecasts, not the least of which saw the NASDAQ market continue, almost indefinitely, on its ascent to new and awe-inspiring levels.

One month later, the NASDAQ index closed at 5,132.52 – the apogee. The subsequent rapid decline from this extreme caused severe financial damage and crushed the hopes of millions of investors who had bought into the "new paradigm" economy based on high technology, an idea that was found to be as wishful as the new theories that had been expounded a short time earlier. The markets collapsed and the cure to this behaviour was once again felt to rest with the lender of last resort, the Federal Reserve, and its ability to lower interest rates and print money. The Fed obliged with vigour and monetary largesse was pumped into the system and overflowed into the world economies.

A debilitating side effect of collapsing markets is the reduced ability to attract sales people from other firms. An investment adviser does not want to aggravate an already testy client by putting them through the transfer procedures, and furthermore probably doesn't even want to talk to the client unless absolutely necessary. This reality curtailed the hopes of enlarging 3 Macs' sales staff during the troubled times of 2000. That summer, Harrison decided that his "best by" date was approaching faster than he had intended and what was needed was a new leader with experience and history within the industry who could manage the firm and attract a sales force. He made the board aware of his thoughts, and after minimal discussion it was decided that a person from outside the company should be found and interviewed.

At the same time, the Toronto and Montreal exchanges convinced their members that the two trading entities would be better prepared for the future as "for-profit" corporations. This presented an unusual problem for 3 Macs, since it was obvious that the exchanges were going to become publicly traded share companies and the resulting fluctuations in value would make the internal transfer price of 3 Mac shares almost impossible to value and might impose significant burden on new shareholders. The solution was to isolate the shares of the exchanges in a separate pool and attribute their value to two classes of preferred shares. These preferred shares were to be held for the benefit of the shareholders of record on 31 October 2000. This isolating of subsequent values proved to be a financial boost for those shareholders in future years.

Over the years Harrison had been on the lookout for a suitable presidential candidate and had quietly talked to many younger rising stars within the industry. Harrison was chairman of the Canadian Investor Protection Fund (CIPF) and the many committees of that organization had put him in touch with a small selection of potential candidates. He turned to his short list but found that the uncertain environment also extended to salaried officers of senior dealers and banks. Eventually, a candidate was found within the ranks of unemployed senior operators of a bank-owned firm. Terry Jackson was interviewed by the board and in early 2001 an offer was made for his engagement. An experienced operator from a Montreal family (with great golfing credentials), he appeared to have the right background to encourage sales people to join 3 Macs and prosper accordingly. His assumption of the role of president elevated Harrison to the role of vice-chairman, a position that allowed him to continue his industry-association work and maintain a chair at the bond desk. It was a difficult time for Micheline Bourque, who had worked as Harrison's personal assistant for years and had kept him (mostly) on schedule and free of distractions. "Miche" moved to work on the burgeoning registration requirements for the sales force but soon decided that retirement held more promise.

The board continued to expand with appointments for Bob McKenzie, Timothy McNicholas, and John Bridgman. Bridgman had come from Dominion Securities and was well known in the business after working for Greenshields for most of his career. He had built a retail practice but had found that the demands of the bank-owned dealer were causing him worry and annoyance.

On 20 January 2001 George W. Bush was inaugurated as the new president of the United States, and he took command of a country reeling from a serious recession and filled with distracted investors. His timing was not great but it was to get worse. When 9/11 arrived that fall, Bush was still trying to figure out what his role was and what he could do about the economy. Of course, the tragedy of that event would cast a huge shadow over his term of office, and, as the years went by, it became apparent that once again the world order was shifting. While President Bush concentrated his administration's attention on his war against terrorism, other countries were pursuing agendas that saw their rise as world powers proceed at remarkable speed.

A coalition of armed forces led by the United States invaded Afghanistan in November 2001 after the Taliban government failed to hand over leaders of the suspected perpetrators of the 9/11 attacks. Later, in March 2003, the United States invaded Iraq with the sole purpose of overthrowing a brutal and apparently nuclear-ready regime. We await the outcome of these two wars against terrorism. But there is nothing like a war and the opening of the federal purse strings to revitalize an economy, and lavish spending, combined with sequential generous tax cuts, soon placed escalators under the American GDP, despite rendering the currency hostage to government profligacy.

Terry Jackson had met with minimal success in attracting new sales people and his more dramatic plans for the company were not inspiring much support. So in May 2002 he left the firm and Tim Price assumed the role of president and chief executive officer. The appointment was greeted with a solid heartfelt cheer by the staff, reflecting their comfort in having a member of the "family" return to the position. Tim had served on the Executive Committee since 1993 and had the distinction of being the only senior officer who had not only obtained his bachelor of commerce degree and qualified as a chartered accountant but had also passed the rigorous chartered financial analyst exams. Concurrent with his appointment, Cathy Watson joined the board and became secretary of the company.

Once in the presidency, Price moved quickly and, through a long relationship with most of the staff, was able to secure the Montreal office of a failing Toronto dealer. The market was still very unsettled and profits were hard to generate for all industry members, and the acquisition of an experienced and productive sales force was a genuine coup for the company. Of course, some of the faces were familiar. Doug Reynolds, Peter Johnson, and Bill Cowen returned to 3 Macs and brought with them Rick Hart, Jerry Semmelhaack, Richard Woo, and Jean Trudeau. In incremental steps, additional space was taken and converted to make room for the tightly squeezed departments that were not directly related to sales.

The fiscal year ending 2002 was a success for 3 Macs considering the state of the economy, the uncertain markets (the NASDAQ market bottomed out in October at 1,108), and unsettling preparations for war. The company recorded a profit equal to the low point in 1992 but was encouraged by the beginning of a period of unusual prosperity within Canada. Slowly at first and then rising rapidly, commodity prices were the focal point of a new and vigorous transition in the way the world thought of Canada. Aided by the emerging demands for raw materials from Brazil, Russia, India, and China, the so-called BRIC consortium, a genuine bull market appeared. The price of oil began a long, steady advance based on demand and uncertain supply. Metal prices followed. Copper, the metal said to have a PHD in economics, set the tone for the entire market, advancing from a low point of about eighty cents a pound to a high five years later of more than $4.00. The Toronto Stock Exchange continued its role as a key market for mining companies and attracted listings from all over the world. Alberta's oil industry embarked upon a massive development of the fabled oil sands and Canada was suddenly in the spotlight of investors looking to cash in on the new next big thing. The Toronto Stock Exchange joined this enthusiasm by filing a prospectus for the issuance of shares and shortly thereafter asked the member firms if they wished to include the previously issued shares they held in the initial public offering. The directors of 3 Macs chose to do so, and shortly thereafter the market welcomed this new listing and the response allowed the shares to be sold at a huge multiple of the value on the 3 Macs balance sheet. The outlook for the exchange, now known as the TSX, was bullish, not only because of the outlook for natural resources but also because of a huge increase in new listings.

The investment industry has an ability to turn dross to gold if given a chance. Right after the collapse of the "dot.com" era and the substantial reduction in interest rates, agile minds went to work and a hitherto benign financing structure was brought to the forefront. The income trust model was formulated to perfection and by 2002 the new issue volumes had overwhelmed traditional fundraising procedures. Over 75 per cent of all initial public offerings were designed as income trusts and the public was greedily purchasing them in amounts that created a $160-billion market value at its highest point. The attraction was the relatively attractive annual payout by the trusts and the comparative values these represented, risk notwithstanding. Investment bankers made fortunes in the process.

During this period, Price was in conversation with Scotty Fraser about starting an investment-counselling subsidiary. Fraser, one of the founding partners of Jarislowsky, Fraser, Montreal's leading money manager, was keen to help create a small retail-oriented facility and joined 3 Macs in late 2002. After a period of registering the facility in Canada and the United States, he was followed by Douglas Buchanan, then by David Stenason from 3 Macs, and MacDougall Investment Counsel (MIC) was created. Buchanan had a successful reputation working for a smaller investment firm in Montreal, the sale of which to a major Toronto-based organization caused him to look for a more comfortable working environment. Stenason was a highly regarded oil analyst with a senior firm and was looking for a change in his hectic life of constant travel and road shows. Exceptionally well regarded in his milieu, he had no trouble performing the double role of gathering assets and providing portfolio management.

The idea of joining with an investment counsellor had been explored before by 3 Macs and grew from the concern that the investment-dealer platform was becoming too restrictive and expensive for the provision of full, profitable services to clients who essentially wanted portfolio management for a fee. The investment-counsel licence is easier to register in both Canada and the United

States and carries with it fewer capital requirements, but also reduced activities. Buchanan and Fraser were looking for a single source for custodial, research, trading, and office facilities. Today, the counsel entity, as well as its records, is located within separate premises. Together, 3 Macs and MIC have the ability to offer clients full services from a shared platform but separately identified business portals.

Despite wars being fought in foreign lands and an uncertain economic outlook, the Dow Jones managed to rally from a low of 8,341 at the end of 2002 to 10,453 a year later. In May 2002 the TSE relinquished the compilation of its traditional 300 Index to Standard & Poor's and a new index was created known as the S&P/TSX. This measurement seemed to give a new dimension to Canada's only stock market and the listed companies responded by beginning a rise of remarkable proportions. From a close of 6,614 in 2002, the market gathered strength through a combination of vastly increased earnings from its three most heavily weighted components (financials, oil producers, and materials) and a rally in the loonie to record heights. As forecast, Canada was indeed the place to be for the accumulation of wealth. It was a happy circumstance for those in the investment industry, and 3 Macs and its clients' portfolios prospered.

The industry was growing once again and the Investment Dealers Association was under pressure from its members to split off the advocacy side of its mandate and hand the regulatory section to the established Regulation Services, which had sprung from the rib of the TSE. This idea was based on the recognition that, although the big bank-owned dealers did the majority of the business in Canada, their agenda was not always the same as that of the other 100-plus individual firms that comprise the industry. A group of regional dealers had formed a loose association within the IDA and had met for years to try and influence the rule making and policy decisions of the national Board of Directors. Tim Price had been active within this group, and when the IDA divided itself and formed the new Investment Industry Association of Canada, he became the second chairman of the organization. Any senior officer of a small firm who gives his time to jobs such as this can vouch for their usefulness but also is aware that the time spent away from the office doing the work is a large sacrifice for the dealer.

A robust market allows a dealer to expand its sales force with a degree of assurance that the expense of the start-up period for the new entrant will be offset by increased revenues from the established sales force. In the case of 3 Macs, it used this time to increase its sales force significantly, with an emphasis on younger talent to assist and then replace the older investment advisers as the years progressed. Accordingly (in no particular order), Bill Black (Ian's son), Eric Bodnar, Guy Cyr, Dominique Vincent, Chris Gillett, David Khazzam (an options specialist), Jason and Sam MacCallum, Peter Quarles, Adena Franz, James Kellett, Wilma Larratt-Smith, David Robinson, Jeff Hewett, Tom Reber, Claude Breton, Fernand Lemay, James Bowey, David MacDougall, and Robert Cundill joined the company.

Cundill, whose uncle Frank had worked for 3 Macs in earlier years, came from a small dealer but brought with him several things: a large clientele, a casual manner, a managerial talent, and a warm personality. His premature death was a sad time for all who knew him and his skills would be hard to replace. The need to service his substantial client base was handed to MIC and the relocation of the accounts there showed the foresight behind the formation of that facility.

The research department, headed by Ian Nakamoto, added Troy Crandall, Richard Woo, and Bill Chisholm to its ranks and continued to focus on a relatively short list of choices. Nakamoto had come from the "buy" side of the business and demonstrated a skill at stock selection and market direction. Crandall had experience as an analyst with one of the rating agencies and this credential added considerable validity to his work. Together with Chris Sears and Rob Mark, the department continued to steer the portfolio managers with conservative investment advice and the occasional punt for the more adventurous client.

To strengthen the board, new appointments were made in the spring of 2005, with Ian Nakamoto, Judy Cochrane, and Marco Ouellet following earlier selections of Derek Rennie, Peter Sears, and David MacDougall. Cochrane, who understood the new complicated trading systems that run parallel to the TSX, was now head trader with responsibility for the money market, the bond desk, the stock desks, and new issues. David MacDougall, son of Bart, had joined the Toronto office in 1999 with no promises of exceptional consideration. He had built his own client base and, working with Tim McNicholas, had learned the role of the investment adviser/ portfolio manager. David is the fifth-generation MacDougall to work at 3 Macs.

To accommodate the growing list of worthy employees and to make the ownership of shares an easier financial burden, the shares of the company were split five for one, with the result that each share dropped to about $500 in value. This was the second stock split on record since 1960 and spoke to the constant concern of allowing employees to feel genuinely involved in the fortunes of the company and proud of their contribution to its welfare.

The Canadian market was extraordinarily buoyant and in 2005, when the S&P 300 index passed the Dow Jones Industrial Average (11,272 vs. 10,717), a smug look, akin to the winning of the Stanley Cup by a Canadian team, appeared on the faces of most local investors. The rise in stock values was also accompanied by a slow but steady increase in the value of the currency, and the much-discussed proposal three years earlier of throwing in our collective lot with the American dollar disappeared from the conversation of leading economists. When the TSX surpassed trading values of $1 trillion in the closing months of 2005, it was apparent that Canada was a playground for international investors and speculators. In short order, some of Canada's leading companies succumbed to takeover bids from foreign entities and such icons as Dofasco and Inco disappeared from portfolios.

Early in 2007, the Bourse de Montréal announced plans to file a document to allow the trading of the shares given to the members in exchange for their "seats." The Bourse had achieved a record of profitability trading options and derivatives and this combination was considered to be the growth area of financial markets. In due course a market was established and 3 Macs, on behalf of the preferred share ownership, sold the shares into the market. The realized gain was large and valued the seat at a multiple of book value undreamed of years earlier. With the sale of the shares, the long-standing relationship with the Montreal Stock Exchange and 3 Macs came to an end and the history of their relationship is now a memory. The front hall of the Bourse for many years had oil portraits of the two original MacDougall brothers and of Ernest Savard, their worthy competitor at the time of establishing the exchange.

By the spring of 2007, markets around the world experienced new record highs, with Brazil, China, and India leading the way. The huge expansion of these economies was the driving force behind the demand for raw resources, and as economic forecasts grew more bullish, the media concentrated on reports of growing shortages. Food prices were buffeted by weather, bee-colony collapses, changing eating habits, and maybe even sunspots or the lack thereof. Oil was running out, metal production could not meet demand, and the future was seen to be one of constant, demand-driven increases in prices. And there was also the 2008 Beijing Olympics, which would show the world what a vibrant, progressive country was hosting this extravaganza. The China stock market was subject to dire warnings (from outsiders) about a bubble, but Chinese investors were emptying their savings and jumping into the stock markets. India was experiencing the same exhilaration and the new wealth of some of its senior business leaders appeared to herald even greater prosperity to come. It was wonderful to behold. Obviously, it was time for Lucy to snatch the ball away, causing Charlie Brown to fall on his back, again.

In July 2007 the money markets in New York and London seized up and the ensuing collapse of market-priced transactions, with resultant losses by the international banking system, was staggering in its magnitude. Oddly, the stock market of North America chose to overlook, for a few months, this unwinding of the serious over-extension of the credit markets and climbed to new highs before the smack-down became too large to ignore. By October 2007, the Dow recorded a high of 14,164 and the S&P/TSX did not top out for another nine months.

The damaged financial stocks, which had formed a core part of all investment portfolios, were marked down with a ferocity that caused suspect banks and investment dealers to seek substantial equity capital. The market had reacted to the unveiling of lending practices that might be considered to be a once-in-a-lifetime exception. It is useful to read a report of Berkshire Hathaway for Warren

Buffet's perspective on the situation: "Our purchases of Wells Fargo shares were helped by the chaotic market in bank stocks. The disarray was appropriate. Month by month the foolish loan decisions of once well-regarded banks were put on public display. One huge loss after another was unveiled, often on the heels of managerial assurances that all was well." Those words were written in the 1990 Annual Report but they applied equally to the economy in 2007–08. Once again the markets were witnessing the excesses of the banking system and its ability to leverage itself and its friends into a state of collapse.

Simultaneously, the TSX and the Bourse de Montréal, after many rumours, agreed to join forces within one group and the TMX was established. The merger of these two historical exchanges was a sensible and timely move. The proposal to consolidate the stock and derivative businesses was achieved, and the Quebec-based exchange was allowed to maintain its presence in Montreal and have the right to appoint directors from that province. Approval was granted by the local authorities and Canada had a single marketplace to show the world.

By the summer of 2008, markets around the world were reacting to selling pressures and the average retreat from their highs was in excess of 20 per cent, which usually signals a bear market. Canada was spared the worst of that sell-off, but as resource prices began to sink back to historical trends, the TSX was losing ground. It looked as though the sceptics who pronounced the takeover of Inco and Falconbridge just another foolish example of inexperienced operators ignoring the long cycles of commodities, and who predicted that the prices paid for these companies would demonstrate how clever the Canadian shareholder had been to sell them at the top, would be proved right. Certainly, the history of Canada does have examples of how the conservative nature of hewers of wood and drawers of water helps them to endure long periods of winter with little complaint. The summers are shorter but can be very, very agreeable and from time to time very profitable.

The history of MacDougall, MacDougall & MacTier has been influenced by many people with many talents and there are many names not mentioned in this attempt to capture the main themes and highlights. To try to list all of them would be folly, because someone is bound to be forgotten or misplaced in time (to say nothing of the possibility of misspelled names). The company is blessed by having a staff that shares the values of the founders and the sequential handing on of those values is the cornerstone on which 3 Macs is built: integrity, independence, service, and performance.

The company has prospered by following that simple, but meaningful, philosophy. During good and bad times, the client has always come first and the steps taken to ensure that this principle is honoured are not obvious on the surface. Investment dealers have many options and the markets will present opportunities to place significant bets to the benefit of the house. Positioning inventories to take advantage of suspected moves in either stocks or bonds is a normal practice for dealers, and the subsequent unwinding of these positions usually creates conflicts, as does the underwriting of securities. Further, the offloading of some issues may cause the sales manager to create incentives for the sales force to sell a mispriced issue. The list of conflicts is short but the consequences can be dire for the retail client if they are not aware of the dealer's agenda.

From its earliest days to the present, 3 Macs (and its antecedents) created an environment of trust and honesty that still prevails throughout the staff and reflects out to the client. The future is probably brighter than ever, and the reasons are obvious. The transferring of wealth that will occur over the next generations will be significant and the client base will be looking for independent advice separate from its banking relationship. The competition for these clients will be formidable and the victors will be those firms that can provide excellent portfolio advice, tax strategies, and estate planning. These attributes fall under the catchphrase "wealth management." The client will be attracted to a company committed to a relationship founded on trust and knowledge, not on a buzzword. The platform that is now 3 Macs is ideally suited to this challenge. The road ahead requires little alteration to its present direction.

NOTES

1 Mann's Most Pleasing of London and Parson's Guide to the Sights (1844), Royal Military Acadeny, Woolwich, http://www.royalengineers.ca/RMA.html.
2 J.M.S. Careless, *The Union of the Canadas: The Growth of Canadian Institutions, 1841–1857* (Toronto: McClelland and Stewart 1967), 25.
3 One of the strangest crops in its day and the most peculiar sounding to modern ears was "ashes." Yet, in its limited time frame, from the mid-eighteenth century to about 1850, it was not only an immensely popular crop for new arrivals clearing land in Upper New York State and bordering areas in Canada, it also significantly changed the landscape of this part of North America.

The ashes came from burning large trees, mainly elms, as the farmers cleared the land in the upper Mohawk valley of New York, as well as land bordering Ontario and Quebec. Millions upon millions of trees were felled in the last part of the eighteenth century and the first half of the nineteenth, not only to clear the land but to make ashes which, after being boiled down and treated, were transformed into the "black salts" – crude potash – that were so sought after in England that they paid for the farmer's newly acquired land. A hundred pounds of potash could fetch $3.00, the price of an acre of land at that time. As much as 200 pounds of potash could be produced from a single tree.

"Potash was eagerly sought after and held a large place in world commerce. It was used in glass and soap making and dyeing, but most of all in the scouring of wool, meaning thereby, cleansing the wool of the yolk, the natural gummy secretions which ordinarily account for more than half the weight of the fleece as shorn" (Jared van Wagenen, Jr, *The Golden*

Age of Homespun, American Centuries Series [New York: Hill and Wang 1953], 165). As fast as it could be shipped to Montreal and New York, says *The Golden Age of Homespun*, it was loaded on boats bound for England, a profitable non-renewable resource for the farmers, brokers (including the MacDougalls), and shippers alike. The making of ash finally stopped when potash was found in Germany in the mid-1900s.

4 *The Shoe and the Canoe or Pictures of Travel in the Canadas* (London: Chapman and Hall 1850), 108.

5 Careless, *Union of the Canadas*, 20–1.

6 Douglas McCalla, "An Introduction to the Nineteenth Century Business World," in Tom Traves, ed., *Essays on Canadian Business History* (Toronto: McClelland and Stewart 1984), 18.

7 Ibid., 21.

8 Henry G. Norman, *Growing with Canada. Speech to the Newcomen Society* (Montreal, 1957), 12.

CHAPTER TWO

1 Toronto: Macmillan 1956 (p. 385).

2 McCalla says in "An Introduction to the Nineteenth Century Business World," 14, that "until 1850, the scale and structure of Canadian business might be said to have been 18th century in nature."

3 Peter Ward, "Courtship and Social Space in Nineteenth-Century Canada," *Canadian Historical Review*, 68, no. 1 (1987): 35–62.

4 For more than one hundred years, the St James Club's ornate Victorian presence was an attractive addition to the new business community that was beginning to form just up the hill from St James Street and just below the mountain. In the 1950s the building was torn down to build Place Ville Marie, which now dominates René Lévesque Blvd (once Dorchester Street), but the club itself continues a few doors away in a more modern building.

   The St James's Club has had many extraordinary visitors over its 150 years of existence, including members of the royal family and various heads of government. But the prize for the most exotic member goes to a senior British military officer, Dr James Barry. The club provided honorary memberships to senior officers of the British military while they were stationed in Montreal, and Barry, the inspector general of army hospitals, was one of them. According to Collard's *The Story of the Beginnings of the St. James's Club*, Barry stood only about five feet tall and looked anything but a military figure, "with small hands, high cheek bones, a high-pitched and peevish voice. His manner was quarrelsome and aggressive." He swaggered around the club and managed to find the largest sword he could for regimental occasions, especially those in Christ Church Cathedral. During his prior posting in Cape Town, South Africa, the governor there had described him as " the most skilful of physicians and the most wayward of men." Montreal society was used to entertaining unusual, even eccentric characters in their drawing rooms and their clubs but it still must have been a shock to the honourable members of the St James's Club – and to many households, the MacDougalls of Outremont included – when they discovered after his death that Dr James Barry was a "she." According to Collard, the post-mortem examination in London, where "she" died in 1864, revealed "one of the greatest masquerades in history." He adds: "How she was able to enter the Army and to advance so far in remained a mystery, though it has been supposed that she must have been aided by influence from very high places."

5 G.M. Young, *Victorian England: Portrait of an Age* (Oxford: Oxford University Press 1936), 44.
6 Ibid., 77.

CHAPTER THREE

1 Stephen Leacock, *Montreal: Seaport and City* (Toronto: McClelland and Stewart 1948), 180.
2 The mother of a friend, then in her eighties, spoke to one of the authors in excited tones in the 1960s about how her grandmother told her in the 1920s about the thrill she and her sister had waiting in the gallery of the Crystal Palace in August 1860 for the prince to call to them to the dance floor. She related that her great-aunt, rather than her grandmother, was eventually picked out of the crowd by Albert Edward during his marathon dance session.
3 C.P. Stacey, "Fenianism and the Rise of National Feeling in Canada at the Time of Confederation," *Canadian Historical Review*, 12, no. 3 (1931): 240.
4 Ibid., 249.
5 Ibid., 238.
6 Elinor Kyte Senior, "Roots of the Canadian Army: Montreal District, 1846–1870," Society of the Montreal Military and Maritime Museum, *Historical Publications*, 87.
7 Ibid., 88.
8 Ibid.
9 Hereward Senior, *The Last Invasion of Canada: The Fenian Raids, 1866–1870* (Toronto: Dundurn Press in collaboration with Canadian War Museum, Canadian Museum of Civilization 1991), 125.
10 Toronto bankers long continued to feel the pain of two major bank failures in the 1860s, failures that they blamed on the aggressive tactics of the

Bank of Montreal. In the late 1860s, a new bank was founded in Toronto, the Bank of Commerce, ironically financed mainly by Montreal investors. It grew in the next few decades to offer stiff competition to the predominance of the Bank of Montreal, marking the start of the movement to dilute that bank's influence.

CHAPTER FOUR

1 Frances Morehouse, "Canadian Migration in the Forties," *Canadian Historical Review*, 9, no. 4 (1948): 26.
2 Alfred Brady and Harold Palmer, "The Snow Shoe Song (c. 1860), "Midi" sequence for *The Great Canadian Songbook*.
3 Charles G.D. Roberts, "The Canadian Guide-book: The Tourists and Sportsman's Guide to Eastern Canada and Newfoundland" (New York: Appleton 1891), 70. Rinks could serve as venues for activities other than skating, as indicated by an account of the Citizen's Ball in the mid-1870s that was attended by the governor general, Lord Dufferin, and his wife. As one observer, George Stewart, wrote: "Grander entertainment had never been given before in that city ... Between six and seven hundred persons took part in the ball, and the dresses worn by the ladies were characterized by that becoming taste which so largely obtains among the fair daughters of Montreal. The occasion was marked by the appearance of much womanly beauty." The vice-regal couple didn't waste any time heading for the next social outing, this one at a skating rink: "On the 30th inst., another social event occupied the attention of the leaders of Canadian society. A Fancy Dress party was given at the Victoria Skating Rink, and at an early hour the grand entry was made. The ladies and gentlemen filed in, and on the arrival of Their Excellencies eight couples advanced in front of the dais and danced a quadrille; a series of waltzes followed. Lord Dufferin took an active part in the masquerade, and was dressed in a pink satin domino. Fully three thousand persons were present." George Stewart, *Canada under the Administration of Lord Dufferin (1872–1878)* (Toronto: Rose-Belford 1878), 98.
4 John Foster, *The Life of Charles Dickens* (Philadelphia: J.B. Lippincott 1874), 412.
5 Donald C. Masters, *The Rise of Toronto, 1850–1890* (Toronto: University of Toronto Press 1947), 211.
6 Leigh married in England in 1879, when he was in his fifties, and died there in 1901.
7 Still another insurance company that had the backing of MacDougall Brothers was Royal Canadian; in a 1885 shareholder's list, MacDougall

Brothers held 95,900 shares of Royal Canadian, one of the company's largest holdings that year.

8 The culmination of the bank failures of the period would come in 1883 when Montreal's Exchange Bank collapsed, an event reported by the New York *Times*: "The Exchange Bank stopped paying its bills today, which is not considered a good sign of its condition." The directors of the bank included many highly esteemed members of the community and one of them, Alexander Buntin, described as one of the wealthiest in the Dominion, ended up in jail, although the judge seemed reluctant to send him there and allowed him some perks. The courtroom was crowded with excited spectators as Judge Monk of the Court of Queen's Bench said he would limit the jail term as much as possible because Buntin had made restitution of the $8,000 he was accused of taking after the bank closed it doors. This is the account of what happened next as described by the *Times*: "The sentence would therefore be imprisonment in the common jail of the district for the period of 10 days. Mr. Buntin was then removed to the jail, where he will be allowed to furnish his own bed, bedding and food; the millionaire convict will not be badly off. Before being taken to jail Mr Buntin was conducted with by the Hon J.W. Ogilvie, Th my Bulmer, and E.K. Green, all ex-directors of the defunct bank, and the Rev. R. Campbell, a Presbyterian divine. In conversation he said he felt he had done nothing to be ashamed of, but he would bow to the law, which last remark was certainly making a virtue of necessity." New York *Times*, 17 September 1883.

9 Second Session of Fourth Parliament, Debate on Stockbrokers Regulation Bill, 602.

CHAPTER FIVE

1 Susanna McLeod, "Melville Bell: A Phone Connection," http://canadianhistory.suite101.com/article.cfm/melville_bell_a_phone_connection.
2 House of Commons, *Debates*, 29 April 1880.
3 Alan Hustak, *Sir William Hingston, 1829–1907: Montreal Mayor, Surgeon and Banker* (Montreal: Price-Patterson 2004), 118.
4 Montreal *Herald*, August 1876.
5 Montreal *Gazette*, 18 April 1885.

CHAPTER SIX

1 Later in life, Hartland was a stalwart member of the Montreal polo team that won the Canadian championship more than ten times. He was recog-

nized as one of the continent's best polo players, challenging American teams at Saratoga, New York, and other east coast cities as well as playing several times in the winter haven for polo, Aiken, South Carolina.

2 Montreal *Gazette,* letter to the editor at the time of Hartland's death, 1947.

3 J. Graham Patriquin, *B.C.S.: From Little Forks to Moulton Hill,* 2 vols. (Sherbrooke, Que., 1978), 82.

4 William Henry Atherton, *History of Montreal, 1536–1914,* 3 vols. (Montreal, Vancouver, and Chicago: S.J. Clarke Publishing 1914), 3: 240.

5 Patriquin, *B.C.S.,* 8.

6 Ibid.

7 Ibid., 9.

8 Molson, born in 1880, was the son of John Thomas Molson and Jane Baker Butler. He went on to become a track star at McGill, captain of its hockey team and a player on its football team, and a racquets player. He was killed near Vimy Ridge during the First World War and McGill's athletic stadium is named after him.

9 Metis Beach was part of a seigneury established under the French regime and owned by a French nobleman who likely never saw it. In the 1820s it was sold to a Quebec City–based Scotsman who brought several shiploads of Scots to settle in the area. Many of the same families remain today as year-round residents with their own school and churches, one of the oldest English settlements in Quebec.

The beautiful piece of land jutting into the St Lawrence and watched over by a lighthouse was then "discovered" by McGill principal Sir William Dawson, a geologist by training, in the 1850s. He saw it as a recreational hideaway so he built a summer home there and was followed by many McGill faculty members and other Montrealers. The summer community has gone through several phases, including one where ten hotels catered to summer guests. They are no more but the old summer houses have passed down three and four generations, and new ones have been added. It is still a lure in the summer for relatives of the year-round residents, for relatives of the original summer residents who come from as far away as the United Kingdom, Texas, and Vancouver, and for newcomers from Toronto, Montreal, Ottawa, and the Maritimes.

10 Robert Reford, Private Diaries, letter to his wife, Katie. Courtesy of Alexander Reford.

11 Ibid.

12 Ibid.

13 Montreal *Gazette,* 27 April 1898.

14 G.M. Grant, *Picturesque Canada* (Toronto: Beldon 1882), 133.

15 Henry G. Norman, "Growing with Canada: The Story of Canada's Oldest and Youngest Stock Exchanges." Newcomen Address, Montreal, 7 November 1957.

CHAPTER SEVEN

1 Adrian Waller, *No Ordinary Hotel: The Ritz Carlton's First Seventy Five Years* (Montreal: Vehicule Press 1989), 34.
2 Charles Beresford Topp, *The 42nd Battalion, O.E.F. Royal Highlanders of Canada in the Great War* (Montreal: Montreal Gazette Printing 1931), 179–80.
3 Hartland C. MacDougall was nicknamed "Tommy" at an early age to avoid confusion with his father. He was always known as Tommy to his friends, although he was often referred to as "H.C." by his business associates.

CHAPTER EIGHT

1 Col. William Wood, ed. *The Storied Province of Quebec, Past and Present (Five Volumes)* (Toronto: Dominion Publishing 1931), 2: 463.
2 Ibid., 2: 765.
3 Iris Clendenning, *The History of the Montreal Polo Club, 1900–1940.*
4 The oldest of H.B. MacDougall's daughters, Grace, was married 5 May 1923 (before Lorna) to Ward Chipman Pitfield. The result of these unions is that the first generation of five substantial Montreal families – the Refords, the MacDougalls, the Prices, the Pitfields, and the Molsons – became cousins and subsequently peopled Quebec City, Montreal, Toronto, Ottawa, and Vancouver as well as points as far away as Singapore and Texas. And, like a medieval pilgrimage, most of them wend their way back to Metis, if not every summer, then every few summers, to this day.

CHAPTER NINE

1 Hartland M. MacDougall was destined for a lifelong career with the Bank of Montreal, where he reached the position of vice-chairman before being appointed chairman of the Royal Trust Company.
2 Ward Chipman Pitfield came to Montreal from New Brunswick just before the First World War and by the early 1920s was second-in-command to Izaak Walton (Ike) Killam. He then struck off on his own in the investment business, forming W.C. Pitfield & Co. in 1928. Half in jest, a few of his contemporaries, including the Major, his father-in-law, called him "an upstart from New Brunswick." Pitfield, who married the Major and Edith's oldest daughter, Grace, died tragically in 1939 at age forty-six from a rare disease contracted from chewing hay. His first son, also Ward C. Pitfield (II), was brought up in Montreal and trained race horses on the family farm, not far from Saraguay. He went to McGill where he starred as a hockey player along with Jack Gelineau. Ward joined Hershey Bears

training camp and played a few exhibition games for the Boston Bruins until injury sidelined him, while Gelineau went on to play a star role as a goaltender on the Bruins. Years later, Ward directed a very successful investment business in Toronto and owned and bred race horses.

3 "Peter MacDougall, the great-great-grandfather of Bart and Marian Mac-Dougall and Sally and Susan Pitfield, although coming to Canada when quite elderly (in the 1850s), hunted with Montreal, so that the MacDou-galls are probably without parallel on the North American continent in having five succeeding generations who have hunted with the same pack," comments John Irwin Cooper in *The History of the Montreal Hunt* (1953), 130.

4 The writer seemed to get carried away. All evidence indicates that he suf-fered his stroke on 2 April 1929, a time of the year when it is unlikely he could have played polo, swam, or played tennis outdoors. But he may well have had a few games of racquets and a swim before he visited his new granddaughter.

5 Eric Kierans, *Remembering* (Toronto: Stoddart 2001), 62.

6 As a reporter in 1960, one of the authors of this book watched in amaze-ment as the telegraph operator at the train station in Saint-Georges de Beauce sent a story of his to Montreal by Morse code.

CHAPTER TEN

1 Alf Dobell, born in Winnipeg, had served in the Royal Canadian Navy and after the war began a career with International Paints (U.K.) as east-ern sales agent for marine services, a position he was not as happy with as he had expected. On the death of his father (a senior executive with Ogilvie Flour Mills), he sought out Colonel MacTier to help him with the terms of his father's will. MacTier recognized a talent for sales in the thirty-year-old veteran and hired him. Alf was required to pass all the nec-essary exams before, as he put it, "being unleashed on the unsuspecting public."

BIBLIOGRAPHY

BOOKS

Bercuson, David J., and J.L. Granatstein. *The Collins Dictionary of Canadian History: 1867 to the Present*. Toronto: Collins Publishers 1988.

Brown, Robert Craig, and Ramsay Cook. *Canada 1896–1931: A Nation Transformed*. Toronto: McClelland and Stewart 1974.

Campbell, Marjorie Wilkins. *The Nor'Westers: The Fight for the Fur Trade*. Toronto: Macmillan 1961.

Careless, J.M.S., ed. *Colonists and Canadians, 1780–1867*. Toronto: Macmillan of Canada 1971.

– *Toronto to 1918*. Toronto: James Lormier 1984.

– *The Union of the Canadas: The Growth of Canadian Institutions, 1841–1857*. Toronto: McClelland and Stewart 1967.

Clendenning, Iris. *The History of the Montreal Polo Club, 1900–1940*. Privately published 1987.

Collard, Edgar Andrew. *Canadian Yesterdays*. London: Longmans, Green 1955.

– *Chalk to Computers: The Story of the Montreal Stock Exchange, 1986*. Montreal: Montreal Stock Exchange.

– *Montreal: The Days That Are No More*. Toronto: Doubleday Canada 1976.

– *Montreal Yesterdays*. London: Longmans 1962.

– *The Story of the Beginnings of the Saint James's Club*. Montreal, 1995.

Colombo, John Robert. *Colombo's Canadian References*. Toronto: Oxford University Press 1976.

Cook, Ramsay. *Canada and the French Canadian Question*. Toronto: Macmillan of Canada 1966.

Cooper, John Irwin. *The History of the Montreal Hunt, 1953.*
– *Montreal, The Story of 300 Years, 1942.* Montreal: L'imprimerie Lamirande.
Creighton, Donald, *The Empire of the St. Lawrence.* Toronto: Macmillan of Canada 1956.
– *The Forked Road: Canada 1939–1957.* Toronto: McClelland and Stewart 1976.
Dafoe, J.W. *Laurier: A Study in Canadian Politics.* Toronto: McClelland and Stewart 1963.
Denison, Merrill. *The Barley and the Stream: The Molson Story.* Toronto, 1955.
– *Canada's First Bank: A History of the Bank of Montreal, Volume One.* Toronto: McClelland and Stewart 1966.
– *Canada's First Bank: A History of the Bank of Montreal, Volume Two.* Toronto: McClelland and Stewart 1966.
Denison, Merrill, W.T. Easterbrook, and Hugh G.L. Aitken. *Canadian Economic History.* Toronto: University of Toronto Press 1988.
Gilmour, Kenneth F. *Memoirs of Rackets in Canada and the Montreal Racket Club.* Montreal: King Press, n.d.
Glazebrook, George P. *A History of Transportation in Canada,* 2 vols. Toronto: McClelland and Stewart 1966.
Gordon, John Steele. *An Empire of Wealth: An Epic History of American Economic Power.* New York: Harper Perennial 2003.
Grant, G.M. *Picturesque Canada.* Toronto: Beldon 1882.
Hustak, Alan. *Sir William Hingston, 1829–1907: Montreal Mayor, Surgeon and Banker.* Montreal, Price-Patterson 2004.
Jenkins, Kathleen. *Montreal: Island City of the St. Lawrence.* New York: Doubleday 1966.
Kierans, Eric. *Remembering.* Toronto: Stoddart 2001.
Leacock, Stephen. *Montreal: Seaport and City.* Toronto: McClelland and Stewart 1948.
MacMillan, David, ed. *Canadian Business History: Selected Studies.* Toronto: McCelland and Stewart 1972.
Masters, Donald C. *The Reciprocity Treaty of 1854.* Toronto: University of Toronto Press 1969.
– *The Rise of Toronto, 1850–1890.* Toronto: University of Toronto Press 1947.
Morton, W.L. *The Critical Years: The Union of British North America, 1857–1873.* Toronto: McClelland and Stewart 1969.
Neufeld, E.P. *The Financial System of Canada: Its Growth and Development.* Toronto: Macmillan of Canada 1972.
Ouellet, Fernand. *Lower Canada, 1791–1840: Social Change and Nationalism.* Toronto: McClelland and Stewart 1983.

Paterson, Alex K. *My Life at the Bar and Beyond*. Montreal and Kingston: McGill-Queen's University Press 2005.

Patriquin, J. Graham. *B.C.S.: From Little Forks to Moulton Hill*, 2 vols. Sherbrooke, Que., 1978.

Proctor, Frank. *Fox Hunting in Canada and Some Men Who Made It*. Toronto: Macmillan 1929.

Royal Montreal Golf Club, 1873–1973. Centennial Edition. Privately published.

Thompson, John Herd, and Allen Seager. *Canada, 1922–1939: Decades of Discord*. Toronto: McClelland and Stewart 1976.

Shortt, Adam. *Currency and Banking, 1840–1867*. In E.P. Neufeld, ed., *Money and Banking in Canada*. Toronto: Macmillan of Canada 1964.

Siegfried, André. *The Race Question in Canada*. Toronto: McClelland and Stewart 1966.

Skelton, Oscar Duncan. *The Life and Times of Alexander Tilloch Galt*. Toronto: McClelland and Stewart 1966.

Stewart, George. *Canada under the Administration of Lord Dufferin (1872–1878)*, Toronto: Rose-Belford 1878.

Terrill, Frederick William. *Chronology of Montreal and of Canada, A.D. 1752 to A.D. 1893*. Montreal: John Lovell and Son 1893.

Timothy, H.B. *The Galts: A Canadian Odyssey, Volume 1, John Galt 1779–1839*. Toronto: McClelland and Stewart 1977.

– *The Galts: A Canadian Odyssey, Volume 2, Alexander Tilloch Galt 1817–1893, Elliott Torrance Galt 1850–1928*. Toronto: McClelland and Stewart 1984.

Topp, Charles Beresford. *The 42nd Battalion, O.E.F. Royal Highlanders of Canada in the Great War*. Montreal: Montreal Gazette Printing 1931.

Tucker, Gilbert Norman. *The Canadian Commercial Revolution, 1845–1851*. New York: Anchor Books 1971.

Tulchinsky, Gerald J.J. *River Barons: Montreal Businessmen and the Growth of Industry and Transportation, 1837–1853*. Toronto: University of Toronto Press 1972.

Waite, P.B. *Canada, 1874–1896: The Arduous Destiny*. Toronto: McClelland and Stewart 1971.

– *The Life And Times of Confederation, 1864–1867*. Toronto: University of Toronto Press 1963.

Waller, Adrian. *No Ordinary Hotel: The Ritz Carlton's First Seventy-Five Years*. Montreal: Véhicule Press 1989.

Wood, Col. William, ed. *The Storied Province of Quebec, Past and Present (Five Volumes)*. Toronto: Dominion Publishing 1931.

Young, G.M. *Victorian England: Portrait of an Age*. Oxford: Oxford University Press 1936.

ARTICLES

Beauregard, Ludger. "Outre Mont Royal 1694–1875." www.Histoire-quebec.qc.ca/pulicat/vol8.

Brown, George W. "The Opening of the St. Lawrence to American Shipping." *Canadian Historical Review*, 7, no. 1 (1926): 4–12.

Careless, J.M.S. "Frontierism, Metropolitanism and Canadian History." *Canadian Historical Review*, 35, no. 1 (1954): 1–21.

Cooper, John Irwin. "The Social Structure of Montreal in the 1850s." Canadian Historical Association, *Historical Papers*, 1956, 63–73.

– "Some Early Canadian Savings Banks." *Canadian Banker*, 57, no. 2 (1950): 135–43.

Creighton D.G. "The Victorians and the Empire." *Canadian Historical Review*, 19, no. 2 (1938): 138–53.

Keesler, Paul. "Mohawk, Chapter 9: They Burned the Woods and Sold the Ashes." Paul Keeslerbooks.com/potash, 2002.

Masters, D.C. "The Establishment of Decimal Currency in Canada." *Canadian Historical Review*, 33, no. 2 (1952).

McCalla, Douglas. "An Introduction to the Nineteenth-Century Business World." In Tom Traves, ed., *Essays on Canadian Business History*. Toronto: McCelland and Stewart 1984.

McKeagan, David. "The Development of a Mature Securities Market in Montreal." MA essay, Concordia University, 21 December 2004.

Morehouse, Frances. "Canadian Migration in the Forties." *Canadian Historical Review*, 9, no. 4 (1948): 129–42.

Norman, Henry G. "Growing with Canada: The Story of Canada's Oldest and Youngest Stock Exchanges." Newcomen Address, Montreal, 7 November 1957.

Pentland, H.C. "The Lachine Strike of 1843." *Canadian Historical Review*, 29 no. 3 (1948): 255–77.

Roberts, Charles G.D. "The Canadian Guide-book: The Tourists and Sportsman's Guide to Eastern Canada and Newfoundland." New York: Appleton 1891.

Senior, Elinor Kyte. "Roots of the Canadian Army: Montreal District, 1846–1870." Society of the Montreal Military and Maritime Museum, Historical Publications.

Shortt, Adam. "Founders of Canadian Banking – Horatio Gates, Wholesaler, Banker and Legislator." *Journal of the Canadian Bankers' Association*, 30, no. 1 (1922).

Stacey, C.P. "Fenianism and the Rise of National Feeling in Canada at the Time of Confederation." *Canadian Historical Review*, 12, no. 3 (1931): 238–61.

– "Fenian Troubles and Canadian Military Development, 1865–1871." Canadian Historical Association, *Annual Report*, 1938, 26–35.

Ward, Peter. "Courtship and Social Space in Nineteenth-Century Canada." *Canadian Historical Review*, 68, no. 1 (1987): 36–53.

ABOUT THE AUTHORS

JAMES FERRABEE

James Ferrabee was born in Montreal and has worked as a journalist for fifty years, forty of them for the Montreal *Gazette* and
Southam News. He has written on provincial and federal politics,
business, and finance, as well as making the occasional foray into
sports and travel writing. He was a foreign correspondent for fifteen years, at various times based in Nairobi, Kenya, Paris, and
London. He reported on the last days of Rhodesia and Idi Amin,
the Israeli invasion of Lebanon in 1981, the collapse of the Soviet
Union, a royal wedding, and the ferry disaster in Zeebrugge, Belgium, in March 1987, when 193 passengers and crew died. For his
reporting on the Zebrugge tragedy, he received the National Newspaper Award for Spot News Reporting, the country's premiere
newspaper award. Since his retirement, he has written a business
column for the *Gazette* for five years and a column on policy issues
for the Institute for Research on Public Policy (IRPP) for seven
years. He served as president of the corporation of Bishop's University between 1999 and 2003. He and his wife, Di, have three children and seven grandchildren. They live in the village of Hatley in
Quebec's Eastern Townships.

MICHAEL ST B. HARRISON

Born in Montreal in 1934 and educated at Lower Canada College, Michael St B. Harrison joined the Bank of Montreal in 1954, Cochran Murray & Co., Toronto, in 1965, and MacDougall, MacDougall & MacTier in 1988. He served on the board of the Investment Dealers Association and as its chairman from 1989 to 1990, was vice-chair of the Bourse de Montréal, 1991–92, and was chairman of the Canadian Investor Protection Fund, 2000–04. Married to Carol Reaper Morison, he has no prior experience as a writer of historical fact, preferring to blog about the markets and inventing most of the references.

INDEX

3 Macs. *See* MacDougall,
MacDougall & MacTier (3 Macs)
3rd Battalion, Victoria Volunteer
Rifles, 47
3rd Canadian Infantry Division,
107
5th Battalion: Royal Fusiliers, 47;
Royal Light Infantry, 47
5th Light Anti-Aircraft Battery, 128
42nd Battalion, 5th Royal
Highlanders of Canada, 106, 107,
108

Abbott, J.J.C., 24, 34, 43
Accident Insurance Company of
Canada, 67
A.E. Ames and Company, 148
Afghanistan: Russia and, 176; U.S.
and, 211
Aiken, Tom, 197–8, 205
Albert, Prince Consort, 29
Alberta: oil and gas in, 132, 139; oil
sands development in, 212
Albert Edward, Prince of Wales,
31, 39
Allaire, Luc, 188
Allan, Sir Andrew, 42

Allan, Hugh, 30, 34
Allan family, 28, 33, 42
Allan's Steamship Line, 30
Amateur Hockey Association of
Canada, 88
American Growth Fund, 147
Ames, A.E., 97, 148
Anderson, Cathy, 188
Anderson, T.B., 42
Angus, R.B., 101
annexation of Canada to U.S., 24,
25, 46
Applegarth, Betsy Geraldine (née
MacDougall). *See* MacDougall,
Betsy Geraldine (later
Applegarth)
Applegarth, Edward Richard D.,
70, 98, 109, 115
Applegarth, Grace, 70
Applegarth, Hartland Leonard St
Clair, 70
Arbuckle, Stewart, 162
Arnold, Thomas, 87
ashes, 221–2n3
Atlantic Acceptance, 151–2
Atlantic provinces, 56, 65
Aubin, Julie, 203

automobiles, 94, 117, 134–5

Baby Boomers, 138–9
Bache, 148
Back River Club, 120
Baird, John, 144, 177, 193, 195
Ball, Ben, 200–1
Ballantyne, Elizabeth, 178
Ballantyne, James R., 162
Bank Act (Canada), 147, 149
Bank of British North America, 16, 42, 56, 82
Bank of Canada, 12, 150, 152
Bank of Commerce, 224n10
Bank of Montreal, 16; Anderson of, 42; Bart MacDougall at, 142; and Bell Telephone Company of Canada, 74; and bond trading, 96–7; Campbell and, 53, 67; and currency crisis, 21; Davidson and, 46; description of, 39; dominance of, 46, 57; establishment of, 4, 12; Hartland B. and, 89, 101, 102; Holton and, 55; in London, 54, 96; Lorn and, 82; MacDougall & Davidson and, 68; in New York, 46, 53, 96; 1930s depression and, 125; Paterson and, 99; and Royal Canadian Bank, 64; and 3 Macs, 147–8; transfer of provincial account from Bank of Upper Canada to, 55, 64; volume of shares in, 57
Bank of the United States, 126
Bank of Upper Canada, 55, 64
banks, 16–17; and bond trading, 96, 97; correspondent links with investment dealers, 147–8; and currency crisis, 21; deposit insurance and, 152; establishment of, 12; failures, 56, 58, 64, 125–6; inflation and, 177; interest rates

and, 177; and investment dealers, 176, 185–6; investments in, 56; Lorn and, 82; MacDougalls and, 132–3; 1960s prosperity and, 146–7; numbers of, 54, 56; Porter Commission and, 149–50; private, 12; public-private relationships, 97; size of, 46; U.S. compared to Canadian, 46, 54, 56–7, 125–6. *See also names of individual banks*
Banque du Peuple, 16
Barbeau, Christina, 202
Barker, Eleanor, 202
Barnoff, Phil, 163, 175
Barry, James, 222–3n4
Barry & McManamy, 168, 200
Beatty, Sir Edward, 119
Beaverbrook, Max Aitken, Lord, 97
Bell, Alexander Graham, 72
Bell, Melville, 72–3
Bell Telephone Company of Canada, 72, 73–5
Benson, John, 176, 188, 199, 200
Bergeron, Michel, 180, 193
Berkshire Hathaway, 217–18
Berlin Wall, 187–8
Berry, Douglas, 203
Bertrand, Luc, 166
Bethune, Strachan, 74
bicycles and bicycling, 85, 93
Bigsby, John Jeremiah, 11
Bishop, Tracey, 188
Bishop's College School (BCS), 86–8, 116, 141, 150; alumni, 204–5, *photo*
Bishop's University, 99, 141–2
Black, Bill, 215
Black, Ian, 152, 167, 168, 193, 194
Black Monday, 184
Black Watch (Royal Highland Regiment of Canada): MacTier

and, 144; Tom Price and, 142, 164. *See also* 42nd Battalion, 5th Royal Highlanders of Canada

Blaikie, John L., 67

Bloomberg information system, 201

Board of Brokers (Montreal), 17, 44

Board of Stock Brokers (Montreal), 44, 54, 57

Board of Trade (Montreal), 15, 16, 26–7, 33, 42, 81, 104

Bodnar, Eric, 215

Bogert, H.S., 155, 164

Bond, Frank, 61–2

Bond, William Bennett, 83

Bond Dealers' Association, 112

bonds: banks and, 96–7; First World War, 112–13; Victory, 131; volume of buying, 127

bond trading, 95–7; brokerage houses specializing in, 113; before First World War, 99; First World War and, 112–13; MacTier and, 143; Montreal's dominance in, 144

Boston, Harriet Lucy. *See* MacDougall, Harriet Lucy (née Boston)

Boston, John, 35

Boston Stock Exchange, 148

Bourassa, Robert, 169

Bourque, Micheline, 210

Bourse de Montréal, 166, 216–17, 218. *See also* Montreal Stock Exchange (MSE)

Bowey, James, 215

Breton, Claude, 215

BRIC consortium, 212, 217

Bridgman, John, 202, 210

Brinco, 158

Britain. *See* United Kingdom

British Columbia: in Confederation, 56; gold in, 53

British North America: federation of colonies of, 52–3; U.S. Civil War and, 40–1

British North America Act, 53, 180

British Petroleum (BP), 182, 183, 185

British Telecom, 182

Brodhead, Cricky, 188

brokers and brokerage business, 33, 54; as bankers, 105; bond trading, 96, 97, 113; characteristics of, 105; 1870 volume of trade, 57–8; relations with politicians, 105; reputation of, 81–2, 104, 105; self-regulation of, 194

Brydges, Charles John, 70–1, 95

Brydges, Grace (later MacDougall). *See* MacDougall, Grace (née Brydges)

Buchanan, Douglas, 213, 214

Buchanan and Company, 19

Budden, Alexander, 46

Budden, John, 166

Buffett, Warren, 217–18

building societies, 54

Buntin, Alexander, 225n8

Burnett, James, 155

Burnett & Company, 155

Burns, Arthur, 165

Bush, George H.W., 191–2

Bush, George W., 211

business: in Canada, 33–4; government and, 15–16; intermediaries, 17; politics and, 15, 43

Cambodia, bombing of, 160

Campbell, Ron, 182, 193

Campobello Island, 49

Canada: annexation to U.S., 24, 25, 46; deficit budgets in, 170;

government debt, 170, 179; government deficits, 179, 199; immigrants in, 4, 21–3, 63, 75–6, 124–5, 131; international investment in, 216; and Korean War, 137–8; population of, 63, 75, 97–8, 138–9, 161, 169

Canada Cement Company, 97

Canada Land Company, 11

Canada Savings Bonds, 148, 166

Canadian Arena Company, 119, 120, 134

Canadian Bank of Commerce, 82

Canadian District Telegraph Company, 73

Canadian Investor Protection Fund (CIPF), 210

Canadian Marine Insurance Company, 34

Canadian Pacific Railway (CPR), 63–4, 70, 93

Canadian Peat Fuel Company, 45

Canadian (ship), 28

Canadian Stock Exchange, 117

Canadiens, 119–20, 133–4

canals, 4, 21, 22, 96

Cantin, Augustin, 43

Cantin, Josée, 203

Carlton Hotel Committee, 103

Carter, Jimmy, 171, 174

Cartier, Debbie, 188, 199

Cartier, Sir George-Étienne, 16, 43

Catholic Church: and fall of Berlin Wall, 188; in Quebec, 138, 139, 140

Cattarinch, Joseph, 119

Central Canada Loan and Savings Company, 97

Central Depository System, 192, 201

Champlain and St Lawrence Railroad, 7

Charles Meredith & Company, 98, 101–2, 103, 109. *See also* Meredith, Charles

Chechnya, 202

Cheney, Richard, 191–2

Cherrier, C.S., 43

Chisholm, Bill, 215

Christ Church Cathedral, 38, 76, 80, 83

Chrysler Corporation, 173

churches, 5, 38. *See also* Catholic Church; *and names of individual churches*

Churchill Falls, 158

City Bank, 16

Clahane, Charlene, 188

Clarke, Ian, 202

Clinton, Bill, 195, 198

closed-end funds, 147

Cobbett, David, 197

Cochrane, Judy, 188, 195–6, 201, 215–16

Cohen, Arthur M., 61–2

Colabella, Toni, 188

Cold War, 155, 188

Collard, Edgar Andrew, 36–7

Collier, Norris & Quinlan, 150

Collis, Ross and Company, 19

Commercial Bank of the Midland District of Ontario, 55, 64

commissions, 181; client fees and, 194; fixed rates of, 150; mutual funds and, 147; negotiated with clients, 167–8; portfolio management vs., 204; quality of stock trading and, 177; and remuneration of retirees, 164; and revenues, 154; tapering schedule of, 167; in Toronto branch, 166

Committee on Trade (Montreal), 15

commodities, 43, 54, 57, 165, 212, 213

Companies Act, 27
computers, 198–9
Confederation, 41, 43, 53, 55, 56, 64, 93
Consolidated Bank, 69
Constitutional Act (1791), 64
Corneil, Robert, 202
Corn Exchange, 44, 54
Corn Laws, 22
Coulter, Bob, 203
Cowen, William, 156, 172, 175, 193, 212
Craig, Rick, 163, 176, 177, 199
Crandall, Troy, 215
Crystal Palace (Montreal), 40
Cundill, Frank, 215
Cundill, Robert, 215
currency: in British North America, 30–1, decimal, 30, 33–4; U.S., 165, 178
Cyr, Guy, 215

Dandurand, Leo, 119, 120
Davidson, David, 46
Davidson, Thomas, 46, 73, 74, 82, photo
Davis, Jefferson, 46
Dean Witter, 148
debentures, 96
DeGrandpré, Denise, 188
Delagrave, M. Gerard, 168
Deveney, George A., 143, 144
Dickens, Charles, 9, 65
Diefenbaker, John, 140
Dinnick, Wilf, 194–5
diseases, 36
D.L. MacDougall Stock Brokers, 84
Dobell, Alfred M. (Alf), 144, 152
Dominion Securities, 97
Dominion Telegraph, 73
Dorval Airport, theft of securities from, 192

Dotzko, David, 188, 199
Doyle, John, 51
Drapeau, Jean, 145
Drexel Burnham Lambert, 187, 191
Duplessis, Maurice, 139
Durham, Lord, 8

economic depressions/recessions: 1840s, 22, 24; 1857, 30; 1876–79, 62–3, 69; 1930s, 123–4; 1980s, 179; 1990s, 191; in U.K., 182
economic growth: 1870s, 62–3, 69; 1890s, 94; 1920s compared with 1930s, 123–4; 1930s depression and, 125; 1950s, 137–9; 1960s, 146, 151, 157; 1970s, 161, 169; 1990s, 198, 200; 2000s, 212; Confederation and, 56; financial panic and, 56, and crisis in market and, 100; after U.S. Civil War, 75
education: in Ontario, 42; in Quebec, 139; Scots and, 42. See also Bishop's College School (BCS)
Edward VII, King, 102
Eisenhower, Dwight David, 138
electricity, 93, 102
Elgin, Lord, 23, 24, 26
Eliock School, 86
Elizabeth, Queen, The Queen Mother, 164, photo
emigrants and emigration: French Canadian, 93, 102, 124; from Nova Scotia, 124; to U.S., 63, 93, 124. See also immigrants
Erie Canal, 4, 22, 25
Ethier, Jean, 202
Exchange Bank, 225n8
Expo '67, 154–5

Farrugia, Michael, 166, 175
Fenian Brotherhood, 48–52, 83
First World War, 106–13

flour, 18–19, 30, 33
football, 85, 86, 136
Forbes, W.H., 74
Forest and Stream Club, 110
Forget, Louis-Joseph, 43, 97, 105
Forget, Sir Rodolphe, 105
Franz, Adena, 215
Fraser, Scotty, 213, 214
French Canadians: emigration to U.S., 93, 102, 124; investment patterns, 140; numbers in Montreal, 66; Scots and, 42–3; in U.S., 11
Front de Libération du Québec (FLQ), 159
Frost, Colonel, 57
Fulford, Francis, 28

Gallop, John, 189, 196–7
Gallop, Mark, 202
Gallwey, Thomas, 61
Galt, Sir Alexander Tilloch, 16, 24, 30, 43, 45, 55, 67, 109
Galt, John, 11
gambling, 117
Gaspé Lead Mining Company, 45
Gault, Hamilton, 120
Geddes, Charles, 57
George Glen (ship), 19
Gillespie and Moffat, 98
Gillett, Chris, 215
Girouard, Desirée, 69
Giroux, Sue, 188
Glass, John, 14, 16, 19, 20, 21, 34, 81
gold: in British Columbia, 25–6, 53; price of, 165, 171
golf, 61–2, 85–6, 121–2, 161–2
Gorbachev, Mikhail, 187, 188
Gordon, Athol, 170
Gordon, Sir Charles, 103, 115, 119
Gordon brothers, 121
Gordon Capital, 202

governments: and bond trading, 96; and business, 15–16; debts, 170, 179, 195, 201; deficits, 170, 179, 199; privatization by, 182, 183
Grace Anglican Church, 95
Grand Trunk Railway, 27, 31, 32, 70, 93, 95
Grant, Ulysses S., 49
Grant, W.L., 93
Grantham, Laird, 189, 192–3, 196, 198
Gratias, Orvald, 154, 189
Greenspan, Alan, 169, 184, 202
Grossman, Anne Dixon, 189
Groves, Shelagh, 188
Grunner, Jennifer, 189
guaranteed interest certificates (GICs), 177, 178, 183
Guarantee Insurance Company, 67–8, 109, 110
Gulf War I, 195
Gundy, J.H., 97

Hamilton, Luther, 16
Hampson, H.A. (Tony), 149
Hanson Brothers, 97
Harrison, Michael St B., 186–7, photo; appointees of, 189; and Bloomberg information system, 201; and Canadian Investor Protection Fund (CIPF), 210; and clients' set fees, 194; and collegiality of sales staff, 189, 193; on commonality of investment opinions, 189; expansion of bond business, 195–6; and information technology, 198–9; and Investment Dealers Association, 187; on portfolio selection, 189; as president and COO, 186–7, 189; steps down, 209; and successor, 210; as vice-chairman, 210; Y2K and, 206–7

Hart, Rick, 212
Hebert, Paul, 189
Hewett, Jeff, 215
Hincks, Sir Francis, 69, 80
Hingston, William, 79
hockey, 87–9, 119–20, 130, 133–4
Holland, Peter, 189
Holton, Luther Hamilton, 43, 55
Hooper, George, 120
horses: Campbell and, 85; Hartland B. and Edith and, 90; Lorn and, 10, 35; McLennan and, 109; polo and, 120–1; racing, 129; St Clair and, 35; Tommy and, 116. *See also* polo
hospitals, 37
hotels, 102–4
Hudson, Elspeth. *See* Meredith, Elspeth (née Hudson)
Hudson's Bay Company, 53, 65, 70
hydroelectricity, 158–9

immigrants, 21–3, 63, 75–6; during 1930s, 124–5; American, 4; English, 4; European, 43; Irish, 4, 22–3; Jewish, 43, 111, 124–5; numbers of, 97; Scots, 4; Second World War and, 131; in U.S., 63, 75. *See also* emigrants and emigration
Imperial Oil, 168
industrialization, 75–6, 93, 98, 102; Second World War and, 131–2
inflation: 1960s, 155, 157, 158, 159; 1970s, 161, 165, 169, 170, 171–2; 1980s, 177, 178, 179, 183; in U.S., 171–2, 174
Info Mac, 208–9
information technology, 201
infrastructure, 45, 95–6
institutional business, 152, 166, 167, 171, 172, 175, 181

insurance companies: and bond trading, 96; investment patterns, 149
Intercolonial Railway, 93
interest rates: 1960s, 155; 1970s, 161, 170, 172; 1980s, 177, 178, 179, 183, 184; 1990s, 191, 195, 213
International Centennial Exposition in Philadelphia, 68
Investment Dealers Association (IDA), 105, 137, 185, 186, 214
investment industry, 105; banks and, 147–8, 176, 185–6; interest rates and, 179; legislation of, 105; numbers of dealers in Montreal, 180–1; privatization and, 182; regulation of, 200, 214; research in, 202; S&L collapse and, 178; takeovers within, 181; U.S., 147
Investment Industry Association of Canada, 214
investments: advice on, 147–8; counselling, 213–14; foreign, in Canadian markets, 147; by insurance companies, 149; by pension funds, 149
Investors Group (Winnipeg), 155
Iranian revolution, 168–9
Iraq: U.S. invasion of, 211; War of 1990, 191–2
Ireland: immigrants from, 4, 22–3; independence from Britain, 48; potato famine in, 22

Jackson, Andrew, 7
Jackson, Peto, Brassey and Betts, 32
Jackson, Terry, 210, 211
Jankey, Carmen, 188
Japan: collapse of real estate bubble, 191; markets in, 170
Jarislowsky, Fraser, 213
Jews, 43, 111, 124–5

J.H. Dunn and Company, 99–100
J.L. Marler & Company, 156
Jobin, Marc, 171, 180, 182, 193
John Paul II, Pope, 172, 188
Johnson, Lyndon Baines, 153,
    157–8, 160
Johnson, Peter, 171, 205, 212
Jones, Hugh A. (Buster): on board,
    156; as CFO, 197–8; joins 3
    Macs, 153–4; and non-directors
    as shareholders, 164; and tax
    preparation, 153–4, 172; and 3
    Macs' financial position, 175, 181;
    as treasurer and secretary, 189;
    as vice-president, 169
junk bonds, 187
Jutras, André, 203

Kadi, Bassam, 203
Kellett, James, 215
Kennebec Gold Mining Company,
    45
Kennedy, Charles, 181, 182
Kennedy, John F., 145
Kent State University shootings,
    160
Kerrigan, John V., 161–2, 167, 185,
    205
Kertland, Kim, 166
Ketchabaw, Bob, 197
Khan, Jawaid, 167, 176–7, *photo*
Khazzam, David, 215
Kierans, Eric, 140
King, E.H., 55
King, William Lyon Mackenzie,
    124
Kingston, capital shifted to
    Montreal from, 21
Kingstone, Herbert, 161
Kingstone & Mackenzie, 161–2
Kinnear, Jim, 177
Korean War, 137

labour unions, 94, 114, 182
Lachine Canal, 4, 10, 29
lacrosse, 86
La Fontaine, Sir Louis-Hippolyte,
    61
Lake Huron Silver and Copper
    Mining Company, 44
Lamontagne, E.-E., 61
land: in Canada, 92–3; immigrants
    and, 11; in Lower vs Upper
    Canada, 6, 10, 11; tenure system,
    10; in U.S., 6, 92–3
Larratt-Smith, Wilma, 215
Laurier, Wilfrid, 92
Law, Tom, 192–3, 196, 200
Leacock, Stephen, 39–40
LeDain, Victor A.B., 116, 131, 141,
    photo
Leddy, Joe A., 144, 162, 169
Lees, Nigel, 166, 175
LeFrançois, Glenn, 207
Legault, Peter, 166, 181
Lemay, Fernand, 215
Lesage, Jean, 145
Letourneau, Louis A., 119
Lévesque, René, 158, 179–80
Linton Apartments, 102
Lipari, Sheila, 188
London (Ont.), 3 Macs office in,
    197, 200
London (U.K.): Bank of Montreal
    in, 54, 96; Canadian government
    borrowing in, 54–5; finance in,
    54; Grand Industrial Exhibition
    (1851), 29; public health in, 37;
    smallpox in, 79; stock exchange,
    26, 59
Lower Canada, 8; creation of, 64;
    land in, 6, 10, 11; political reform
    in, 7–8; population, 10–11;
    seigneurial system in, 7; wheat
    in, 18

Lucas, R.A., 74
Lusitania (liner), 106

Macaulay, Bruce, 188
MacCallum, Jason, 215
MacCallum, Sam, 215
Macdonald, Sir John A., 65, 70,
  75, 92
MacDonald Currie, 153
MacDougall, Ada, 70
MacDougall, Alicia Dora, 17, 35
MacDougall, Bartlett Herbert
  (Bart), 109, 129, *photos*; and Bank
  of Montreal, 142; at Bishop's
  College School, 142; on Board
  of Directors, 152; as chairman,
  204; and hockey, 134; joins Mac
  & Mac, 142; as non-director
  shareholder, 150, positions with
  3 Macs, 189; at Royal Military
  College, 142; and Toronto office,
  156, 158, 181; as vice-president,
  169
MacDougall, Betsy Geraldine
  (later Applegarth), 70, 109
MacDougall, Bobs. *See*
  MacDougall, Robert R. (Bobs)
MacDougall, Campbell (George
  Campbell), *photo*; arrival in
  Montreal, 34–5; and Bank
  of Montreal, 53, 67; and Bell
  Telephone Company, 72; and
  Brydges, 70–1; death of, 87, 98;
  education, 35; during 1870s, 70;
  and 5th Battalion, Royal Light
  Infantry, 47; and horses, 35, 85;
  Lorn and, 82; and MacDougall
  Brothers, 66–7, 84; marriage,
  71; and snowshoeing, 60; and St
  Clair, 111; as widower, 85
MacDougall, David Martin, 215,
  216, *photo*

MacDougall, Dora Lucy, 70, 76
MacDougall, Dorothy (née
  Molson), 108–9, 122, 128, 129,
  132, 204, *photo*
MacDougall, Edith Eleanor (née
  Reford), 90–2, 132
MacDougall, Elizabeth (née
  Smith), 70
MacDougall, Florence (later
  Wilson), 70, 76
MacDougall, Geraldine Jane (later
  Paterson), 35, 98
MacDougall, Grace (Edith Grace;
  later Pitfield), 108, 132
MacDougall, Grace (née Brydges),
  71, 85, 95
MacDougall, Harriet Lucy (née
  Boston), 35–6, 70, 82–3
MacDougall, Hartland Brydges,
  72, *photos*; and Back River Club,
  120; and Bank of Montreal,
  89, 101, 102; and banks, 132–3;
  at BCS, 86–7; birth of, 71; and
  Black Tuesday, 125; and Britain,
  128; career, 132–3, 135; and cars,
  134–5; characteristics, 132–3, 135;
  connections, 119; death, 133; and
  Edith, 90–2; at Eliock School,
  86; in England, 89–90; in First
  World War, 106–9; and football,
  86, 136; and golf, 85–6; Hartland
  Molson named after, 130; and
  hockey, 88–9, 119–20, 130, 133–4,
  136; homes, 101, 104; and horses,
  85, 90; known as "the Major,"
  108; life of, 85; and MacDougall
  Brothers, 98, 115; and Mac &
  Mac, 115; and Meredith, 98, 101–
  2, 109, 129; and Montreal Forum,
  136; and Montreal Victorias,
  88–9, 136; and MSE, 102; and
  polo, 136; Price and, 118–19;

and rackets, 136; and R.E.
MacDougall, 86; reputation,
135; and Ritz-Carlton Hotel, 103;
and Saraguay, 129, 132; sense
of humour, 135; and sports, 101,
135–6; suffers stroke, 122–3, 136;
Tommy and, 132–3; and United
Financial Corporation, 115; in
Washington, 107–8, 115

MacDougall, Hartland Campbell
(Tommy), 108–9, *photos*; at
Bishop's College, 116; and
Britain, 128–9; and Canadian
Arena Company, 134; at
Canadian Staff College, 129;
as chairman and president,
159; death, 204; and Dorothy
Molson, 122; and employees'
pension plan, 157; and horses,
116; and Mac & Mac, 116, 131;
and merger with Kingstone &
Mackenzie, 162; and Montreal
Hunt, 132; in Ottawa, 129–30;
and polo, 121, 132; as president
of 3 Macs, 144; and Racket
Club, 205; reduction of role
in company, 163; retirement,
169; at Royal Military College,
Kingston, 116; at Saraguay, 129,
132; and Second World War,
128, 130–1; and skating, 132; and
tennis, 116, 122; travels, 128

MacDougall, Hartland Molson,
129, 134

MacDougall, Katherine Lorna
(later Price). *See* MacDougall,
Lorna (Katherine Lorna; later
Price)

MacDougall, Leigh (Hanbury
Leigh): arrival in Canada, 17;
and Budden, 46, 54; business
life, 67; on committee of brokers,
17; and commodities, 57; homes,

34; and horses, 35; partnership
with Lorn, 20, 34, 45–6; and
polo, 35; portrait in Bourse de
Montréal, 217; and rackets, 61;
social life, 35, 36; and St James's
Club, 36; younger brothers and,
53–4

MacDougall, Leonard (Hartland
Leonard), 98, 109, 115

MacDougall, Lorna Elizabeth, 122,
129

MacDougall, Lorna (Katherine
Lorna; later Price), 108, 118, 122

MacDougall, Lorn (Donald Lorn),
3, *photo*; and Accident Insurance
Company of Canada, 67;
achievements, 32–3, 81; advertising by, 21; and Annexation
Manifesto, 24; arrival in
Montreal, 8; as banker, 82;
and Bank of Montreal, 82; and
banks, 82; and Bell Telephone
Company, 72, 74–5; and Board
of Stock Brokers, 44, 54, 57; and
Board of Trade, 15, 81, 104; and
Boston, 35; business life, 12–13,
14, 32–4, 67; business style, 82;
on Canadian commission for
the International Centennial
Exposition in Philadelphia,
68; and Canadian Peat Fuel
Company, 45; career, 81–2;
and charities, 82–3; charter of
vessels, 19, 33; children of, 70;
on committee of brokers, 17;
and Davidson, 46, 82; death,
80–1; and decimal currency,
30, 33–4; and 1840s depression, 22; and Fenians, 51–2, 83;
as financial sage, 68; financial
success, 34; generosity, 82; and
Glass, 14, 16, 19, 20, 21, 81; and
Guarantee Company, 67; homes,

34, 68–9; and horses, 9, 10; and
Hunt Club, 41, 47, 83; infra-
structure investment, 45; and
Lake Huron Silver and Copper
Mining Company, 44; as leader
of brokering industry, 33; and
MacDougall Brothers, 45–6;
and MacDougall & Davidson,
54, 75; meets and marries Lucy
Boston, 35–6; military training,
9–10; and Montreal Investment
Association, 45; and Montreal
Mountain Boulevard Company,
45; and Montreal Plumbago
Mining Company, 45; and
Montreal Railway Terminus
Company, 45; and Mount Royal
Cemetery, 29; and MSE, 44, 57,
81, 104; and North British and
Mercantile Insurance Company,
54; and Oxford Mining and
Smelting Company, 44–5; parents and siblings, 8–9, 53–4, 82;
partnerships, 20, 34, 44, 45–6;
and politicians, 16; portrait in
Bourse de Montréal, 217; and
rackets, 61, 83; reputation, 81–2;
and Royal Guides, 47, 51–2, 83;
and shipping business, 33; and
skating, 59, 83; and snowshoeing, 83; social life, 35, 36; and
St James's Club, 36; and stocks
vs commodities, 57; trading in
flour and grain, 18; trustworthiness of, 14; weekly updates for
Gazette, 21
MacDougall, Lucy (née Boston).
See MacDougall, Harriet Lucy
(née Boston)
MacDougall, MacDougall &
MacTier (3 Macs): Alberta oil
sands development and, 212–13;
annual distributions for staff
and shareholders, 149, 151, 152,
156, 181, 187; Bank of Montreal
and, 147–8; Barry & McManamy
and, 168; bond trading by, 154,
195–6; and Burnett & Company,
155; chief financial officer (CFO),
197–8; client services department, 155–6, 172; cost control
within, 201; directors, 144, 152,
164, 171, 182–3, 196–7, *photo*;
Executive Committee, 189;
financial reporting system, 197;
forecast seminars, 209; formation of, 143–5; information
technology and, 198–9, 201;
institutional accounts, 152, 166,
167, 171, 172, 175; and investment counselling, 213–14; and
Kingstone & Mackenzie, 161–2;
London (Ont.) office, 197, 200;
Morning Room, 164; and MSE,
206, 216; numbers of employees,
162, 164, 170; October 1987 crash
and, 185; operating regulations and, 200; operations area,
200, 201; overhead expenses,
187; pension/retirement plan
for employees, 157, 205; political unrest in Quebec and, 163;
portfolio management, 195, 204;
Price Room, 204; Quebec City
office, 168, 171, 180, 193, 203;
research/research department,
154, 189, 192–3, 202, 208–9, 215;
revenues and profits, 151, 156,
159 (1960s), 166, 167, 172, 173,
175 (1970s), 179, 181, 182–3, 186
(1980s), 201 (1990s), 212 (2000s);
sales people, 152, 166, 178, 193–4,
202–3, 209, 211, 215; shareholders, 164, 171, 175–6, 182–3, 193,
216; sources of revenue, 154; on
St James Street, 145; and stock

exchanges as for-profit corporations, 210; and surcharges on larger trades, 167; syndicate participation by, 154; tax-preparation services, 153–4, 172; theft of securities from Dorval Airport, 192; Toronto branch, 156, 158, 163, 166, 172, 175, 177, 181, 198, 200, 202, 203; trading staff, 177; wealth management by, 153; Y2K and, 206–7

MacDougall, Marian Edith, 129, 134

MacDougall, Peter L., 108, 121, 132, *photo*

MacDougall, Peter (Major; 1774–1861), 9, 34, 82, *photo*

MacDougall, Robert E. (Bob), 86, 88–9, 115, 131, 133, *photo*

MacDougall, Robert R. (Bobs), 108, 121, 132, *photo*

MacDougall, Somerled (Lorn Somerled), 70; and D.L. MacDougall Stock Brokers, 84; moves to New York, 84; in South Africa, 84

MacDougall, St Clair (Hartland St Clair), 61–2, *photo*; appearance, 110–11; arrival in Montreal, 34–5; and Bell Telephone Company of Canada, 72; in business, 53–4; and Campbell, 111; and Canadian Sports Hall of Fame, 89; death, 110–11, 115; and 5th Battalion, Royal Fusiliers, 47; and Forest and Stream Club, 110; and golf, 86, 99, 110; and Guarantee Insurance Company, 68, 109, 110; homes, 99, 110; and horses, 85; and Hunt Club, 110; and Jockey Club, 110; Lorn and, 82; and MacDougall Brothers, 66–7, 84, 109; marriage, 70; and

Mount Royal Club, 110; and MSE, 57, 84, 99; and Paterson, 98; and Polo Club, 85, 99; semi-retirement of, 109; and St James's Club, 110; and 3rd Battalion, Victoria Volunteer Rifles, 47

MacDougall, Tommy. *See* MacDougall, Hartland Campbell (Tommy)

MacDougall Brothers: and Accident Insurance, 67; advertising, 21, 66; Applegarth and, 70, 115; and Bell Telephone Company of Canada, 75; Campbell and St Clair comprising, 66–7; after death of Lorn, 84; formation of, 20; and Guarantee Company, 68; Hartland B. and, 115; Lorn and Leigh compromising, 20, 34, 45–6; as managers of wealth, 133; St Clair and, 109

MacDougall & Budden, 54

MacDougall & Davidson, 54, 67; advertisement for, 66; and Bank of Montreal, 68; Bell Telephone Company and, 75; "correspondence" relationships with British banks, 96; formation of, 46; and municipal bonds, 96; and North British and Mercantile Insurance Company, 67; and Scottish American Investment Company, 67

MacDougall Investment Counsel (MIC), 213–14, 215

MacDougall & MacDougall (Mac & Mac), 86, 115–16; Bart MacDougall joins, 142; Christmas dinner party (1953), *photo*; as managers of wealth, 133; merger with MacTier &

Company, 143–5; 1930s depression and, 125; 1940s–50s profits, 136–7; in 1960s, 140–1, 142; Price joins, 142; Second World War and, 131
MacDougall & Prentice, 67
Mackay, Hugh, 74
Mackenzie, Alexander, 8, 72
Mackenzie, Philip, 161
MacTier, W. Stuart M. (Stuart), 143–4, 150, 159, *photo*
MacTier & Company, 143–4
Maritimes. *See* Atlantic provinces
Mark, Rob, 202, 215
Marler, Leslie, 156
Mary Brock (ship), 19
Masson, Joseph, 43
Mather, Betty (née Molson), 141
Mather, Larry, 141
Mathers, Suzanne, 189
Maxwell, W. and E.S., 110
McGill, Peter, 14–15, 16
McGill University, 4, 35, 38, 42
McInnes, Donald, 67
McKenzie, Bob, 200–1, 210
McKiee, Reid, 152, 156
McLea, Ernest, 88–9, *photo*
McLennan, Bartlett, 108–9, 120, 129
McMaster, A.R., 67
McNicholas, Timothy, 200, 210, 216
McNicol, Nicol, 181, 182, 185
Mechanics Bank, 69
Merchant's Bank, 101
Merchant's Exchange Building, 44
Meredith, Charles, 101–2, 115, 119, 129. *See also* Charles Meredith & Company
Meredith, Elspeth (née Hudson), 101
Meredith, Sir Vincent, 119
Merrill Lynch, 148

metal business, 31
Metis, 90, 108, 121–2, 162, *photo*
militia, 47
Milken, Michael, 187
Miller, William, 174
Mills, John, 23
mining, 44–5, 118, 146
Mitchell, Denham, 201
Mitchell, Ken, 197
Molson, Betty (later Mather). *See* Mather, Betty (née Molson)
Molson, Dorothy (later MacDougall). *See* MacDougall, Dorothy (née Molson)
Molson, Hartland de Montarville, 120, 129–31, 143
Molson, Herbert, 106, 108, 119, 122, 130
Molson, John, 87
Molson, Percival, 89
Molson, William, 42
Molson family, 5, 6, 12, 42
Molson's Bank, 69, 82
Montreal, 3–6; in 1840s, 21–2; in 1850s, 30–1, 37–8; as banking centre, 57; Board of Trade, 15; as capital, 21; churches, 5, 38; clubs in, 4–5; Committee on Trade, 15; construction in, 29; and Expo '67, 154–5; as fashion centre, 38; as financial centre, 99, 127, 139–40, 144, 145–6, 172, 180–1; growth of, 111; harbour, 41–2; hotels in, 102–4; inclusion in Upper Canada, 12; industrialization of, 102; infrastructure, 95; Irish immigrants in, 22–3; Jews in, 43, 111; living conditions in, 36, 95; and Ontario hinterland, 65; Parti Québécois government and, 169–70; political uncertainty in, 179–80; population, 6, 10, 25, 31, 65, 66, 97, 102, 111, 127;

Prohibition and, 114–15; Quebec City vs, 12; reputation of, 11–12; Scots in, 42–3; Sherbrooke Street, 102–3; shipping and, 28; smallpox in, 78–80; social scene in, 36; sports in, 5; street railway, 45; strikes in, 114; theatre in, 5; Toronto vs, 12, 64–6, 99, 139–40; tourism in, 5; trading of stocks in, 13–14; *Trent* affair and, 46–7; U.S. Civil War and, 46–8; U.S. dealers' offices in, 148; Victoria Bridge, 29, 31, 32, 36, 46–7; wealth creation in, 180; Winter Carnivals, 61, 78

Montreal Amateur Athletic Association (MAAA), 86, 136

Montreal Bank. *See* Bank of Montreal

"Montreal Brokers Circular," 17

Montreal Curb Market, 117

Montreal Exchange, 33, 43–4, 57. *See also* Montreal Stock Exchange (MSE)

Montreal Forum, 119, 132, 133–4, 136

Montreal General Hospital, 4, 37

Montreal Hunt Club, 34, 41, 47, 83, 110, 132

Montreal India Rubber Company, 32

Montreal Investment Association, 45

Montreal Jockey Club, 110

Montreal Maroons, 119–20, 134, 136

Montreal Mountain Boulevard Company, 45

Montreal Museum of Fine Arts, 102

Montreal Neurological Institute, 135

Montreal Ocean Steamship Company, 28

Montreal Plumbago Mining Company, 45

Montreal Polo Club, 120

Montreal Racket Club, 136, 205

Montreal Railway Terminus Company, 45

Montreal Royals, 133

Montreal Skating Rink, 59, 83

Montreal Stock Exchange (MSE): Black Tuesday and, 123; Board of Stock Brokers and, 57; and Boston Stock Exchange, 148; cost of seat on, 99, 118; and 1879 depression, 69; expansion of, 95; First World War and, 109–10; FLQ bombing of, 159; as for-profit corporation, 209–10; Hartland B. and, 102; history of, 44, 57; information technology and, 199; Kierans and, 140; Lorn and, 44, 57, 81, 104; MacDougall Brothers and, 67, 84; Meredith and, 101; and Montreal Curb Market, 117; New York and, 100; 1930s depression and, 126; during 1960s, 145–6; numbers of members, 58, 104–5, 145–6, 151; Paterson's seat on, 98–9; Second World War and, 126; St Clair and, 84, 99; and St James Street, 151; and surcharges on larger trades, 167; 3 Macs and, 216; as trading market for options and derivatives, 206; trading staff on floor of, 177; TSE and, 58, 59, 137; volumes of trading, 59, 131, 136–7, 147. *See also* Bourse de Montréal

Montreal Telegraph Company, 73

Montreal Victorias, 88–9, 136, *photo*
Montreal Waterworks, 32
Morgan, C. Powell, 151
Morgan Stanley, 158
Mount Royal Cemetery, 29
Mount Royal Club, 102, 110
Mouvement souveraineté-association, 158
Mulroney, Brian, 188
Murray, Herman, 192
mutual funds, 147, 155

Nakamoto, Ian, 215
NASDAQ, 205–6, 209
National Bell Telephone Company, 73
National Energy Program, 176
National Policy, 75
natural gas. *See* oil and gas
Nazarewicz, Troy, 200
Nelson, Wolfred, 23
Neville, Joan, 196
newspapers, 93, 118
New York: Bank of Montreal in, 46, 53, 96; and Canadian bond trading, 97; Canadian federal government borrowing in, 111; MSE and, 100; population, 6, 10, 25; smallpox in, 79; stock exchange, 26, 59, 147, 153, 166, 167–8; Toronto and, 65; TSE and, 100
Nixon, Richard, 160–1, 166
North American Free Trade Agreement, 188
North British and Mercantile Insurance Company, 54, 67
Northey, William, 120
Norton, J.G., 83
Notman, William, 70
Notre Dame Church (Montreal), 39

O'Connor, Bill, 171
October Crisis, 162
Ogilvie, A.E., 120, 121
Ogilvie, Alexander W., 30
Ogilvie, G.L., 120, 121
Ogilvie, John, 30
Ogilvie family, 33, 42
O'Handley, Colin, 188, 199
oil and gas: in Alberta, 132, 139; federal government and, 168; Mackenzie valley pipeline, 168; National Energy Program, 176; in Ontario, 30; in Russia, 202; TSE and, 146; U.S. investment in Canadian, 138
oil prices: 1970s, 168, 170, 173; 1980s, 179, 183; 1990s, 191, 195, 201–2; 2000s, 212
Olympia & York, 195
Olympic Games: 1980, Moscow, 176; Winter games 1948, St Moritz, 130
Ontario: creation of, 64; education in, 138; industrial expansion of, 138; mining industry in, 146; Montreal-Toronto competition for hinterland, 65; population, 65, 137
Organization of Petroleum Exporting Countries (OPEC), 165, 170, 183
Osler, F.G., 99
Ouellet, Marco, 189, 193, 215
Outremont (house), 34, 35, 36, *photo*
Oxford Mining and Smelting Company, 44–5

Papineau, Louis-Joseph, 7
Parizeau, Jacques, 149
Parti Québécois, 158, 162, 169, 176
Paterson, Alexander (son of Alexander Thomas), 98–9

Paterson, Alexander Thomas, 35, 98
Paterson, Geraldine Jane. *See* MacDougall, Geraldine Jane (later Paterson)
Paterson, Hartland MacDougall, 132
Paterson family, 132
Paton, Thomas, 42
Patriotes, 7–8
Pearson, Lester, 140
Penfield, Wilder, 123
Penmans, 102, 132
pension funds, investment patterns, 149
Perrone, Jim, 198, 202
Perry, Diane (later Stoneman), 203
Perry, Lynn, 203
Perry, Merne (later Price). *See* Price, Merne (née Perry)
Peters, Jennifer, 203
petroleum and natural gas. *See* oil and gas
Petry, H.J.H., 87
Pitfield, Edith Grace (née MacDougall). *See* MacDougall, Grace (Edith Grace; later Pitfield)
Pitfield, Ward Chipman, 227–8n2, 227n4
Pitfield, Ward Chipman II, 134, 228n2
Plante, Jacques, 133
Plourde, Marc-André, 202
Pollitt, Murray, 166, 181
polo, 35, 85, 99, 120–1, 132, 136
Porter, Dana, 149
Porter Commission. *See* Royal Commission on Banking and Finance (Porter Commission)
portfolio management, 149, 194, 196, 204, 213, 215
Power, Michael, 23

Prefontaine, Raymond, 95
Price, Joan. *See* Price, Lorna Joan
Price, John Herbert ("Jack"), 118–19, 122
Price, Katherine Lorna (née MacDougall). *See* MacDougall, Lorna (Katherine Lorna; later Price)
Price, Lorna Joan, 141
Price, Merne (née Perry), 142
Price, Sir William, 118
Price, Thomas Evan, *photos*; at Bishop's College School, 141; at Bishop's University, 141–2; and Black Watch, 142, 164; career, 203; as CEO, 203–4; as chairman, 169, 186, 189, 203; characteristics, 141, 203; death, 203; as executive vice-president, 152; heart attack, 187; in insurance business, 142; and Investment Dealers Association, 185, 186; and Mac & Mac, 142; and Merne Perry, 142; and Montreal Racket Club, 205; as partner, 143; as successor to Tommy, 163–4; and 3 Macs' financial position, 181
Price, Timothy Evan, 188, 205, *photos*; elected to board, 198; and IDA, 214; and Investment Industry Association of Canada, 214–15; and MIC, 213; as president and CEO, 211–12
Price Brothers, 118, 132
privatization, government, 182, 183
produce brokers, 16–17, 19, 54
Province of Canada, creation of, 64
public health, 37
pulp and paper industry, 93, 118
Putin, Vladimir, 202

Quarles, Peter, 215

Quebec Act (1774), 64
Quebec Bank, 12, 16
Quebec City, 5; Montreal vs, 12;
  population, 10; 3 Macs office in,
  168, 171, 180, 193, 203; timber
  trading and, 19; wealth creation
  in, 180
Quebec (province): Bank of
  Montreal and, 96, 97; Caisse
  de Dépôt et Placement, 159;
  Catholic Church in, 138, 139, 140;
  creation of, 64; Duplessis and,
  138; education in, 139; emigration from, 63, 93, 102; hydroelectricity in, 158–9; industrialization policy, 138; investment
  patterns in, 140; October Crisis,
  162; Parti Québécois government in, 169, 701; population,
  65, 137; Quiet Revolution, 145;
  sovereignty movement, 162, 169,
  173, 176, 201; Toronto and, 65
Queen's University, 42

rackets, 61, 83
railways, 6–7, 29, 31–2, 37, 41;
  transcontinental, 63–5, 75
Rappaport, Eric, 197, 205
Rawlings, Edward, 67, 109
Raymond, Donat, 119, 120, 134
Reagan, Ronald, 178, 187
real estate, 177–8, 191
Rebellion Losses Bill, 23–4
rebellions of 1837–38, 19
Reber, Tom, 215
Reciprocity Treaty, 29–30, 49, 52
Redpath, Peter, 30
Redpath family, 42
Redpath Sugar Refinery, 30
Reford, Alexander, 92
Reford, Edith Eleanor (later
  MacDougall). See MacDougall,
  Edith Eleanor (née Reford)

Reford, Kate, 90, 91
Reford, Robert, 90–1
Reichmann family, 195
Reid, Parker B. (Banty), 140–1,
  144, 148
Renaud, Louis, 34, 43
Rennie, Derek, 203, 215
resource industries, 118, 131–2
Reynolds, Doug, 176–7, 193, 205,
  212
Richard, Maurice "The Rocket,"
  133–4
Ritz, Cesar, 103
Ritz-Carlton Hotel (Montreal),
  102–4, 119, 132
Roberts, Charles G.D., 60–1
Robertson, Alexander, 73
Robertson, Andrew, 74
Robinson, David, 215
Robinson, John Beverley, 32
Root, Norman, 116, 131
Rose, James, 67
Ross, James G., 67
Ross, Robert G., 150–1, 189
Royal 22nd Regiment ("Van
  Doos"), 114
Royal Bank, 196
Royal Canadian Bank, 64
Royal Canadian Insurance
  Company, 225n7
Royal Commission on Banking
  and Finance (Porter
  Commission), 149–50
Royal Guides, 47, 50–2, 83
Royal Military Academy,
  Woolwich, 9–10
Royal Military College, Kingston
  (RMC), 116, 142
Royal Montreal Curling Club, 5
Royal Montreal Golf Club, 61–2,
  85–6, 99, 110
Royal Securities, 152, 156
Royal Trust, 157, 196

Rugby School, 87
Russell, Sir William Howard, 36–7
Russia: default on debt, 201; invasion of Chechnya, 202; oil and gas industry, 202; Revolution, 114

St James's Club, 36–7, 77, 110, 222–3n4
St Laurent, Louis, 138, 140
St Lawrence and Atlantic Railroad, 27, 34, 41
St Lawrence River, 4
Salomon Brothers, 191
Samson, Olivier, 168, 180, 200
Saraguay, 101, 129
Savard, Ernest, 217
savings and loan (S&L) business, 177–8
Sclater, C.P., 74
Scots: and education, 42; and French Canadians, 42–3; as immigrants, 4; success of, 42–3
Scott, Barbara Ann, 130
Scottish American Investment Company, 67
Sears, Chris, 202, 215
Sears, Peter, 195, 215
Second World War, 126–7
Securities and Exchange Commission (U.S.), 167
Semmelhaack, Jerry, 212
Seward, William, 41
shareholder value, 185–6
shipping business, 6, 10, 12, 28–9, 33, 37, 41–2
Shultz, George, 165
Sidey, J.G., 62
Simpson, George W., 57
Sise, Charles Fleetwood, 73–4, 75
skating, 5, 59, 60–1, 83, 130, 132
Skinner, Paul, 197
smallpox, 62, 78–80

Smith, Elizabeth (later MacDougall). See MacDougall, Elizabeth (née Smith)
snowshoeing, 59–61, 83
South African war, 84
Soviet Union. See USSR
Spanakis, Maria, 202
Spanish influenza, 112
sports, 5, 59–62, 83, 85–6, 116
Sports Hall of Fame, 89, 135–6
Squire, William, 29
Squires, Janice, 188
Stanley Cup, 88–9
Starnes, Henry, 51
Stenason, David, 213
Stephen, George, 65
Stephenson, Robert, 32
Stevenson, David, 197, 205
Stimson, G.A., 97
stock brokers and brokerages: in early Quebec, 12; Mac & Mac as, 143; regulation of, 58, 69
stock exchanges: bond trading and, 96, 113; "call" system, 94–5; 1870s depression and, 69; London, 26, 59; New York, 26
stock markets: 1929 collapse, 123; 1987 collapse, 184–5; 2000 collapse, 209, 213; Second World War and, 131
stocks: commodities vs, 57; trading, 13–14, 16, 99, 177, 178–9
Strathy, H. Gordon, 73
street railway, 45
Stuart, Frank L., 161, 162, 173
Sulpicians, 5, 39
Sun Life Assurance Company, 169–70
surety bonds, 110

tariffs, 22, 75
tax preparation, 153–4
Taylor, J.W., 57

Taylor, T.M., 57
technology: and bond trading, 99–100; information, 201; Second World War and, 126–7
telegraph, 7, 33, 37, 73, 168
telephone, 72–5, 117
tennis, 116, 121–2
textile industry, 111
Thatcher, Margaret, 181–2
Theatre Royal, 5
Thibaudeau, J.-R., 74
timber trade, 19, 26
TMX, 213
tobogganing, 5
Tomacs. See MacDougall & MacDougall (Mac & Mac)
Toronto: banks in, 55; Dickens on, 65; and Maritimes, 65; Montreal vs, 12, 64–6, 99, 139–40; and New York, 65; population, 10, 31, 65, 66, 97, 127; and Quebec, 65; 3 Macs branch in, 156, 158, 163, 166, 172, 175, 177, 181, 198, 200, 202, 203; U.S. Civil War and, 47–8
Toronto Stock Exchange (TSE): and Alberta oil sands, 212–13; Black Tuesday and, 123; cost of seat on, 99; and 1879 depression, 69; as for-profit corporation, 209–10; founding of, 58; information technology and, 199; and mining companies, 212; MSE and, 137, 206; New York and, 100; during 1960s, 146; and oil and gas industry, 146; and S&P 300, 214; and surcharges on larger trades, 167; Toronto branch of 3 Macs and, 163; trading staff on floor of, 177; as TSX, 213; volumes of trading, 147, 165–6, 183
Torrance family, 5, 12

tourism, 5
Trans Canada Pipelines, 168
transportation, 6, 94
Trent affair, 46–7
Trottier, Richard, 200
Trudeau, Jean, 212
Trudeau, Pierre Elliott, 157
trust companies, 105, 196
TSX: formation of, 213; joins with Bourse de Montréal, 218

unemployment, 179
Union Act (1840), 64
United Financial Corporation, 115
United Kingdom: Corn Laws, 22; Fenians in, 48; investment in Canada, 96, 127; Irish independence from, 48; Jewish immigrants in, 124; privatization in, 182, 183; recession in, 182; Spanish influenza in, 112; Thatcher in, 181–2; trade with U.S., 19; and U.S. Civil War, 40–1; U.S. relations with, 48
United States: and Afghanistan, 211; annexation of Canada to, 24, 25, 46; banks in, 46, 54, 56–7, 125–6; and Britain, 19, 48; and Canadian bond trading, 96, 97; Canadian emigrants in, 63, 124; Canadian relations with, 94; Civil War, 36, 40–1, 46, 47–8, 63; currency, 161, 165, 178; dealers' offices in Montreal, 148; Drawback Acts, 22; economy, 22, 75, 123, 125, 157–8, 165, 211; emigrants to Canada, 4; expansion of, 63; Federal Reserve, 174, 178, 184, 209; and Fenians, 48, 52; French Canadians in, 11, 93, 102; gold reserves crisis, 161; government debt, 195; Great Depression in, 125–6; Great

Society agenda, 158; immigrants in, 63, 75; inflation in, 171–2, 174–5; interest rates in, 195; investment in Canada, 127, 138; and Iraq, 191–2, 211; Irish in, 23; Jewish immigrants in, 124; Kennedy and, 145; land in, 6, 92; and Moscow Olympics, 176; 9/11 and, 211; oil prices and, 171; population, 63, 75; Prohibition in, 114–15; and Reciprocity Treaty, 29–30, 49, 52; relations with Canada, 48, 188; shoppers in Montreal, 38; s&l business in, 177–8; smallpox in, 78; Spanish influenza in, 112; tariffs, 22; unemployment in, 179; Vietnam War and, 157–8, 160–1
University Club, 102
Upper Canada, 8; creation of, 64; inclusion of Montreal in, 12; land in, 6, 10; population, 10–11; wheat in, 18
USSR, 155; and Afghanistan, 176; collapse of, 187–8, 202; and Czechoslovakia, 157

vaccination, 62, 78–9
Vail, T.N., 74
Vega, Fedi, 188, 199
Victoria Skating Rink (Montreal), 88
Vietnam War, 153, 157–8, 160–1
Viger, Danielle, 195

Vincent, Dominique, 215
Volcker, Paul, 174–5, 178, 184
volunteer regiments, 47

Waite, Peter, 42
Walwyn Stodgell Cochran Murray, 186
War of 1812, 21
Watson, Cathy, 200, 211
W.C. Pitfield & Company, 152
wealth management, 133, 153
Weber, Brian, 202
Western Rail Road Company of Canada, 70
Weston, Donny, 188
Whalen, Donna, 188
wheat, 11, 18–19, 26, 33, 98, 165
Whitestone, Bruce, 156, 166, 189
Wilson, Reid, 76–8
Wilson, Walter, 76–8
Winnipeg: General Strike, 114; population, 98
W. John Price Joint Stock Company, 118
Wojtyla, Karol, 172
Woo, Richard, 212, 215
Wood, E.R., 97
Wood Gundy, 156
Wurtele, M., 97

Y2K, 206–7, 209

Zirpollo, Tony, 199